P9-DMR-516

THE 20-MINUTE VEGETABLE GARDENER

Gourmet Gardening
for the Rest of Us

Illustrations by Steven D. Guarnaccia

RANDOM HOUSE • NEW YORK

The
2⊙-MINUTE
VEGETABLE
GARDENER

Tom Christopher
and Marty Asher

Library of Congress Cataloging-in-Publication Data

Christopher, Thomas.
The 20-minute vegetable gardener; gourmet gardening for
the rest of us/Tom Christopher and Marty Asher.
p.   cm.
ISBN 0-679-44815-2 (alk. paper)
1. Vegetable gardening.   2. Herb gardening.   3. Low maintenance gardening.
4. Organic gardening. I. Asher, Marty. II. Title.
SB324.3.C48   1999
635—dc21   98-38175

Random House website address: www.atrandom.com

Printed in the United States of America on acid-free paper

24689753

FIRST EDITION

Book design by Carole Lowenstein

For Suzanne, who kept her sense of humor;
for Matthew, who was appallingly honest
in his critiques of the recipes;
and for Madeleine, who each day teaches us
the true meaning of tofu.

Acknowledgments

Putting a book together is not a 20-minute project, and this one in particular reflects the generous help of many people. Our wives, Suzanne and Judy, provided encouragement, critical readings, help in the garden and the kitchen, and a pinch of sanity, when needed. Marty wants to thank his son, Dan, for all the heavy lifting; Tom thanks his son, Matthew, for reminding him that gardening is supposed to be fun and for helping to make it so. The librarians of the New York Botanical Garden continue to amaze us with their command of the garden's resources and their unwavering patience. Dora Galitzki, horticulturist extraordinaire, purged many an error from the manuscript, and she even laughed at our jokes. And how do you thank an editor like Sean Abbott, who showed us how to cut the fat and tune the prose with so little pain?

Contents

THE 20-MINUTE VEGETABLE GARDENER

Chapter 1
The Challenge

"Pass the cucumbers," said Tom.

Marty obligingly slid the dish across the red-checked table-cloth.

Tom peered at the slices inside and grunted. "That's interesting."

Marty lifted a slice of whole-grain to inspect his bean sprout–avocado sandwich.

"I said, that's interesting."

"Yeah, I think the sprouts are a *little* wilted," Marty replied.

"No—I mean the cucumbers. Did you know that Tofu to Go serves 'Fordhook White Spine' cucumbers? You hardly ever see them anymore. They're a real antique."

"I told you this is a good place." The two differently abled gardeners were celebrating the completion of their last book, *The 20-Minute Gardener,* with a luncheon at Marty's favorite bistro. The manuscript was edited, the galleys were corrected, and there had been no violence (well, there was that incident with the copy editor, but Marty had warned her what would happen if she politically corrected Tom's prose). Marty picked up his sandwich, sniffed it, and bit off a corner.

"I'll bet you didn't know that's a 'Bacon' avocado," Tom added helpfully.

Marty gagged and spat out the offending mouthful. "This is supposed to be a vegetarian restaurant," he yelped. "What the hell are they doing, counterfeiting avocados from nitrited pork?"

"It's okay, it's okay—it's not a bacon avocado, it's a '*Bacon*' avocado." Tom shooed away an anxious waitress, who kept chirping that Hi, her name was Cindi, and she was their server for today and could she help them? "See, 'Bacon' is the name of the type of avocado—it's a standard variety among commercial growers in California. Personally, I prefer the nutty flavor of 'Mexicola'."

Marty glowered at Tom. Maybe it wasn't too late for a little mayhem after all. "Tom, did you ever consider eating a vegetable without discussing its pedigree? I mean, cucumbers are just cucumbers, and who wants to be on a first-name basis with their sandwich?"

"But, Marty, it's really interesting. Besides, vegetables are not all the same. You should try growing them, that's the best way to get to know them. Maybe you can't grow your own avocados in Connecticut, but you *could* sprout your own beans. Those are mung-bean sprouts you're eating—pretty bland. You should try radish-seed sprouts; they would give your sandwich a really interesting, spicy flavor. Or mustard sprouts—they're more peppery. And when it comes to cucumbers, well, these off-the shelf slices can't possibly compete with the yard-long Armenian cucumbers I grew last summer."

"Tom," said Marty, pointing with his fork. "Look, we got through the compost book together. And we figured out how to fill the yard with flowers in twenty minutes a day. Actually, *I* figured that out, but you really were a help. Really. But there's no way you are going to persuade me to grow my own fruits and vegetables. That's a lot of work: digging, planting, hoeing, chasing deer and woodchucks and the neighbor's kids, swatting bugs, spreading manure. Why bother with all of that when I can drive down to the local Stop & Shop and get a head of lettuce for a buck?"

"Money's not the point," Tom insisted, pointing his own fork and punching up the volume. "It's the different colors, aromas, and tastes, all the fascinating ways that Nature has seen fit to give us such an abundant world. Do you want to spend the rest of your life eating hydroponic iceberg and romaine—textured water—when there are dozens of better alternatives? There are gourmet French lettuces, antique Italian types, sweet-leaved mint lettuces, crisp-heads, deer tongues, and oak leafs. Life can be so much more interesting. Besides, you'll never taste any of these lettuces at their best until you have them fresh from your own garden.

"And what about arugula? The arugula you buy, it's always been picked too late; the leaves are big and tough and bitter. Grow arugula yourself, pick the leaves while they are still small and sweet and tender, and you won't believe how good it is. You'll realize it really isn't just some yuppie scam. Then, of course, there are home-grown tomatoes, sweet corn, real Irish potatoes, fresh-picked peas, even beans—I'm planting three different kinds of beans this spring that you will never see in the store."

"Right, right, but it's all so complicated. My agenda already needs an air-traffic controller. No, the only way I'd go near fruits and vegetables, at least before they are picked and shrink-wrapped, is if someone figured out an easy way to grow them. You know, like we did for flowers in *The 20-Minute Gardener*. But that's impossible. No one would be stupid enough to try and grow fruits and vegetables in twenty minutes a day."

Marty saw a crazed smile spreading over Tom's face.

"No," Marty said. "Absolutely not. No way."

The woman at the next table shushed *her* server ("Hi, I'm Bob"). "I'll have whatever they're *not* having," she said.

Marty's Manifesto

Marty doesn't care for blind commitment. After Tom agreed to pick up the check for lunch, Marty agreed to help Tom reinvent vegetable gardening. But before he started, he insisted on a contract. Marty had worked with Tom long enough to know that Tom often mistakes hard labor for fun. Besides, Marty knew that Tom's horticultural enthusiasm is likely to run away with him. Grabbing a pen from a passing waiter, Marty started scribbling terms onto his napkin.

The basis for their new method of vegetable gardening, Marty

said, had to be the same rule as the one he had invented for *The 20-Minute Gardener*: they would garden for just twenty minutes each day. Unless, Marty added, the weather was glorious and he didn't want to go inside and face the vacuuming; then he should be allowed to garden longer. Tom agreed to that, and added some fine print of his own: he might have to garden more than twenty minutes in one day to finish some essential task, like picking the apples for his hard cider, that could not be put off. In that case, he would receive a credit for the extra time, a credit that he could redeem in a vacation from gardening on succeeding days. And what about days when the weather was really foul, Marty added, or days on which his boss had left him with a worse than ordinary case of post-traumatic shock disorder? He should be allowed to take those days off. However, the essential point was, they both agreed, that the *average* daily gardening time should be twenty minutes.

In marked contrast to the kind of vegetable gardening that Tom had always practiced, this new method would allow you to have a life outside the garden. In fact, it would require that. What's more, those twenty minutes that he did spend in the garden, Marty insisted that they had to be fun. He wasn't going to waste his time perfecting another system of drudgery. There was plenty of that around already.

Ultimately, after much discussion, a few more napkins, and several double mochaccinos (at Tom's expense), the two horticultural pioneers perfected the following:

Marty's Ten-Point, 20-Minute Fruit and Vegetable Pledge of Allegiance

1. *The 20-minute gardener makes every minute count by growing high-impact crops.* One cayenne pepper can make a whole dinner exciting. And when the first spear of asparagus pushes its way up out of the soil in springtime, it's not a harvest, it's a pagan fertility rite.

2. *The 20-minute fruit and vegetable gardener gauges success not by the size of the crop but by the amount of pleasure it delivers.* This pleasure comes not only at the dinner table but also in the garden: a 20-minute fruit or vegetable is *fun* to grow.

3. *A 20-minute fruit or vegetable must offer a significant improvement over the store-bought alternative.* American farmers, for example, have never heard of Malabar spinach, but the 20-minute gardener knows that unlike traditional spinach, which needs cool weather, Malabar spinach loves heat and it delivers real spinach-flavored greens right through the summer, long after traditional spinach poops out. A 20-minute fruit or vegetable may also be some superior variety of a familiar crop, one that does not adapt to the marketing process. A tomato with flavor, for example.

4. *Twenty-minute gardeners don't fight Nature (they know who will win that battle).* Their fruits and vegetables are chosen to suit *their* climate and *their* soil; that's why they are so easy to grow. The 20-minute gardener doesn't insist on snow peas in Arizona, or on heat-loving eggplants in Vermont. Fussing is fun in the kitchen, but it's counterproductive in the garden.

5. *Twenty-minute gardeners plant in rows only when planning to harvest by tractor.* They know that arranging their plants in a linear fashion is boring and inefficient, the first step toward traditional agriculture and its stoop-labor slavery. Twenty-minute gardeners prefer to plant in blocks or swathes, or even decorative patterns (Tom is really compulsive about that). They may even, like Marty, mix seeds in a homemade shaker and scatter them like salt. Nonlinear planting is more fun and more efficient in its use of space. Twenty-minute gardeners harvest more vegetables per square foot and so get a bigger return for their investment of work and compost.

6. *Twenty-minute gardeners nurture their dirt.* They can plant more densely than other gardeners because the soil in the 20-minute beds is superb. Twenty-minute gardeners don't coddle

their plants. They don't have to, because they have coddled their soil.

7. *Twenty-minute gardeners don't weed.* They have no need to weed, because they never let weeds into their gardens. They leave weeds no opportunities, and if a weed should find its way in, the 20-minute gardener develops a recipe and transforms the weed into a vegetable.

8. *The 20-minute gardener never applies anything to his garden that he would be afraid to get on his hands.* (Tom's note: except for manure.) (Marty's note: especially manure.)

9. *The 20-minute gardener can do this because she rarely has to confront bugs.* Instead, she ignores, avoids, or excludes them.

10. *The 20-minute gardener recognizes that the hose is his most important gardening tool, and so wields it with the care it deserves.* How you water not only determines the health of your plants and their resistance to pests and diseases, it even dictates the size, quality, and flavor of the harvests.

And because Marty always has to have the last word, we spoil the symmetry of our manifesto and add the following:

11. *Mellow gardeners grow better-tasting vegetables.* Stay cool. God created supermarkets for a reason.

Chapter 2

The Method, or Tom and Marty's Prescription for Farming the Suburbs

When in the course of horticultural events . . . Pompous, way too pompous. Maybe *These are the plants that stir men's souls.* . . . Weird, way too weird, and no punch. It's gotta have punch. Hey, Tom, what about this? *Gardeners of the world, unite! You have nothing to lose but your* . . . uh . . . *hoes?*

Marty was working up a preamble for his new vegetable gardening manifesto. He had explained to Tom that he, Marty, would be the Marx *and* Engels of this revolution, while Tom, he added grandly, could be the Stalin and attend to the dirty work.

Suddenly, though, a thought struck Marty. Stalin—hadn't

he had something to do with long vacations in unpleasant places? Marty vaguely recalled some professor back at Brooklyn College quoting Comrade Stalin (or was it Comrade Trotsky or Comrade Mao? Or maybe Spiro Agnew?), something about the "dignity of labor." That's a word which makes Marty nervous. He decided he'd better check what Tom was up to.

He found Tom surrounded by stacks of seed catalogs, busy inking in a sheaf of order forms. In response to Marty's question, Tom explained that he was starting a vegetable garden the way you always start a vegetable garden. This did not surprise Marty, that Tom intended to grow this stuff the way he always had. (Shoot, Tom does everything the way he always has—that's why he feels so at home in New England.) Unfortunately, though, further questioning revealed that this traditional approach was going to involve a catastrophic quantity of hard, physical labor. And besides, it didn't promise much of a harvest.

What Tom proposed (and he insisted that this was standard practice nationwide) was to set aside a weekend in early April. With a rented rototiller the size of a Land Rover, he and Marty would work from dawn to dusk ("from can to can't," as the old farmers say) through Saturday and Sunday plowing up a huge tract of soil. The next step would have to wait at least a week, however, because it would take that long for Tom and Marty to recover so that they could even walk again.

Once they were ambulatory, the two gardeners would mark out with stakes and strings the broadly spaced parallel rows for planting. That's why they had to dig up so much area, Tom added, because the rows would be set as much as a foot and a half apart. Even the radishes and lettuces would be lined out that way, like lonely ranks of Foreign Legionnaires at Fort Zinderneuf. When they had the planting lines marked, they would sow the $150's worth of seeds that Tom orders each year from the blizzard of nursery catalogs that drop into his mailbox around January 1st.

Having accomplished this, Tom admitted that he (and surely Marty, too) would become overwhelmed by the commitment they had made to watering, weeding, spraying, etc. How could he and Marty possibly manage this enormous agribusiness while still holding down day jobs? It would be impossible to keep up with all the gardening work. Recognizing this was important, because it would free them. They could give up, retire to the porch for a beer, and surrender the garden to the woodchuck and the pigweed.

Marty's reaction to this plan was pure scorn.

"Why don't we cut right to the chase and just open the beers now? That way, we can skip the grubbing around in the mud, send out for Chinese, and let that woodchuck starve. I never liked him anyway."

This was unfair. Not to the woodchuck (who had it coming), but to Tom. For in fact, the plan, though ridiculous, was in the best traditions of American vegetable gardening. The problem is that, in this field, our best traditions are none too good.

Most likely this is because until this century (the twentieth, that is) vegetables were not something that Americans ate much of. Lumped together under the label of "sass," vegetables were boiled thoroughly ("cooked down," as they still say in rural Texas) and then deposited about the dinner table in little bowls. Fried or roasted meats, breads, biscuits, pies and cakes were the staples; aside from a few starches such as corn and potatoes, vegetables were an afterthought.

Not surprisingly, vegetable gardening itself was also an afterthought in early America. Where vegetables have been the dietary foundation, as among the peasant populations of Europe and Asia, vegetable growing developed as a fine art. In our country, however, it was just something you did when you were caught up with the farm work. Naturally, you organized the garden just like you managed your farm. The plots were smaller in vegetable gardening, and so were the tools, but the basic strategies were the same as those found beyond the garden fence, out in the fields.

That's why our vegetable gardens are designed for machines, not people. This is an attitude picked up from farming, which in the United States has concentrated on mechanization and mass production for a century and a half. We've transformed the landscape, leveling it, draining it, filling in low spots, and cutting it up into broad rectangles so that it's comfortable for tractors and combines. We plant in rows because that makes cultivation easy for machines, and we space the rows to suit the machines' wheelbase.

Besides transforming the landscape, we've also transformed the food plants, so that they lend themselves better to mechanical handling. We value uniformity in vegetables because variety upsets machines.

A century and a half ago, a packet of turnip seeds was full of individuals. Though the turnips were all of the same strain, they were not hybrids. The pollination that produced the seeds had been done randomly by bees, not by some guy with a white coat and a camel hair brush. This meant that there was considerable genetic variation from seed to seed. As a result, the plants that sprang from the seeds varied in vigor. Each plant grew at a somewhat different rate. This was good, because it meant that plants matured at different rates, which made for a longer harvest. Your turnip crop came in gradually over a period of many weeks, so that you had fresh turnips most of the summer. But you had to hunt through your patch each night to find the plants that were ready for picking. Machines (and gardeners who were trained by them) don't have the patience for that. They want a crop they can pick all at once.

The lack of uniformity in old-time vegetables also meant that a single planting could satisfy many needs. A single planting of onions, for instance, would produce large bulbs for slicing, smaller ones for nestling in around the pot roast, and maybe even some tiny ones for your martinis. That kind of thing upsets machines, though; it's liable to choke them.

So, to suit our machines, we have bred our vegetables for uniformity. That's led to the bumper harvests with which American farmers fill tables all over the world. But in the backyard plot, these regimented vegetables have fostered the nemesis of the home gardener: the glut. Garden by the old rules, and you'll never harvest just enough greens to fill a pot. Instead, you'll have nothing for weeks and then, all of a sudden, basketfuls. You'll go straight from famine to a solid-waste-disposal crisis. Even now, Tom (who remains a traditionalist at heart) insists that you aren't a real gardener unless by July, your friends run and hide when you ring their doorbells. They *know* you have a bushel of zucchinis hidden behind your back.

Marty can deal with gluts (he has a teenage son) but he really hates another aspect of the traditional, borrowed gardening style. He hates the emphasis on hard work. On the farm, fields are planted without much regard for the sheer brute force that will be required to maintain them. What does that matter? A machine is going to supply this. A tractor doesn't mind the labor-intensive inefficiency that's typical of mechanized cultivation: the widely spaced plantings, for example, that invite weeds and so necessitate constant cultivation of the soil between the rows. Keep pouring in the fossil fuel, and a tractor will drive up and down, scratching up the soil between the rows forever. But in the home garden, your muscles take the place of the tractor engine. And eventually, you might get tired of hoeing.

"So forget the hoeing, Tom. I told you, I tried that already. It's right there in the preamble to the manifesto: *no hoes allowed.*" Then, in his usual masterful fashion, Marty began to sketch in the outlines of *his* kind of vegetable garden.

- It must be quick and easy to create. There would be no weekend-long orgy of digging and tilling. "Remember: twenty minutes a day."
- The soil must be perfect, because in Marty's garden the plants would have to grow themselves. And the soil had to be perfect from day one; Marty wasn't going to spend five years composting, liming, digging in this and forking in that to transform the compacted clay in his backyard. He demands instant gratification.
- The garden must look nice. Tom kept insisting that vegetables

need sun, and the only sunny spot in Marty's yard lay right in the middle of the back lawn. "I'm not doing any weird, funky number there where I have to look at it every night when I sit on the patio drinking my Chardonnay. This is a good neighborhood. As you know," Marty added, dropping the name with a clang, "Martha Stewart lives just down the road."

· The design must be easy to duplicate. If they were going to launch a vegetable revolution, the concept had to be easy for anyone to grasp. "Remember: gardens to the people."

Tom tried sarcasm. "So you want something you can take out of a box, slap down in your backyard, and voilà! Gourmet vegetables."

"Exactly!" Marty answered, the relief plain on his face.

"An off-the-shelf, instant garden," Tom sneered.

"Precisely."

Tom subsided into a grumble. He told Marty that the rototiller was nonnegotiable. They had to have a rototiller. And that he better keep next Friday morning free. Then he gathered up his catalogs and stalked off.

Friday

April the 24th was clear, cool, and sunny. It was perfect weather for garden making, and Tom should have been happy. But Marty kept whining about property values. Again and again, he kept telling Tom that he wasn't going to have any horticultural eyesore depreciating his equity.

When Tom asked about the rental of a rototiller, Marty became evasive. Every time Tom tried to pursue this further, Marty's cell phone would ring, and he would excuse himself. Keeping in touch with the office, Marty explained. But which office? Didn't Marty work at a publishing house? What was this about "point spread" and "first race at Aqueduct"? Technical terms, Marty explained. He was talking to the guy who makes the books.

Then with a crunch of gravel, the truck from the discount home center pulled into Marty's driveway. As the driver tossed down bags from the truck bed, Tom checked items off his list:

3 8-foot-long cedar 2 × 8's
4 strap hinges
11 bags of topsoil (total: 7 cubic feet)*
11 bags of "sharp" builder's sand (total: 7 cubic feet). This is the coarse, gritty type of sand used in concrete mixes.
1 4-cubic-foot bale of sphagnum peat or 6 bags of compost
5 bags of composted cow manure (total: 3 cubic feet)

As Marty's son, Dan, shifted bags from the driveway to the backyard, Tom and Marty chose the spot in which to install the garden. The site must be open to the south, Tom explained, since that is the direction from which the sunlight comes in North America, and most vegetables need full exposure to the sun for at least six hours a day. Marty insisted that he knew where south was, because he was sure the sun set right over the neighbors' bedroom window he watched that every evening. He seemed quite annoyed when Tom pulled a compass out of his pocket and located true south, on the opposite side of the yard from the neighbors' boudoir.

But Marty regrouped quickly, declaring that the spot directly underneath the branches of the hemlock hedge was the sunniest in the yard. Tom looked up and, referring to his compass again, he settled on an area underneath and slightly to the north of the largest gap in the canopy of tree branches. Marty immediately an

---

* When Tom had stopped by the store to order the materials, the store salesman had insisted that each of their bags held 2 cubic feet of soil. A few minutes with tape measure and some high school mathematics had revealed that the actual capacity was two-thirds of a cubic foot. Tom had expected this discrepancy. For years he has bought trees and shrubs advertised as "5-gallon-sized," which meant that they had been grown in containers of 5-gallon capacity, when the actual capacity of the containers in which they were planted was closer to 5 quarts. A "1-quart" perennial comes in a pot that holds barely a cup. Tom figures that nurserymen operate according to a different system of measurement, sort of like a metric system created by capitalists.

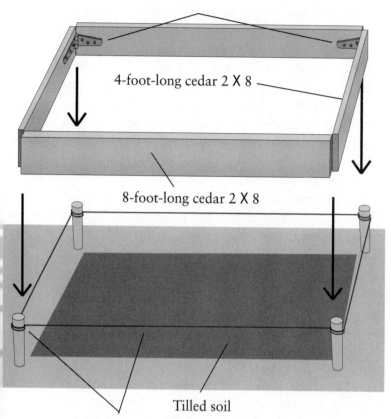

4-foot-long cedar 2 X 8

8-foot-long cedar 2 X 8

Tilled soil

stakes and string marking perimeter of garden bed

nounced that *that* spot, and in fact, virtually any other spot in the yard except for the one under the hemlock hedge, lay directly over his heirloom sewage treatment system. He described in lurid detail what would happen if they tapped that. Tom explained that they were going to build up, not dig down, so the cess pit would remain as safe as the mummy's tomb.

With stakes and string, Tom marked out a rectangle that measured 8 feet long and 4 feet wide, orienting it so that the long sides of the rectangle faced south and north. In this way, he ensured that the sun would pass over the bed from side to side rather than end to end. This would help to keep any tall plants in the bed from shading all of their fellows. Marty would have helped with this, except that he was on the phone, negotiating terms on what he said was sure to be a blockbuster. Personally, Tom didn't think that "Daily Double" was such a great title for a book of poetry.

As soon as the stakes were in and the string stretched, Tom demanded the rototiller. Marty announced that actually, he didn't have it, but he could get it. It was down the street at his neighbor's house. "Never rent if you can borrow—the watchword of the twenty-minute gardener."

The tiller proved to be something that looked like an eggbeater with a little gasoline engine grafted on to it. To Marty's amazement, Tom announced that it was perfect.

Cranking up the mini-tiller, which leaped and tugged like an eager puppy, Tom quickly scrambled the lawn within the string-and-stake rectangle. The tiller wouldn't bite deeper than an inch or two, but that was enough. Breaking up the turf was all that was needed.

When that task was completed, Tom set the tiller aside, and with Dan's help ("It's the *Boss*," Marty whispered as he pressed his ear to the phone, waving off all interruptions), Tom cut one of the 8-foot-long cedar boards in half. With the hinges, he next linked the four lengths of a 2 × 8 at the corners to make a collapsible 4-foot-by-8-foot bottomless box. He and Dan then dropped this over the rectangle of scrambled turf. Then, as Dan dumped bags of sand, manure, and topsoil into the box, pausing from time to time to toss in a chunk of the compressed peat, Tom ran the eggbeater tiller back and forth, mixing the contents as they rose ever higher.

Soon the cedar box was full to the brim. Tom sprinkled 4 cups of ground dolomitic limestone, and 2 cups of 5-10-5 fertilizer over its surface, mixed them in, and then turned off the tiller. There, in the middle of the lawn, stood a ready-to-plant raised bed.

"Oh, come on, give me a break!" Marty shouted. "No, no, not that kind," he whispered into the phone, his hand slipping down protectively over his kneecap. "I'll have it for you, I promise. Next week. Really." Then, switching off the phone, he sighed, and strolled over to inspect.

"Neat enough—that cedar is kind of country casual, you know? How's the soil?"

"It's as close to perfect as anything you can find. Really, what we created here is a good potting mix. The texture's nice and light, easy for the roots to penetrate, and there's lots of air but enough substance to anchor the plants well. With all that sand and the elevation of the raised bed, the drainage will be perfect. Water will soak right in, the peat will absorb as much as the plants need, and any excess will run down and out.

"The peat could make the soil too acidic, but the lime I added will take care of that. It will raise the pH so that the soil is just slightly acidic, and that's ideal for most vegetables. There's an extra benefit, too. I used dolomitic lime, which also adds a trace of magnesium to the soil, and most vegetables need that.

"The fertilizer will provide enough nutrients to get your first planting off to a good start. Its effect won't last long; synthetic fertilizers like that are fast-acting but they wash out of the soil within a month or two. By then, though, the plant roots will have found the manure, and they can feed on that."

"Well, I hope they're happy," Marty muttered, "given what it cost me to build this vegetable Xanadu. The bill from the home center came to $206.60, what with the delivery charge, and those are dollars I badly need just at the moment."

"You could have cut that bill by fifty dollars if you'd been willing to use pressure-treated lumber instead of cedar."

"Yeah, right," Marty snapped, "and fill my soil and vegetables full of the heavy metals and arsenic they use in that pressure-treated stuff to keep it from rotting. No, thank you."

"There's research that says the preservatives don't move out into the soil."

"And I'll just bet those studies were all funded by the companies that inject that stuff into lumber in the first place."

"So maybe you were right to pay extra for the cedar," Tom admitted. "Anyway, you saved some money by borrowing the rototiller. If you had rented it, though where you could rent a rototiller like that, I don't know, the fee would have added maybe forty dollars to the total.

"Actually, that's not much more than you would have paid to do a proper job of creating a conventional, in-the-ground vegetable patch. You still would have needed a rototiller, and you would have needed a larger one, which might have cost more. In most cases, you still would have had to buy the fertilizer and lime, peat and manure, and probably the sand, since the average suburban soil is nothing but a nutrient-poor, organic-deficient, compacted clay. So all you would have saved by doing things the hard way would have been the cost of the lumber and the topsoil."

"What do you care what this garden cost me?" Marty complained. "And what about all the work I've had to put in here today?"

"Marty, we saved hours and hours by adopting this prefab approach. If we had started your garden the old-fashioned way, it would have taken us most of the weekend to break up that hard-packed soil beneath your grass. And you'll save even more time in the future. Unlike an old-fashioned, do-it-yourself vegetable plot, the soil in this one is entirely free of weed seeds. If you mulch the bed after you plant it, it will stay that way, too. That means your vegetables will grow better because they don't have to compete with the weeds, and you won't spend any time doing what you like least: hoeing.

"You'll also save time on the watering, because this made-to-order soil with its perfect structure will absorb more easily any rainwater that falls on it. This soil won't crust over, and so the rain won't run off across the surface and be wasted. That means Nature will do most of your watering for you, here in Connecticut. When we do hit a stretch of dry weather, you'll find that the water you apply with a hose or sprinkler is also absorbed most efficiently, and the peat in the soil will act like a sponge to soak up the moisture and hold it until the plant roots take it. Even during a drought you'll water this garden far less than you would the average home-made bed.

"Here's a bonus: I made the bed narrow enough so that you can do all the planting, digging, and harvesting without ever stepping into it. You just reach in from the side. Not stepping on the soil means you won't compress it. The soil will stay light and loose. That means you won't have to dig it up again every time you re-plant. You'll save work and time that way, too.

"As for duplicating this, well, anybody can do it. You just call the home center and order up a delivery. The only hand tools you need are a handsaw, to cut that one two-by-eight, and a screw-driver to attach the hinges. The beauty of this design is that if you want to expand, you just drop in another identical bed beside the first one. You can keep adding others, too, until you reach the limit of your time and interest.* Once you've had some practice, I'll bet the installation would go faster, too. Even today, all it took us was—"

"Two hours and fifteen minutes," Marty said, looking at his watch and smiling. "At twenty minutes a day, that means we just used up a whole week's worth of gardening time. Looks like I'm due for a vacation."

* In fact, Marty did later install a second bed in his backyard, with Dan and Tom's help.

A Very Personal Yardstick

If 20-minute gardeners don't lay out their gardens to suit a trac-tor's wheelbase, what unit of measurement do they use? They use the natural unit; they use the length of their reach.

Think about it: where do you want to plant a vegetable? Where it matches some number on a tape measure, or where you can reach it without straining when you need to weed or sprin-kle fertilizer around it?

If you fit the average profile, you can reach about 2 feet easily, and 3 feet if you have to. But maybe you aren't average (nearly all of us are above average). To find out what your reach is, stretch a measuring tape out on the ground, kneel by one end of it, and see how far out along it you can put your fingertips without straining. That's your reach. Then see how far you can reach along the tape without falling on your face or throwing out your back. That's your stretch. Make a note of both these numbers.

These numbers are important because they define the dimensions of any garden bed you create. When you are laying out a bed that is accessible only from one side (as with a bed that lies at the foot of a fence or wall), then it should ideally measure no farther across than your reach, and never more than your stretch. If the bed you are making is accessible from both front and back, then it should measure twice your reach and not more than twice your stretch. In both cases, your goal is to design the bed so that you can reach into every part of it without stepping into it. Stepping on a bed compacts the soil in it, and plants don't grow well in compressed soil.

You'll save yourself lots of work just by keeping your feet out of the beds. Turn your soil thoroughly when you make a new bed, mix in lots of compost, and then keep the bed covered with some organic mulch. *Never, ever* step on that soil, and chances are you won't ever have to dig that bed again. Tom knows one great gardener who hasn't dug his vegetable garden in fourteen years.

Aesthetics may play a role in the way you lay out your vegetable garden, and this may cause you to vary from the ideal outlined above. When designing a bed for the foot of a tall wall, you may find that making the bed just a reach across leaves it looking anorexically skinny. In that case you may want to make the bed a full stretch across. Maybe, for some reason, you want to make a bed that's really wide, so wide that you can't reach all the way into its center while standing outside of it. That's okay—run a line of stepping stones or a path made of wooden boards down the middle of the bed, and stand on these when you need to work on the bed's center. That's fine; but don't step off the stones or path onto the adjacent soil.

Shopping for Soil

You may have grown up with the expression "cheap as dirt," but if you are still talking that way, it only shows how out of touch you are. Soil, and the ingredients of which it is composed, are not cheap these days. Also, unless as the buyer you beware, you are going to end up not with healthy soil but with used dirt. There's a big difference.

Soil is a complex blend of different sizes of rock particles, organic matter (humus), and a variety of minerals and salts from which the plants draw their nutrients. For healthy plant growth, the soil must contain not only all the essential nutrients, it must also have an acceptable texture. There must be air pockets between the clumps of soil particles so that air and water penetrate down to the plant roots.

This sounds complicated, and it is, but Nature will make all the arrangements for you if you give her a chance. Start out with a good mix of the basic ingredients, and bugs, worms, and microorganisms from your yard will move into your new garden bed and do the rest.

1. Sand. The function of this ingredient is to ensure a nice, loose texture in your soil. To accomplish this, what you want is the stuff that masons call "sharp" sand. They call this sand sharp because the grains have sharp angles; sharp sand feels gritty when you roll a pinch of it between your fingertip and thumb. Sharp sand is also coarse—the individual grains are large.

What you want to avoid when buying sand is what the local home center will be most anxious to sell you: fine-grained sand that was mined from some tropical beach. This sand is cheap, but in the centuries of rolling around in the surf, the individual grains have had all their corners rubbed off. This sand feels silky smooth between your fingertips, which sounds nice, except that this beach sand won't contribute much toward loosening your soil.

2. Soil. What most gardeners specify when they purchase a load of soil is topsoil. This is a term with wonderful connotations: it summons up visions of the black, rich cake that turned up as your horse-drawn plow busted the prairie sod. And that is topsoil, but so are a lot of other, less desirable soils.

Legally, topsoil is any soil that has been stripped off the surface of the ground, so it can range from a wonderful loam to a worn-out clay. Besides, since there is no regulation of this product, "topsoil" generally means any kind of soil that the supplier could get cheap and stuff into a plastic bag.

If you buy topsoil in bulk, by the truckload, or by the cubic yard from one of the guys who advertise in the local want-ad press, what you will probably get is the stuff that came out of a cellar hole at a construction site. This is passed through a mechanical sifter before it is delivered to you, so that it will be nice and fluffy. Until the first rainstorm, when the "topsoil" will compact into something very like concrete.

What are you to do? Forget topsoil. Instead, aim your shopping at the purchase of a good loam, an intermediate soil that is at once heavy enough to anchor your plants against the wind and retain the required nutrients and moisture, and loose enough so that roots, air, and water can penetrate. To make sure that what is billed as a loam is in fact that, demand a small sample. Moisten a handful of this—the soil should be thoroughly damp but not soaked, sort of like a wrung-out sponge. Squeeze the handful into a ball and drop it from waist height onto pavement. If the soil is a loam, the ball will shatter and the bits partially crumble. If the ball disintegrates entirely, the soil is too sandy to qualify as loam; if the ball hits with a splat, then what you've got is a clay or dense, heavy silt.

3. Sphagnum peat. This is the proper name for the brown, fibrous material that is more commonly called peat moss. It's important to get the name right, though, because there are two kinds of peat on the market, one good and the other bad.

The bad kind of peat is, alas, the American product, which is commonly called Michigan peat. Like all peat, this is the partially decomposed remains of organic materials that have marinated in the acidic waters of a bog. In the case of Michigan peat, the organic materials are sedges, twigs, reeds, or even ordinary humus that washed into or blew into a mixed wetland. This peat may be as little as 20 percent organic material and up to 80 percent ordinary soil. It has limited value as a soil additive, and to harvest it involves the strip-mining of the bog.

The good kind of peat is sphagnum peat, virtually all of which comes from northern Canada. This, as the name suggests, derives from partially decomposed sphagnum moss. What you get in a bale of sphagnum peat is 95 to 99 percent organic. It helps to break up dense soils into smaller crumbs, and so improve its drainage. Yet at the same time, sphagnum peat will absorb and hold thirty times its own weight in water, so it is the best material to correct a sandy soil's tendency to dry out. What's more, the Canadian-peat producers have organized themselves into a professional association which, among other things, has been working to ensure that the sphagnum-peat bogs are given a chance to renew themselves, and are not exhausted.

The one disadvantage of sphagnum peat is that it is sterile, completely lacking in nutrients, which brings us to the next-to-last soil-making ingredient.

4. **Compost.** Everybody knows what this is, right? Except that to define compost exactly gets a little tricky. It's the decomposed remains of organic debris. In a backyard heap, you know what sort of debris went into the making of your compost. But in a commercially produced compost, the debris can be anything from leaves to food wastes to manures to factory by-products. This makes the quality of commercial composts uneven and unpredictable.

Those composts that have been approved for home landscaping are free from dangerous toxins, but they may be relatively rich in nutrients, or they may be nearly as sterile as peat. They may not even be real compost. Some producers have been known to bag their compost before the materials in it have finished the decomposition process. You won't be able to tell this by looking at the product. You'll know it when your plants turn into slackers. They'll fail to grow and sometimes turn yellow. That's because the immature compost is finishing up its decomposition in your soil and to do this it grabs the nutrients that the plants would otherwise use. Eventually, when the compost really is compost, it will start re-releasing those nutrients, but that's small comfort to you when you have lost a season's vegetables.

Other than the compost you make and age yourself, the safest variety is the type your town makes (if it is smart) from stacking the leaves it collects from your curb. Usually, town residents may have that compost for free. If you buy the bagged sort, mix it into your soil well before you plant. If, for example, you dig the compost into your beds in the fall, after your last harvest, it will have several months to mature before your spring planting.

2🕐-MINUTE PROJECT:
Farming the Heap

When confronted with the facts, Tom had to admit that Marty was right. The gardening style Tom had grown up with was misguided. But as Tom later learned from his wife, Suzanne, it can be made to work.

She grew up in the hills of western Massachusetts, on eight bucolic acres surrounded by farms. It was a landscape filled with rural icons: the perfume of manure, scratching chickens eyed by skinny, predatory barn cats, whitewashed tractor tires planted with petunias, and here and there the rusting carcasses of tractors and pickup trucks.

Suzanne's father was a schoolteacher, but also a gardener of the old school. He had clearly studied with the same traditionalists who indoctrinated Tom. Every spring Suzanne's father would plant a huge garden and then abandon it. Even now, many years after the roar of the rototiller has been stilled, Tom and Suzanne still come across lonely, stubborn sprouts of asparagus and rhubarb when cutting brush around the family home.

Suzanne's father enjoyed his gardening, and his six daughters and wife enjoyed watching him have a good time. Besides, they did reap a harvest every year, though not from the garden.

Instead, it came from the compost heap, which Suzanne's father established as soon as he began to garden. This wasn't a high-tech, fast-composting heap that steamed and cooked; this was a garden-variety pile of yard debris and vegetable waste from the kitchen. Given that Suzanne's family is Irish, the latter included lots of potato peelings, and even a few potatoes that had languished in the bottom of the bin until they were no longer fit for the pot. Along with everything else, these went onto the heap, only to be buried by subsequent deposits.

In the loose, moist heart of the heap, the spoiled potatoes would sprout. These new plants flourished. Maybe this compost wasn't "mature" but there was so much of it that the little potato plants still found all the nutrients they needed. As their shoots lengthened, the family would unintentionally hill up around them by dumping on more kitchen and yard waste. Suzanne still recalls the day every fall in which she would attack the heap with an old coal shovel—the heap was loose and easy digging, luckily—to turn up the new tubers that the discarded potatoes had made.

Tom has used this same style of cultivation to raise melons and pumpkins. These were horticultural lagniappe—the plants sprang up unexpectedly from seeds that had found their way into the kitchen waste. Though this sowing was unplanned, it proved very successful. The decomposition of the materials in the compost heap not only produced an abundance of nutrients, it also generated heat, gently warming the plants' roots and the air around their leaves. Both melons and pumpkins are warm-weather crops, and they clearly appreciated the southern ambiance that the compost heap injected into a New England landscape.

Are there any secrets to farming a heap? Moisten the heap by watering it whenever it dries out—this will speed the composting as well as benefit the plants. Be sure also to put the compost heap out in a sunny spot rather than hiding it in the bushes behind the garage like you usually do. Actually, the middle of your vegetable garden is an excellent location; if you have located your garden properly, that spot will be sunny and, of course, it will also be convenient. Disposing of garden wastes won't involve a trek to the back forty, and bringing compost to the garden will be just a matter of dipping your shovel into the heap and then flinging.

One problem with setting the compost heap out in midyard or midgarden is that most heaps are just that: an untidy dump. But you can easily remedy that by enclosing the compostables in a cylinder of wire fencing. The cylinder should measure 3 to 4 feet in diameter and be 3 to 4 feet high. If you use fencing with a coarse mesh, you can plant right through it and let your plants clamber up the outside of the heap. Tomatoes particularly like this treatment. They'll usually hide the heap entirely by midsummer if you give the lengthening stems some support by tying them to the wire with soft twine.

Crops that respond well to this lazy man's garden include not only potatoes, tomatoes, melons, and pumpkins but also cucumbers, zucchinis and squashes, and sweet potatoes. For the best results, plant only the old-fashioned "vining" types of these plants (you'll find these in the heirloom seed catalogs listed in "Sources for Plants and Seeds"). These make long, sprawling stems that are natural climbers. Most modern varieties of these vegetables have been specially bred to produce "bush" plants. That is, they grow into tight little clusters of short stems. These fit more neatly into a conventional garden of broadly spaced rows. Bush plants don't wander irresponsibly into a neighbor's space, nor do they sprawl over the paths.

If neatness is important to you, by all means plant those new bush vegetables. But don't expect them to clamber up a compost heap, turning it into a mountain of lush greenery and effortless harvest.

MARTY'S FIRST 2🕐-MINUTE VEGETABLE PROJECT

Marty remembers as his proudest moment his discovery of the law of relativity. Actually, Marty didn't really discover this. Some guy named Albert Einstein did. But Marty *was* the first to apply this branch of theoretical physics to garden design.

Marty's breakthrough came when he recognized that most people let the size of their yard dictate the amount of gardening they do. If they have a little yard, they fill it up by planting a few plants. And if they have a big yard, then they plant a lot of plants. In other words, they let space be the decisive factor in the gardening equation.

Marty realized that for him (and for anyone without an inherited income and a staff), time was actually the fixed number. He knew that during the average day, all he could reasonably give to his garden was the amount of time he would otherwise spend watching the rerun of a sitcom. If you leave out the ads (and who wants to include them?) that comes to twenty minutes. That should be enough. After all, on television, that's enough time to fall in love, solve a mystery, shoot a bunch of bad guys, and save the free world.

But to do all of your gardening in twenty minutes a day, you have to design a garden differently. You design it to fit the time, not the space. That means you plant only as many plants and fill only as much space as you can reasonably manage in the allotted time. Later on, if you really get on top of the first planting, you may have time for a second one. But you build the garden incrementally, project by project.

For his first solo vegetable-gardening project he decided against filling any of the space in his yard (an Einsteinian coup!). Instead, Marty was going to stay where there were no bugs and no rabbits or deer, where it was always cool and never rained. In short, he was going to stay in the kitchen and raise designer sprouts.

Marty promised to keep notes. Tom knew that Marty was sincere, but that he was also wrong. Left to himself, Marty would forget the record keeping for a week, then reconstruct a bunch of recollections in a hurry, and finish by crashing his computer and wiping the whole mess (along with everything else) off his hard drive. So Tom asked his truly organized scientist-wife, Suzanne, to supervise Marty's research.

She began by insisting that they create a computer spreadsheet on which to record the data. This she did on her own machine, which Marty was not allowed to touch, or even be in the same room with. Suzanne knew that Marty's most notable achievement as a computer programmer had come when he installed Lotus Notes in the laptop his boss gave him for working at home. Marty swears that he followed the directions exactly, but every time he tried to check his e-mail, his computer would dial 911 and the police would come. Suzanne didn't want any electronic emergencies, so she handled the inputting.

After setting up the record keeping, Suzanne told Marty that he needed a half dozen 1-quart canning jars, a box of rubber bands, and a yard of cheesecloth. These things are fundamental to what she calls the "old hippie method" of seed sprouting. Nowadays, you can buy an expensive electrical sprout maker (it'll fit onto the shelf right beside your bread machine and your gelato maker), but a machine lacks the charm and the memories. Besides, Suzanne figured that anything reminiscent of the summer of love was sure to appeal to Marty.

Actually, the shopping list only upset Marty. He informed Suzanne that as far as he knew, there was no cannery in Westport, and that he didn't know how to weave cloth out of cheese. So Suzanne made a trip to the hardware store and one to the fabric shop, and picked up the jars and cloth. Marty brought rubber bands home from his office.

When Suzanne asked Marty what he was planning to sprout, he showed her an old packet of marigold seeds that he had found in his garage. Suzanne then borrowed a *Johnny's Selected Seeds* catalog from Tom, and ordered a collection designed for sprouting: seeds of wheat, alfalfa, broccoli, canola, kale, onions, and radish. She bought a quarter-ounce packet of each type.

As soon as her seed order arrived, she showed Marty how to start the sprouting. She dumped 2 tablespoons of wheat seeds into a jar, added a cup of water, then covered the jar's mouth with a square of doubled-over cheesecloth. She stretched a rubber band around the neck of the jar to fasten the cheesecloth in place. The seeds were left to soak for twenty-four hours. Then Suzanne swirled the water around in the jar and dumped it out into the sink; the cheesecloth ensured that the wheat seeds stayed in the jar. After washing the seeds once more in this fashion, she set the jars full of moistened seeds in the oven of Marty's stove—she explained that the pilot light would keep the seeds slightly warm, which encourages sprouting, and that the darkness would make the resulting sprouts more tender.

Loading up the other jars took a bit more than twenty minutes. Marty forgot to stretch a rubber band around the cheesecloth covering one jar's mouth, and it took a while to clean up the seeds he splashed all over the sink and counter. Then, too, there was some discussion about the amount of seed to add to each jar. Marty was all for filling the jars with seeds and getting the whole project over with all at once. Suzanne, however, had actually read the instructions that came with the seeds and she knew that aside from the wheat seeds (which expand only modestly as they sprout), you shouldn't add more than 1 tablespoon of seeds to a quart jar, because that 1 tablespoon would expand into a cup or more of sprouts. Crowding the sprouts would inhibit their growth and encourage molds and other unwanted visitors.

A minor setback occurred the next morning when Marty made muffins. He told Suzanne that he wasn't angry, he was sure it was just an innocent oversight on her part, but she had not told him that he had to remove the sprouts from the oven before turning the heat up to 350°. By now, though, Marty had the opening step of sprouting down cold, and Suzanne hardly had to explain anything as she prepared the second generation of jars.

Once in the morning and again in the evening, Suzanne poured a cup or so of water into each jar to rinse the seeds, and then strained it out through the cheesecloth. Marty got to be quite handy at this, and really was a help. Rinsing seven jars of seeds took only five minutes or so each time, ten minutes total each day. As Marty pointed out, he was saving half of his 20-minute allotment of daily gardening time. That should be plenty of time, he observed cheerfully, for Suzanne to type her observations into her computer.

We won't share her spreadsheet printout with you, as even Tom finds it overwhelming. Instead, we'll just hit the high spots.

Overall, this was as quick and easy a type of gardening as could be had. The wheat, alfalfa, broccoli, and radish seeds all began to send out shoots within a day of the initial soaking. Actually, the wheat and radish seeds had virtually all sprouted within two days, whereupon Suzanne moved their jars from the oven to a windowsill so that they would turn from albino white to a more appetizing green. As soon as the sprouts colored, she'd store them in the refrigerator.

The alfalfa seeds were ready for salads and sandwiches within four days; the kale and canola took seven, and the onions came in last at twelve. All of these had their season on the windowsill, too, where they stayed for a day so that the sunlight could give them a more appetizing green hue. Then they were stored, ready to eat, in the refrigerator.

The increase was impressive. The original tablespoon or 2 of seed produced jars filled with 1 to 1½ cups of sprouts; alfalfa was the winner here, a tablespoon of its seed yielding 2 full cups of sprouts. What was really remarkable, though, was the range of flavors and textures. The wheat sprouts were pale green and chewy, sugar sweet; the broccoli, canola, and kale differed only subtly, all having a mild flavor of broccoli. Of these Marty preferred the broccoli sprouts, because he had read about research at Johns Hopkins University which indicated that making these a regular part of your diet would protect you against tumors, something that is on Marty's mind a lot.

Tom liked the tangy, peppery flavor of the radish sprouts; he had to admit, though, that Suzanne's onion sprouts were by far the most elegant. These had smooth black seeds the size of peppercorns, and when spread over a salad, the sprouts looked almost like caviar. The flavor was like a milder, more delicate onion, a sort of essence of onion. They were particularly beautiful spread over a cracker topped with chèvre cheese and a sweet red pepper slice. Suzanne brought this arrangement to her son's opening at the local pottery gallery.

Marty judged this sprouting project to be a great success, and said that he would repeat it anytime, as long as Suzanne did her part. Going without muffins for a couple of weeks was a small price to pay for safety from cancer. Suzanne, however, took her seeds and jars home, and has set up business for herself. Marty still enjoys a share of the harvest, but at a price. He has had to promise that he will never, ever go near Suzanne's lab, her computer, or her sprout factory. That's okay with Marty; he's too busy with e-mail, anyway.

A 2🕐-MINUTE FOOTNOTE

Marty isn't the only person farming a Connecticut kitchen. Our friend Sydney Eddison is doing the same thing out west in Newtown, except that she's doing it with an English twist.

Sydney is a horticultural national treasure, an expert gardener and accomplished writer who has the gift of sharing not only information but also excitement. In books such as *A Passion for Daylilies* and *The Self-Taught Gardener,* she manages to communicate not only how to raise all manner of plants, but also makes you understand why you want to. She, with the help of her husband, Martin, also makes a memorable cress sandwich.

Though long ago transplanted, Martin's roots are English, and he maintains certain traditions. Teatime, for example, is observed in the Eddison household. Part of this observance are sandwiches filled with fresh cress. And because fresh cress—not watercress, but curly cress (for the distinction between these two, see Chapter 4, page 80)—is not available in the local markets, the Eddisons raise their own. They grow it indoors, so that they have cress on tap year-round.

The necessary equipment couldn't be simpler: all that is

needed is a baking sheet with a raised lip, a roll of paper towels, a clean plastic spray bottle, and a packet of cress seeds. To economize, you can order the cress seed by the quarter pound. That seems like a lot of seed, but you'll use it all once you taste the results.

Line the pan with a triple layer of paper towels. Next, wet the towels thoroughly and pour off any excess water. Sprinkle cress seed thickly into the pan, and set it in a warm spot. Be sure to keep the seed-encrusted toweling moist; a daily or semi-daily misting with water will take care of that.

Within a day, the seeds will cover themselves with a gelatinous coat and you will smell the distinctive, slightly sour odor of germination. Little white hooks will emerge from the seeds—these are the cress roots. Within another day or so, shoots will emerge from the seeds, and in about ten days, the cress will stand about 2 inches tall. That means it's time to harvest your crop, which you do with a pair of ordinary household shears.

To turn the cress clippings into sandwiches, take very thin slices (one-eighth inch thick is ideal, if you can manage that) of good white bread, and butter each slice on one side. Then pile a half-inch layer of cress onto the buttered side of one slice, and cover with another slice set buttered side down. Gently compress the sandwich, cut off its crusts, and slice it diagonally into two triangles.

To properly enjoy your cress sandwiches, Sydney says, a cup of good tea is essential. Rinse the inside of your teapot with boiling water, empty it, and dump in a teaspoon of loose tea leaves for each cup of tea to be made. Then fill the pot with water that has just come to a brisk, rolling boil. Cover and let steep for three to five minutes. Place teapot and teacup on a tray with your plate of sandwiches and a white linen napkin. Take this over by the fire, pull up a chair, and enjoy English gardening at its very best.

Chapter 3

Winners and Losers

There's no point backing a horse that can't or won't run, Marty says with a weary sort of wisdom. Similarly, a busy or lazy gardener (and we admit to being both) would never give space in his plot to a vegetable underachiever. To garden in twenty minutes a day, you have to be elitist.

But how do you handicap a vegetable? How can you tell the winners from the losers? Size of harvest alone is not a reliable guide. If it were, then the zucchini would be the only vegetable worth growing, whereas actually, the real skill in growing zucchini lies in frustrating its procreative urge (see page 53).

Obviously, a winner crop does have to be a reliable bearer.

You want to have something to show for your work at the end of the day. But often, a small harvest is preferable, as long as the crop is easy to grow and matures quickly. Arugula, for example, looks like the old 20-pound weakling on the back cover of a comic book. It makes a scrawny tuft that the botanical illiterate might mistake for dandelion leaves (or vice versa—ask Marty). One plant of arugula will never fill a salad bowl like a healthy head of lettuce will. But whereas that lettuce is likely to need ninety days to reach picking time, a sowing of arugula will start providing fresh greens in three weeks. This quick growing habit makes arugula an especially flexible crop: you can tuck a few seeds into a spot left by some other crop you just pulled, and keep your garden in full production. We will always grow lettuce, but we rely on arugula.

Another mark of a fruit or vegetable winner, at least for the 20-minute gardener, is impact. By that we mean gustatory impact, though we have happy boyhood memories of the other kinds of impact a vegetable can provide: the grenadelike explosion of a tomato on the seat of your sister's jeans, or the thrilling death-splat of a neighbor's pumpkin when hurled off a stoop. But to return to the present: a winner vegetable has to have exceptional gustatory impact, and that means it must offer a particularly distinctive flavor.

This flavor may be so powerful that just a little bit of the vegetable will transform your whole meal. An example of that is those bird's-eye peppers Tom likes to grow. These are wild peppers from south Texas that bear fruits no bigger than a pea. Just one, though, is enough to add an unforgettable rush to an otherwise prosaic meal.

Equally, a winner's flavor may be subtle, but still so memorable that just a bite or two can change your whole day. Such a flavor may even come to define a season. Fresh asparagus has that effect on Tom. When early spring brings the first delicate, straw-thin spears, he is immediately twenty years old again. He's broke but hungry in a way he never will be again, and shopping at the Italian market in the Bronx where the year's first asparagus sold for 60¢ a pound. With an egg, lemon, and butter to make hollandaise sauce, he has a $2 dinner that distills the flavor of April.

In addition, the winner vegetable may offer quality that you cannot find in the store. Besides the notorious example of tomatoes and apples, there are countless less obvious ones. Chinese cabbage, for instance, bok choy, is just filler in the form you get it from the grocery. It's green, crispy stuff to fill out a stir-fry, a vehicle for sauces and spice. Grow the different varieties yourself, though, and you will be reassured that the people who invented cash and explosives had another hot idea when they took up cabbage. If you are willing to start your own plants from seed, you'll find that there are many different permutations of the basic bok choy, and that each has a distinctive flavor. In fact, if you are like Marty, you'll soon become the sort of bok choy gourmet who uses his knowledge to make a fuss at restaurants and thoroughly overawe colleagues at business lunches.

One last quality that every winner shares: it's easy to grow. This means that the winners list changes from region to region. You can grow apples in the Deep South, for example, but these Northern trees aren't happy there. They are extra-prone to diseases, and they miss the winter cold—only a few lackluster varieties of apples will set fruit and bear at all where frost is uncommon. That means *you* are a loser if you grow apples in Alabama. The winners in your neighborhood are growing 'simmons.

The winners list will vary not only with climate but also with the local soil. This may vary from nearly pure sand to a dense clay or a sticky silt, but that really doesn't matter as long as you add enough compost—Irish potatoes are martyrs to scab in alkaline (limy) soils. If your soil is alkaline, however, you have an advantage as a cabbage and broccoli grower, because the worst disease of that family of crops, clubroot, doesn't thrive in alkaline soils. Of course, if you took our advice and built an out-of-the-box garden, your garden soil won't match the stuff in the ground all around the bed. But soil pH—its acidity or alkalinity—tends to be broadly regional, with the tendency toward one extreme or the other remaining typical throughout a geologic district that may cover several states. If you live in a region of alkaline soils, the bagged stuff at the local discount center is likely to be alkaline, too, since it was probably collected not too far away.

Anyway, even if you start with a nonalkaline soil mix, in such a region, alkalinity will gradually creep in. It's in the water from the local reservoir or your well, so you add alkalinity every time you water. Alkalinity will also wash into the bed with runoff from the surrounding soil when it rains, and it will percolate up from below as the sun draws moisture up and out through the surface of the soil on hot days. So wherever you are, try to go with whatever grows well locally. Remember the 20-minute gardener's mantra: only the hyperactive and truly stupid try to outwit Nature.

The Acid Test of Successful Gardening

Gardening gurus are always advising their audiences to have a sample of their soil analyzed at a soil testing laboratory, and no one ever does. It's the audience's loss, because sending a soil sample off to a testing laboratory will get you a detailed prescription for how to handle your garden soil. That will save you money and time that would otherwise be wasted on unnecessary fertilizations, and it will also guarantee bigger and better harvests.

Well, so what? *We* are not going to waste our time giving you good advice that you will ignore. But we are going to plead with you to perform one simple soil test yourself—a pH test. You can get the necessary materials at any garden center or nursery; they'll cost you just a few dollars, and the work will take only a few minutes. In return, you'll reap an essential clue about what you should grow in your garden, and how to treat your soil.

This "pH" is a chemist's term, which we won't bother to explain (Marty's note: Be honest, Tom—you *can't* explain it). In practice, though, it is a measure of the relative acidity or alkalinity of the soil. Those terms you should remember from Mr. Wizard. He would mix an alkaline such as baking soda with an acid such as vinegar, and the result would be some violent foaming reaction.

You won't be having any fun like that in the garden. But the plants care about the pH of the soil, even if you don't. Some plants like alkaline soil, while others like an acid one, and if you mismatch the plant and soil, you won't get much of a harvest.

So how do you tell what the pH of your soil is? First you take a sample. To do this, you first scrape aside any surface debris from three different spots in your vegetable bed. Then dig a 6-inch-deep hole in each with a stainless steel or plastic trowel, and collect a long, vertical slice of soil from the side of each hole. Mix all these soil slices together in a clean plastic bucket. That's your soil sample.

How you test this sample depends on the type of testing kit you buy. Generally, you mix a prescribed amount of the soil sample with water and then add a few drops of some reagent. This causes the soil and water suspension to turn color, and by matching the color to the right one on a chart that the kit provides, you get a fairly accurate reading of your vegetable garden's average soil pH.

This pH is expressed as a number ranging from 1 to 9, with numbers below 7.0 indicating an acidic pH and numbers above 7.0 indicating an alkaline pH. The farther the number is from 7.0 (which is a neutral pH), the more acidic or alkaline your soil is. A pH of 6.0, for example, indicates a very mildly acidic soil, while 4.5 indicates a soil so acidic that little besides blueberries will grow in it.

Most fruits and vegetables are fairly adaptable plants. Certainly, all of the ones we recommend fit that description. As a rule, vegetables and fruits grow well in a soil whose pH falls between 6.0 and 7.5. If your soil's pH falls outside of this range—that is, if it is more acidic or alkaline—you can do one of two things. You can select acid-tolerant or alkaline-tolerant crops from the lists we have included below. Or, you can moderate the pH of your soil.

If your soil is excessively acidic, you can raise its pH by mixing in ground limestone. The amount you'll need to add will vary with the type of soil, but on average, digging in 5 pounds of ground limestone per 100 square feet of bed (1.5 pounds for one of our 8' × 4' beds) should raise the pH one full point (from 5.0 to 6.0, for example). If your soil is excessively alkaline, you can lower its pH by digging in sulfur; 1 to 2 pounds of powdered sulfur per 100 square feet of bed (one-third to two-thirds pounds in our 8' × 4' beds) should lower the pH by one point. When in doubt, err on the side of caution. Overdosing the soil is only going to cause the pH to swing toward the opposite extreme. And don't expect instant results—depending on the weather, it may take weeks or months for your additives to change the soil chemistry.

Because this process of adjustment is an imprecise one, you should check the results. After adding sulfur or limestone, water the bed well, wait a month, and then test the soil again. You may find that your initial treatment was too conservative, and that your bed needs a bit more lime or sulfur.

Usually, the effects of this kind of soil treatment last several years, especially if you have followed our advice and built one of Marty's no-fuss raised beds. By holding the soil separate and somewhat above the surrounding soil, a raised bed slows the invasion of acids or alkalinity from adjoining soils. But if left to itself, your soil will gradually revert to type. So every couple of years, test the pH again, and re-treat as necessary.

Vegetables and Fruits That Tolerate Alkaline Soils

Apples	Carrots	Peas
Asparagus	Corn	Spinach
Cabbage	Lettuce	Tomatoes

Vegetables and Fruits That Tolerate or Prefer a Distinctly Acid Soil (pH 5.5 or Less)

Beans	Peppers	Strawberries
Blueberries	Radishes	Sweet potatoes
Irish potatoes	Squash	Tomatoes*
Mustard		

*Prefer a neutral to slightly alkaline soil but tolerate acidity.

We've described what separates the winners from the losers in the 20-minute garden, but because you may still be confused by this concept (Marty is, but in his case it's hard to distinguish the horticultural confusion from general confusion), we've decided to illustrate with examples. That way, you can see what make a particular plant qualify for the winner's circle.

The only problem with this plan that we can see is that Tom and Marty cannot agree on what qualifies as a winner. Tom, for example, finds beans fascinating. That, as far as Marty is concerned, says all that need be said about Tom. Marty feels that a winners list could begin and end with cherry tomatoes. That, says Tom, is because cherry tomatoes are the beginning and end of the list of vegetables Marty can grow. So we've actually settled for two lists of winners: five of Tom's and six of Marty's (he always has to have the last word).

To these we've added a third list: six vegetables so difficult to grow or so culinarily unsatisfactory that even Tom and Marty can agree that these are losers. As Marty points out, it's always easier to pick losers than winners.

Tom's List of Garden Champions

1. Asparagus. You may not have spent your student days in the Bronx, but the year's first, pencil-thin spears of asparagus still can be the high point of your spring. You'll never find a flavor or a texture like theirs in the sumo wrestler asparagi (asparaguses? asparageese?) you'll get at the local supermarket. The homegrown type combines tenderness with snap and has a taste of green that is as essential a pleasure of the spring season as crocuses, Easter eggs, and the contract disputes of baseball players.

Nothing could be easier to grow, either. We'll deal with this at length in a future chapter (see "Perennial Pleasures," pages 173–77). Still, we must note here that asparagus flourishes almost everywhere in the United States except along the Gulf Coast. What's more, it really is what all those flowers you order from the glossy catalogs are supposed to be: genuinely perennial. Planting a bed of asparagus roots takes a bit more work than the planting of most other 20-minute vegetables, but do it right and you'll still be picking baskets of spears when your grandchildren are grown (if they haven't moved you to a home, put your faithful dog in the pound, and sold the homestead out from under you, the rats).

This plant suffers from one serious disease, asparagus rust, which (Marty's idea to the contrary) has nothing to do with the iron in your plants and which cannot be cured by scraping and painting. It's a fungal infection, and the best way to fight it is to avoid it by planting disease-resistant types of asparagus such as 'Jersey Knight'. There's also a beetle that specializes in afflicting this crop (called, you guessed it, asparagus beetle), but a dusting or two of a natural plant extract called rotenone will quickly kill it. Also be sure to remove all the asparagus stems after they brown in the fall, since they provide a haven in which beetles like to winter.

A bonus: the spears you don't pick will grow into 4-foot-tall, lacy, fernlike things that are truly beautiful, and that make a wonderful backdrop for flowers, yard statuary, or whatever. Tom would grow asparagus even if it weren't so good to eat.

2. Hot peppers. When Columbus discovered America (much to the surprise of all the indigenes), he didn't find the gold he was looking for, nor the East Asian spices. He did, however, find something he promptly mislabeled pepper. In fact, *Capsicum annuum,* the plant he borrowed from the "Indians" (who had been growing it for thousands of years), has nothing to do with the stuff that the waiter with the phallic grinder inflicts on you at restaurants. Just what a winner it is, though, can be deduced from the fact that within fifty years of its "discovery," it had been adopted by Old World gardeners as far away as China, Africa, and Southeast Asia.

It was hot peppers, of course, that all the nonindigenes wanted. Green peppers seem to be an invention of 1950s America, something to stuff with minute rice and hamburger and set out on a school cafeteria tray. Without proper trays (or even cafeterias, for that matter), the foreigners couldn't appreciate green peppers. What they craved was the excitement of chilies.

Jogging, finally, taught WASP Americans to appreciate chilies too. For a long time, Tom couldn't figure out why people like Marty were always dressing in Lycra to trot along the local roadways. Then he read in a magazine that prolonged exercise ("excessive" is Tom's word for it) causes the brain to release endorphins, opiatelike chemicals that dull the pain caused by this behavior. Endorphins not only dull pain, however, they also induce a sense of well-being. It seems that endorphins are actually physically addictive.

Just say no. Tom does. Instead, he gets his endorphins from chilies. The searing heat they inflict fools the brain into thinking that you are jogging, even when you are stretched out in an easy chair with a beer in your hand, and the brain reacts accordingly. Besides, hot peppers offer all sorts of health and spiritual benefits. We deal with those elsewhere (see Chapter 5, pages 112–14).

In general, peppers are one of the most accommodating crops, flourishing in a sunny, well-drained bed or a tub of rich potting soil or even a window box. When in fruit, peppers are handsome, too. Set a plant of 'Cayenne', 'Thai', or bird's-eye peppers amid your flowers, and the fruits will function there much as they do in the pot, adding a warmth that you'll find addictive.

Caution: Marty insists on adding a warning here. He tells a long, sad story, most of which we will spare you, but the gist of it is this. A smitten young man once invited the love of his life over for dinner, and to impress her, he cooked the meal. Given that he a) did not make a habit of cooking, and b) was (and is) averse to reading directions, this young man made an inadvertent substitution in the recipe. In place of the cup of chopped green pepper he was supposed to add to the main dish, he added a cup of chopped jalapeños. As a result, the dish was incandescent.

Worse yet, Marty claims that the young man was so embarrassed by the mistake that he pretended to like the dish that way and actually consumed a portion (the lady, apparently, had more sense). The essential oil from the pepper, the capsaicin that gives peppers their heat, permeated the young man's whole body so that for days afterward he could be handled only with pot holders.

Tom figures he will take his chances.

3. **Alpine strawberries.** The flavor of homegrown strawberries is great, but the common, garden varieties are a pain in the neck to grow. Like something from an old horror movie, their hobby is self-cloning. Garden strawberries send out long, creepy shoots ("runners," these are called, and they do move fast) along the surface of the ground that root at the tips and sprout new plants. Sounds useful, right? Yeah, except that soon you have strawberries where you don't want them and none of the plants are making much fruit because they are devoting all their energy to making even more plants.

At that point, the traditional gardener institutes an elaborate scheme of strawberry discipline. He's on his hands and knees, snipping off most of the shoots as they appear, and training the rest to make "daughter" plants in the right places. After a full year of training, the traditional gardener gets a summer of berries and then he has to dig the whole thing up and start over again with new plants. This is why strawberries are most often grown by migrant laborers.

Meanwhile, the 20-minute gardener is picking strawberries with a better flavor every year, and without replanting or worrying about shoots and daughters (except, maybe, of the human kind). That's because the 20-minute gardener grows alpine strawberries. These are an older, European relative of the modern garden strawberry. They have smaller fruits—the berries measure a half inch or less across—but the flavor is more intense, and alpine strawberries bear throughout the summer and early fall. Most kinds, including 'Alexandria', 'Charles V', and 'Ruegen', as well as those sold generically as 'Alpine Strawberry', produce no runners, and these plants are truly perennial, continuing to flourish and bear for many years. What's more, alpine strawberries are relatively shade tolerant, bearing fruit even in spots where they receive no more than four hours of sun a day.

Actually, these neat, compact tufts of foliage and fruit are ideal for sticking into odd corners of the garden. Tom has used them to edge flower beds, and they are perfect for this since they like a loose, organic-rich, fertile soil—the same type of soil that most flowers prefer. Or tuck alpine strawberries into the empty spots around the base of deep-rooted shrubs, or at the foot of a sunny fence or wall. By filling the soil with their roots, the alpine strawberries will keep such areas weed free, and they provide fruit as a bonus.

Most likely, little of that fruit will make it into the house. Alpine strawberries are something you pick and eat in passing. If you do manage to collect a cup, however, eat them the way they do in Rome. Wash the berries, put them in a cut-glass dish, and moisten them with a light and fruity white wine.

One last tip: there is a white-fruited alpine strawberry, 'Pineapple Crush'. The berries are supposed to have a pineapple flavor, but the real advantage is that the birds do not recognize them as strawberries and so do not molest them.

4. Gourds. Tom first planted bottle gourds and their southern Italian relative, *cucuzzi,* because (as described in *The 20-Minute Gardener*) they are one of the few flowers whose schedule matches his own. Unlike most flowers, which bloom during the day while Tom is always working, gourds wait until evening to unfurl their flowers. He really enjoyed the perfumed, white blossoms, which is good because the gourds were soon an important presence in his yard.

Tom planted his gourds on the south side of his house, at the foot of a trellis that separates the kitchen and living room door from a black-topped driveway. That spot is a real sun trap and the gourds responded by growing like kudzu. Sometimes the vines would extend themselves by twelve inches in a single night. In a matter of weeks they had buried the arbor, and had gone on to swallow up the kitchen door—to go in or out, you had to swing hrough the vines like Tarzan. One cucuzzi vaulted up into a earby tree, and soon climbed to the top of that, too.

This suggested another use for the gourds, as a sort of vegetable whiteout. Every gardener makes mistakes from time to time. You plant a shrub that, in fact, isn't hardy enough to withstand the ocal winters. Or you plant a bed of annuals too early in the spring nd a late frost kills them all. Such blunders leave embarrassing aps that are going to excite comment. Unless you get smart. Do vhat you do at the office: if you can't blame a blunder on someone lse, hide it fast. And the best thing for hiding almost anything in he garden is a gourd. It'll bury the mistake in a matter of weeks, nd when it has made its lush blanket of leaves and night-blooming lowers, you can claim you did it all on purpose. That's what your oss does, isn't it?

Given all of these virtues, it seems excessive that gourds should lso be good to eat. But they are, and we have included recipes at his chapter's end (see page 60). What's more, the birdhouse gourds ou can dry and turn into (what else?) birdhouses. Tom and his son Matthew are gradually developing a bird condominium around the ront yard with theirs.

. **Radishes.** If Marty had his way, there would be no radishes, or t least no radish roots. He'd sprout all the seeds rather than plant hem. Tom likes radish sprouts, too; they're great in salads and andwiches. But he finds radishes too valuable an aid to gardening o waste them as sprouts.

There are two types of radishes: spring and winter radishes. Winter radishes are the Asian kinds that are often called daikons; hey are well worth growing, but spring radishes are the real win-ers. This group includes the familiar red, globular rooted kinds, hough there are also spring radishes with thumb-shaped white oots, and a globe-rooted strain called 'Easter Egg' that produces oots in pretty shades of pink, purple, and white as well as red.

The real virtue of spring radishes is that they grow in fast for-vard. Spring radishes sprout just a couple of days after you sow the seeds, and are ready for picking in four or five weeks. Thi makes radishes an ideal understudy. You can fill the spot you ar saving for tomatoes with an early planting of radishes, and hav them all harvested before it's time to set out the tomato seedlings Or you can mix radish seeds with the seeds of slow-germinating crops such as beets. The radishes spring up to mark the plantings so that you don't accidentally plant something else there while yo are waiting for the beets to appear. When they do, you pull th radishes. That loosens the soil around the beet seedlings, making i easier for air and water to penetrate to their roots. In addition, you can cook the young radish leaves, steaming them like mustard o turnip greens.

Marty's Top Five

Tom offers all sorts of convoluted rationales for his fruit and veg etable favorites. That's fine. But in making my selections I used a simpler criterion, one that *normal* people can identify with. Wher I plant a fruit or vegetable, it actually has to come up in some form That test eliminated 90 percent of the possibilities. From the shor list of plants that qualified, I then selected the five that returned th most reward for the least work.

1. Cherry tomatoes. The overeducated (you know who I mean may sneer, but this is definitely the best thing in my garden. If yo live in North America, it will be the best in yours, too. You buy these plants as seedlings, so you don't have to fart around with messy little pots of seeds and ruin the paint on your windowsill You buy the seedlings at the garden center, or supermarket, or ou of the trunk of somebody's car, and you just stick them in th ground. If your soil is halfway decent, the plants will grow. This i simple gardening for real people—all you absolutely have to do i remember not to step on the plants.

Of course, you can complicate even cherry tomato growing. You can fertilize the plants, stake them, sing Bach cantatas to them nder the August moonlight, and they will come in great. But who's that fussy?

Unlike Tom, I don't get personal with my vegetables, so I don't keep track of exactly what types of cherry tomatoes I grow. I just get whatever I can buy locally. It doesn't seem to make much difference. No matter what I plant, I always get some great-tasting tomatoes that can go straight into the mouth without slicing, cooking, broiling, or any additional steps. And no matter what I plant, I always end the season with a crop of unripe green tomatoes, probably as many of those as I have picked ripe all summer. This leads me to doubt the local wisdom about waiting until Mother's Day to plant tomatoes; I think I should be setting out my seedlings earlier. But who am I to argue with the greeting card industry?

Tom insisted that I try white tomatoes and black tomatoes and yellow tomatoes, leaving me no space last summer for any red ones. They all came up, too. We'll deal with them in the chapter about tomatoes (see page 94). But they weren't as easy and bug-proof as the cherry tomatoes I grew in tubs.

. **Potatoes.** I seem to be on some sort of alliterative jag here. Actually, I grew potatoes under duress. Tom made me do it, even though I pointed out that this is not my dream vegetable (the name is Asher, not McAsher).

Before I grew potatoes, I actually thought it was a federal law that they could be grown only in Idaho and Maine. But once you get the spuds in your raised bed, they require very little labor. In fact, soon after the plants sprouted, I lost track of them. There was all this competing herbage, and I couldn't tell one type from another, so I decided to go with the huge, healthy plant that was taking over the bed. Months later, I discovered that this was a weed (Tom, no doubt, will tell you all about this later).

No matter. When I finally pulled up the weeds in October, they brought up a half bushel of potato tubers with them. There were red potatoes, gold potatoes, and purple ones. Who would have imagined that potatoes, the dietary lowest common denominator, could be so exotic? Each type had a subtly different, truly distinc tive flavor, too, so that a dish of spuds became a culinary adven ture. Best of all, the tubers that I didn't find and so left in the bed survived the winter and sprouted the next spring to give me an other crop.

I have renewed respect for the Irish.

3. Garlic. Again, before I met Tom, I thought garlic grew in little cellophane-wrapped boxes. I was perfectly happy thinking that too. But now I know that garlic is really a bulb and if you plant it in the fall, the following summer you are rewarded with more than enough garlic to do wonderful things with all the tomatoes you harvest. You hang it up to dry and your friends think they've stumbled into some Soho pasteria when they come visit you. Turns out there are dozens of different kinds, each with its own flavor. I'm becoming a bad breath connoisseur. And the vampire count in our house was virtually nil this summer—a real achievement, considering the family visits.

4. Lettuce. I have to mention lettuce because I know that Tom would never deign to put anything so common in his top five (uh, let me guess: Dutch/Swahilian eggplant; watermelon hops; tangerine okra; spontaneously generating beer cactus; and vines that can be used simultaneously as pasta while they destroy the growth hormones in deer).

Anyway, we tried about six different kinds of lettuce and in spite of what the seed packets say (the type is too small to read anyway) it didn't seem to matter much when we planted them, except in the hottest part of the summer. Right now, the first week of January, I still have lettuce sprouting that I planted in October (okay, it's been an El Niño winter here, but still . . .). With all the news about *E. coli* bacteria being found in California lettuce, why not grow your own?

5. Beans. Again, these are so stupidly simple to grow that I know Tom won't mention them. I do a mix of yellow and green. I never emember to stake them until it's too late,* so that I always lose a few pods, because they get muddy from lying on the ground and they rot. Still, there are so many pods, who cares? Only problem? You have to keep picking the pods as they mature or the plants will stop producing, and when the bean plants are really going good in midsummer, that means you may be harvesting more than you can eat. What do you do with all the extras? Too bad you can't bake them into breads, like zucchini bread.

Which brings us to

5. **Zucchini.** Any sane reader is now putting this book back on the shelf. Most people regard zucchini as just a sign of the season, sort of like the swallows at Capistrano. Summer comes back and so do the zucchinis. Besides, you are probably insulted that I'm offering advice on growing this. After all, if you can't grow zucchini then you're probably incapable of breathing, let alone walking and talking.

So I'll offer only one tip. The essential thing about zucchini is to remember that you've planted it while the fruits are still small enough to harvest. And always practice birth control. For the plants. To avoid the zucchini tsunami that will otherwise wash over your garden by July, try my wife Judy's recipe for battering and frying the blossoms (page 64). This is how the Italians eat zucchini, and there's a reason. It tastes good; it's hot and crispy and gives you the perfect thirst for a glass of cold, dry white wine. More important, though, the more blossoms you eat, the fewer zucchini squashes you'll have to deal with later.

Still, our best efforts didn't stop us from having more zucchini squashes than we could eat or give away. My daughter baked a mean zucchini bread, and that took care of two. Then there was the mother that we kept outside the front door to discourage salespeople. Many of the rest ultimately ended up in the compost pile. I'm thinking of an exhibit of zucchini art next year. Any other suggestions will be graciously received.

* Tom's note: Marty plants bush-type beans, which don't need staking. In fact, you can't stake bush beans. Procrastination rules!

The Losers

1. Onions. These are a vegetable that we love to eat, but on which we won't waste garden space. To begin with, the flavor of the onion bulbs depends largely on the chemistry of the soil in which they are grown. You can grow 'Grano' onions, but your digging won't taste like the 'Granos' that come from Vidalia, Georgia. The reason that Vidalia onions are so sweet is that the soil of that region is particularly low in sulfur, the mineral which lends pungency to the onion bulb. Unless you have Vidalia soil, you won't harvest Vidalia-quality onions.

The other problem with onions is that the ways they are commonly grown in the home garden are ridiculously inefficient. Starting onions from seed opens up a wide range of different types to you, but you have to sow onion seeds indoors as much as three months before the date of the last frost in your area. In most areas north of the Mason-Dixon line, that means you'll be catering to onion seedlings from mid-January until midspring.

Alternatively, you can also grow onions from the "sets" that you'll find at the garden center. These are nothing more than small onions that you plant and eventually harvest as larger onions. Given that usually only mundane types of onions are available as sets (generic yellow, white, or red), this exercise seems like much work for little profit to us.

Where winters are mild, you can grow onions by sowing seeds directly into the garden. You plant in fall for a spring harvest, and in such regions, onion growing would make sense for the amateur. Otherwise, we advocate harvesting your onions with a cart at the supermarket. No doubt this position will attract a lot of abusive letters from do-it-yourselfers with bad breath, but so what?

2. Cauliflower. As far as flavor goes, we rate this stuff with Wonderbread and processed cheese. Why *anyone* would want to grow cauliflower baffles us. But only a complete masochist would try to raise it in a backyard patch.

This vegetable is the ultimate prima donna. Any slight misstep by the gardener, and cauliflower sulks, yielding no harvest. For example, in most areas of the country you have to start the plants from seed indoors in late winter or early spring, and if you do, you must be careful about "hardening off" the seedlings when time comes to move them outdoors. To do this, you have to set the seedlings outside in a sheltered spot for gradually increasing periods of time over a period of up to a week, and if you get this process wrong, hardening off too fast or too slow, no harvest. Plant the seedlings too deep in the garden, and no harvest. Nature deals you some unseasonably hot, dry weather, and—no harvest. Forget to water, and no harvest. Then, if by some miracle you do persuade the cauliflowers to head up, you have to blanch the curds. This involves tying the leaves up around the edible part so that it is deprived of sunlight and goes pale like a cave fish. Forget to do this, and the curd turns brown and inedible.

If you must grow cauliflower, try a purple-headed type such as 'Purple Giant'. This can be grown as a spring or fall crop, whenever the weather is cool, and is satisfied with the same care as are broccoli. It tastes like broccoli, too. Which raises an obvious question: why not grow broccoli instead?

3. **Celery.** Growing celery requires more fussing than any other garden vegetable. Actually, celery takes more fussing than all sorts of far more interesting plants—orchids, for instance—so why do it?

This is another crop that won't stand for high temperatures. Celery won't tolerate cold ones either, for if temperatures drop below 55°F several nights in a row, the plants go to seed, which stops the production of edible stalks. If you don't keep these thirsty little plants as well watered as they like, the stems go tough and stringy, developing a bitter flavor. You have to fertilize celery every two to three weeks, and most types taste better if you blanch the stems by providing each plant with a collar of roofing paper.

You may want to grow this crop just once (Tom did) to develop an appreciation of what a bargain the grocer's celery is.

4. Spaghetti squash. This crop is relatively easy to grow; you treat it like any other squash. The problem comes with the harvest. Once the novelty of spaghetti squash wears off, you'll realize that the only thing this dish has going for it is the stringy texture. The flavor is mediocre at best, and not at all like pasta. Anyway, since when was stringy a virtue in a food?

5. Cherries. This fruit is delicious, and cherries would be a must if the trees were not heir to more diseases, pests, and tribulations than Job. Even if you do beat all of these, an accomplishment that will come only with continual applications of toxic sprays, the birds will eat your whole harvest unless you swathe your tree in netting. So if you do plant a cherry tree, plant a dwarf, tart-fruited type such as 'Meteor' or 'North Star'. These stand no more than twelve feet tall, so you won't need the help of a cherry picker crane to slip on the hood of netting. Besides, the tart cherries are self-pollinating, so you needn't worry about finding sexually compatible mates, as you must with sweet cherries. That process is really tiresome—remember?

6. Lima beans. What is the point of writing a book if you can't vent your spleen? Tom hates lima beans. He hates them so much that he won't let Marty even try to come to their defense.

Lima beans are actually fairly easy to grow, and also unusually productive, but these qualities are defects in this instance. Because nobody could actually like the flavor of these bland, pale-green blobs. Indeed, they have a unique ability to neutralize other flavors, so that a small helping of limas can steal the pleasure from a whole meal. They are like a culinary black hole.

Lima beans may have some value as a means of disciplining children—Tom's father used to threaten him with dishes of succotash when he was obstreperous—but surely there is a kinder way? Like beating the kid with a leather strap or sending him to military school.

In short: you should be ashamed of yourself, growing lima beans.

A 2🕐-MINUTE EPIPHANY

To partake of a meal cooked by Italian ladies is, for Tom, a sacrament. Tom has eaten many fine meals prepared by male chefs, even Italian male chefs; those were good. Tom's a skilled cook himself, and makes a memorable osso buco and a passable risotto al Milanese. But none of this can begin to compare with dishes nurtured to perfection by females of the Italian peninsula.

Tom learned this during his semester as a student at an institute for classical studies in Rome. The institute was housed in a convent, and every night Tom would sit down to three courses crafted by the nuns. This became the spiritual part of Tom's day, and it is an experience he has struggled to re-create throughout his life since.

The city in which Tom now lives is actually a wonderful hunting ground for his kind of cook. Middletown, Connecticut, boasts of its New England heritage, but as near as Tom can tell, the city appeared all on a single day when the entire population of the Sicilian village of Melilli decided to emigrate together. When he joined this band of expatriates, Tom hoped that his cute, blond son would serve as bait. In the end, though, gourds have proven much more effective.

We have already described how useful the gourds of the species *Lagenaria siceraria* can be. But much as Tom had come to rely on his gourds' ability to cover for his mistakes, and much as he enjoyed their nocturnal displays of perfumed flowers, still Tom had not an inkling at first of how essential a 20-minute plant they would prove to be.

They are ridiculously easy to grow. Prepare the soil in a sunny spot by digging up an area 3 feet square. Turn it to a depth of 10 inches and mix in a bucket of compost and a half bucket of dehydrated manure. In the South, you can sow the seeds directly into the prepared soil as soon as all danger of frost is past. In the North, where summers are shorter, start the seeds indoors a couple of weeks before the last frost date, sowing them into 4-inch peat pots full of a commercial seed-starting mix. Actually, you can use any kind of pot to start these seeds, but peat pots eliminate much of the trauma you cause the plants when you move them out into the garden. That's because seedlings grown in peat pots are planted pot and all and so no damage is done to the roots. Set the pots on a sunny windowsill and keep them moist. Plant the seedlings outdoors about a month later, or as soon as the weather has warmed up and nighttime temperatures aren't dropping below 50°F.

Gourd cultivation involves nothing more than twice-weekly waterings during dry weather and a monthly feeding with a tablespoon of soluble fertilizer dissolved in a gallon of water. This took Tom almost no time. But the fruits—bottle gourds and cucuzzi—did. *Lagenaria* gourds need a growing season of ninety to one hundred frost-free days to mature, which means that even though Tom had started the seeds in pots indoors, it was late August before the vines started to set fruit.

When they did, though, they seemed intent on making up for lost time. Little high-waisted fruits popped out all over the bottle gourd vine that blocked the kitchen door, and gradually swelled into vessels a foot or more tall. Meanwhile, the vine on Tom's sourwood tree sprouted sausage-shaped cucuzzi's that grew longer, and longer, and longer—one reached 34 inches before Tom lost his nerve and picked it.

Tom planned to turn the bottle gourds into birdhouses, with Matthew's help. Accordingly, he left them on the vine to ripen and dry. The cucuzzi, though, he knew should be eaten—his neighbors told him so. No one offered to help with cooking it, however, until one day when Tom was picking up a fax at his wife's place of employment. Tom happened to mention his dilemma to one of the telephone switchboard operators, Genevieve Aforismo, and she took charge.

She shared with Tom her recipe for cucuzzi soup (we've included a copy below) and she put him in touch with a lady in the physics department, Ana, who in turn took Tom's problem home to her mother, Vincenza Milardo. Signora Milardo learned how to cook cucuzzi from her mother as a child in Melilli. She knew what Tom really wanted, and she sent him not only a recipe, but also a casserole full of her cucuzz' to inspire him.

Because he is married, Tom had to share this. What he got to eat was heaven. He couldn't really begrudge his wife, Suzanne, her portion. The look on her face suggested that she was experiencing the same emotions of reverence and awe.

Tom has timed the preparation of Signora Milardo's recipe and found that it takes about fifteen minutes of actual work—of course, it is even more efficient to persuade a real maestra to do it for you, and the results will be far better. Cucuzzi soup takes longer to prepare, about twenty-five minutes, but you end up with a hot dinner. Anyway, take it from Tom, this is the most pleasurable kind of gardening you will ever experience.

And now for the lagniappe:

One day as Tom was admiring his ripening bottle gourds, one of his wife's colleagues, Indira Karamcheti, stopped by.

Indira is a professor of literature who is a native of the Indian state of Andhra Pradesh, and she told Tom that in India, bottle gourds are grown not for birdhouse making, but for eating. A few days later, Indira dropped by a packet of spices with instructions for their use. Tom faithfully did as he was told, and twenty minutes later he had a dish so pungent and savory that he spent the whole of his remaining eight minutes of gardening time pondering what his life would have been like had he studied in Hyderabad rather than Rome.

So many gourds, so little time.

Signora Milardo's Cucuzzi

Try to harvest fruits before they grow too large—the smaller fruits, those 10 to 12 inches long, have a crisper flesh and taste best. Peel cucuzzi and split them lengthwise. Scoop out seeds from center, cube, put in a colander, and wash in cold water. While the cucuzz' is draining, dice onions and fresh tomatoes—allow one medium-sized onion and 2 to 3 plum tomatoes for each cucuzz'. In a large saucepan sauté onion and tomato in a couple tablespoons of olive oil over a medium flame until the onion is transparent and the tomato is reduced to a sauce (this takes 5 to 10 minutes). Add four or 5 fresh basil leaves and cucuzz' and a little bit of water, too, if the mixture seems dry and threatens to burn. Continue cooking until cucuzz' is tender. Top with grated cheese—"whatever kind you have got"—and serve as a side dish or mix with cooked pasta.

Gen's Gourd Soup

Peel cucuzz', cut into cubes, and set aside. Then chop an onion and a couple of ripe plum tomatoes and sauté in a tablespoon of olive oil. When onion is beginning to turn transparent, add the cucuzz'. Continue to sauté for a couple more minutes, then add chicken stock until the squash is just covered. Bring to a boil and simmer until tender.

In a separate pan, boil noodles until done and drain. Add to soup and cook for about 5 minutes. "If you wish, you could add a raw scrambled egg. When you serve it, add Italian grated cheese."

Indira's Bottle Gourds

Peel a young gourd and cut into cubes, removing and discarding seeds and pulpy center. Heat 1 tsp. vegetable oil in a saucepan and add 1 tsp. black mustard seeds, 1 tsp. black gram (*urad dahl*), and a little cumin (if you wish). Crumble in two dried chilies. Cook over a medium flame until the mustard seeds start to pop and the black gram turns reddish. Add cubed gourd, cover pan, and reduce heat; cook until gourd is tender.

2🕐-MINUTE PROJECT:
Judy's Fried Zucchini Blossoms

You can grow zucchini. No matter how nonexistent your skills as a gardener, you can do this without breaking a sweat. As Marty has already indicated, the only real difficulty of zucchini growing is dealing with the consequences.

What's the drill? Unless you intend to grow your zucchinis on the compost heap (see pages 27–29), and zucchinis do very well there, order seeds of bush-type plants. We particularly like the varieties 'Clarimore' and 'Raven.' The advantage of the bush types is that they have what horticulturists call "a compact habit." This means that unlike the old-fashioned, vine-making zucchinis, the newer, hybrid-bush types aren't going to smother all their neighbors.

Start the seeds indoors (see page 102 for a guide to this), in 3-inch peat pots filled with seed-starting mix, three to four weeks before the last frost date for your area. Of course, you can also do as Marty does and wait until it's time to put the plants out in the garden and then just buy whatever anonymous zucchini seedlings you find at the local garden center. Tom hates to admit this, but in fact it doesn't make much difference. Actually, in the South, where summers are long, you might as well wait until the outdoor planting time and just poke the seeds into the soil. You won't harvest zucchinis as soon as your harder-working neighbors, but you'll still get as much as you want.

Then, in late spring (two weeks or so after the last frost date in your area), find a sunny spot in your garden and with a stick draw two 2-foot-wide circles in the earth. If your garden is a small one and already planted up with spring salad greens by this time, don't worry. Zucchinis are hot-weather crops, so you can wait to plant them until some cool-weather crop such as spinach has finished its harvest and you have pulled it out.

Prepare each circle for planting by digging into the soil a bucket full of composted manure. Then plant one zucchini plant at each circle's center. Southerners may plant two seeds one inch deep at each circle's center. The extra seed is insurance, and if two seedlings emerge in either circle, pinch off one of them.

Water well and deeply, thoroughly moistening the soil around the plants twice a week in dry weather. East of the Rocky Mountains, guard against squash vine borers. This is actually a kind of moth that lays its eggs at the bases of the squash plants in early summer. From these hatch fat, tallowy grubs that burrow into the stems. Draping the young plants with row covers will ward off these and other insect pests that like zucchinis. Or you can spread out sheets of aluminum foil under the spreading zucchini stems and leaves. Apparently, the borer moths are poor navigators, and the reflected light from the foil convinces them that up is down and vice versa, and they just can't cope.

You'll know you've failed to keep away the borers when a whole section of your zucchini mysteriously wilts. The treatment for this is surgery. With a single-edged razor blade, slit the affected stem, starting near the base. You'll find a trail of chewed plant debris and at its end the grub, which you remove and leave out at the garden's edge for the birds to eat. You bandage the zucchini stem by heaping soil over the wounded part. If this is kept moist, the plant will re-root from the stem and recover.

Large yellow blossoms will start appearing within a month or so of when you set your zucchini plants out in the garden. At first you'll be delighted with the fruitfulness of your plants, and the uninitiated may be tempted to leave all of these blossoms in place. If you do, make sure to pick the zucchini squashes when they are still young and just a few inches long. This is the fashionable way to eat zucchinis. It's also a basic safety measure. If you leave the zucchinis on the plants, they'll swell in a matter of days to something that looks like a cross between a baseball bat and a watermelon. What you do with that is a problem. We've heard frightening rumors of cars left unlocked in our downtown in midsummer, whose owners returned to find the backseats full of orphaned, obese zucchinis.

If you are smart (and we assume you are, since you bought this book), you'll develop a taste for fried zucchini blossoms. When you do, you'll discover the contradictions that a single vegetable can encompass. There is a ponderous earnestness to the steamed slices of the zucchini squash that no sauce can hide. To dine on flowers, though, perfects a summer.

Battered Blossoms

Zucchini blossoms	*2 tablespoons all-purpose*
1 egg	*flour*
2 tablespoons beer	*Vegetable oil*

Pick zucchini blossoms while newly opened and still fresh. Beat the egg in a mixing bowl with the beer, sifting in the flour. Heat ½-inch of vegetable oil in a large frying pan over a moderate heat. Take care not to overheat the oil—it should not get so hot that it smokes—but it must become hot enough that a drop of the egg-beer-and-flour batter turns golden brown almost immediately when dripped into the pan.

As the oil is heating, rinse blossoms in cold water and pat dry gently with paper towels. When oil is sufficiently hot, dip blossoms into the batter, coat them thoroughly, and drop them into the pan. Do not crowd the pan; you probably won't be able to cook more than three or four blossoms at a time.

Cook blossoms until golden on the bottom side, then turn them over so that the other side may cook. When golden all over, remove the blossoms from the pan and set on paper towels to drain. Sprinkle the cooked blossoms with salt, and serve hot with a glass (or two) of cold Frascati wine.

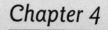

Chapter 4

The Salad Course

Having finished the installation of his garden bed, Marty was hot to start planting. He was dreaming, he said, of the most extraordinary salads. That made Tom anxious. Marty always makes Tom anxious, but in this case, Tom had reason. It was already mid spring in southern Connecticut (the average date of the last frost in Westport is April 11th). That means it was already late to plant the spring greens that, to Tom's way of thinking, are the basis of the best salads.

Actually these greens are not just spring crops. Traditionally, they have been grown in the spring, at least in the Northern states and the upper South, because they love cool, moist weather. With a few adjustments, though, they can be made to flourish in the fall, too (see page 208), except in the Deep South. There, where winters are mild and provide the only cool weather of the year, these greens are commonly cultivated as winter crops.

"Yeah, well, what about summer?" Marty demanded. "Do I put the salad bowl away and look forward to enjoying three months of scurvy?"

Tom thought he could recommend a few crops that would keep the salad bowl busy over the summer, but the peak seasons were spring and fall, and they had to hurry if they were going to take advantage of what was left of spring.

Calibrating the Calendar

Gardening is an intensely seasonal craft; most often success depends more on doing things at the right time than on following exactly the right procedure. Just scratch your lettuce seeds into a bed in early spring, and you are almost sure to get a few pickings, even if you aren't meticulous about preparing the soil and watering. Wait until late spring, though, and in most parts of the United States the lettuce seeds won't sprout, and if they do, the plants won't make any sort of head of edible leaves but instead will move right into producing a tall, skinny, bitter seed stalk.

In short, the plants are going to observe Nature's seasonal schedule, so you better work from the same agenda. The trick is, though, that this natural calendar may seem identical to the one the insurance company sends you, but depending on where you live, the two may not match well at all. Both will be divided into four seasons, but in most parts of the United States, spring isn't going to start on March 21st.

Think about it: does spring start on the same day in Duluth and Atlanta? So this leaves you with another question: how do you know when spring (or any of the other seasons) begins or ends in your region? The answer lies in the dates of the last and first frosts, the last frost of spring and the first frost of fall.

These frame the growing season and are the easy—and natural—way to fix the boundaries of the gardening year. In the case of spring, it is the last frost around which the season revolves. Figure that spring, as one of four seasons, lasts approximately twelve weeks (a quarter of the year). And the last frost marks the midpoint of spring. So once you know that date, the arithmetic is simple. Count back six weeks from the date of the last frost and you have the beginning of spring in your area. Add six weeks to the date of the last spring frost, and you know when spring ends.

Any local nurseryman can tell you when, on average, the last frost occurs in your area. Or you can call the local office of the Cooperative Extension Service. Every state has some version of this agricultural and horticultural educational organization, and it is usually headquartered at the state's land-grant university. As a rule, each state's Cooperative Extension Service maintains offices in every county, and you can generally find the telephone number of the nearest office under the county-government listings in your telephone book.

You'll find that instructions for spring planting are usually tied directly to this date. "Plant seeds two weeks before the last frost," a seed packet may advise, or "Plant when all danger of frost is past." The schedule for starting seedlings indoors is also based on frost dates; tomato seeds, for instance, should be sown into their peat pots (we always use peat pots, to reduce transplanting trauma) four to six weeks before the last spring frost, while peppers, which are slower growing, should be sown seven to nine weeks before that date.

While you are checking out the date of the last spring frost, you should also inquire about the average date of the first fall frost in your area. This is the date that fixes the sowings of fall crops, a type of garden reincarnation that will be described in Chapter 9.

When they got to the seed display at Thee Plante Shoppe, Westport's Garden Emporium, Marty immediately started complaining. Seeds of every edible plant known to man (and most of those known to women) were there on the rack, but to Marty's eye, they were arranged in no perceptible order.

"It's alphabetical," Tom explained.

Marty dismissed this with a snort. "All I know is that to find lettuce, I have to go to kohlrabi and then scramble around amid lamb's quarters and leeks and legumes. For radishes, I've got to wade through radicchio, rhubarb, rutabaga, and, God help me, rape."

"That's how we've always done it," Tom had begun, when Marty launched into a plan for a new seed-marketing strategy. He would pack all the seeds you needed right into a salad bowl (made of plantation-grown, not wild-harvested, teak) along with fertilizer, and when you got home, you'd just dump the contents on the garden, use the big fork and spoon to toss your soil, scatter water from a cruet, and there you were.

Tom, who had been gathering up a selection of appropriate seeds, never suspected that Marty was serious.

Actually, this wasn't the first argument of the morning. Marty had begun the day by insisting that he would plant only what he could find as ready-started seedlings. Why fuss with seeds when for a few dollars you could escape all the work of sowing seeds, waiting for germination, and nurturing infant seedlings? To start the plants from seeds yourself was as ridiculous as buying your clothes as bolts of cloth. Worse—because in Marty's experience, hungry birds usually made sure that any seeds you did sow never germinated.

In fact, Tom had to admit that Marty had a point. Like the TV dinners that saved Tom and his son, Matthew, from starvation when his wife went off on her last expedition to the Antarctic, ready-to-plant seedlings are a lot better than the alternative: nothing at all. If, like Marty, you are so busy extorting a living from a hostile world that you have hardly any free time, then off-the-rack seedlings may be the only kind of gardening you have time for. At 75¢ apiece or more, seedlings may seem expensive, but if you value your time at more than minimum wage (which is what the nursery industry pays the people who actually grow the seedlings), then the time the seedlings save makes them a good deal.

But if the advantages of seedlings are like those of TV dinners, so are the disadvantages. Designed to appeal to a horticultural lowest common denominator, seedlings are boring. The plants are of the most common types, and foolproof counts for a lot more with seedlings than does the flavor of the harvest.

By contrast, starting from seeds opens up to you a huge selection of diverse vegetables. Every conceivable culinary bias is catered to by some seed catalog. There are catalogs that specialize in vegetables for traditional Italian cuisines, various Asian cuisines, even Native American cuisines. Likewise, there are catalogs tuned to the needs of the different regions: vegetable seeds for Southern gardeners, Northern gardeners, Western gardeners, and desert gardeners.

And as for those birds, it's easy enough to frustrate them. There are two ways of accomplishing this. The first of these is what Tom calls "the lazy way": you just drape a fine plastic net over the newly planted area. Garden centers sell this stuff as "garden netting" and you unroll it, stretch it over your bed, and then weight each corner down with a rock. You can lift this net off easily once the seedlings are up and growing, and in the meantime, the birds won't go near the bed because they interpret the netting as a potential trap. Watching the birds frustrated by their own cynicism is one of the great pleasures of gardening, Tom admits.

Still, he prefers the second method of dealing with birds because, though it involves more work, it provides additional benefits. So Tom covers his new plantings with tents of a coarse, plastic cloth that garden centers sell as "floating row cover" (Reemay is the most common brand). A porous, translucent fabric of plastic fibers, this stuff lets sunlight, air, and water through, but keeps out birds, insects, and the wind. You can buy rolls of this material in various widths; however, you want the 6-foot width so that you

Starting Right with Seedlings

Stocking the garden with nursery-grown seedlings can be a genuine shortcut to a homegrown harvest. Or it can be a source of disappointment and frustration. The outcome depends on what you buy, when you buy it, and how you treat it afterward.

To begin with, think small. Those impressively large vegetable seedlings that are already blooming right there in the plastic tray—forget them. They've been in the pack too long, and as a result they are permanently stunted. The jumbo seedlings look good when you plant them, but they'll look just about the same a couple of months later.

What you want are the smaller, stockier seedlings that have not yet produced any flower buds. The color of their leaves should be a rich green, and there shouldn't be any roots emerging from the holes in the bottom of the container. Check underneath the leaves, too, to make sure there are no bugs or other pests lurking there; you don't want to bring these home.

Don't try to force the seedlings to make up for your procrastination. If you have missed the spring planting season, let it go. Don't spend the last Saturday in May rushing from garden center to garden center, buying up the last tired lettuce seedlings. If the label says to plant in early to mid spring, take it at its word. Any crop planted after the recommended season is just going to take up space in the garden without returning any significant harvest.

When you get the seedlings home, don't plant them right into the garden. Chances are they have just come out of a greenhouse, and they need a period of adjustment before they face life in the great outdoors. In gardening jargon, this is called "hardening off."

You begin by putting the seedlings outside for just a couple of hours in a semi-shaded spot that is protected from the wind. Then you bring them indoors, and set them by a sunny window. The next morning you put the seedlings outside in the same semi-shaded spot for a couple more hours, and then bring them inside again. On the third day, you set the seedlings in a sunnier spot. It'll be four or five days before the seedlings are ready to go into the ground.

Don't let the seedlings dry out while they are still in the nursery packs. You'll find that they suck the water out of their potting soil quickly when they are sitting in the sun. When you do plant the seedlings, do it in the evening so that they will have several hours of cool darkness to recover. Water the seedlings immediately after planting with a half-strength solution of some balanced, water-soluble fertilizer. If the next day is sunny, stake sheets of newspaper loosely over the seedlings to act as a protective awning. You don't have to leave this screen in place more than a day or so, but it will help ease the transition from container to bed. Giving your plants some extra help during this vulnerable period will help them take root and resume growth faster; any shock to the young plants is likely to detract not only from the size of your harvest, but even its flavor.

can drape lengths of row cover loosely over your beds, leaving plenty of slack so that as the seedlings grow, they can push up the cover. Cut the cloth strips to length, and tuck their edges into the soil just inside each bed's framework. By keeping out the wind, such a cover keeps the soil surface from drying and so protects the seeds from dehydration, and increases the percentage of germination. You can remove your row covers once the seedlings are well established, though some gardeners prefer to leave them in place to repel bugs (more on that in Chapter 11, page 258).

In the end, Tom and Marty compromised. They agreed to plant a mixture of seeds and nursery-grown seedlings so that they could combine choice with convenience. For the first spring salad planting, though, Tom insisted on starting from seed. Marty agreed, because these seeds are sown right into the garden, "so you won't be ruining the paint on my windowsills with your soggy peat pots."

You start these early-spring crops outdoors because they need the cool, moist weather they find there at that season. But you

Getting Good Seed

The local hardware store or garden center does offer convenience when you are shopping for seeds, Shepherd Ogden concedes. You walk in, pick up whatever the manager has set out on the shelf, pay your money, and leave. The whole process of selecting and buying a garden's worth of seeds takes maybe ten minutes this way, and no planning. But, Shepherd adds, this convenience comes at a price.

Poet and former market gardener Shepherd Ogden is also the founder of *Cook's Garden,* Tom's favorite mail-order source of vegetable seed. Shepherd insists that the committed gardener has no choice but to shop for seeds by mail. We would broaden that category to include 20-minute gardeners, too. Because the kind of convenience that you get by shopping at a local retail outlet is going to cause you lots of work later on in the gardening season, and maybe disappointment, too.

Why is this? Economics, according to Shepherd Ogden, prevent the local retailer from carrying anything but a sampling of best-sellers. For example, you may find only one kind of lettuce seed in the rack at the hardware store. At most, there will be two or three. *Cook's Garden,* in contrast, currently offers forty-three.

"So what?" says Marty (and maybe so do you). Who grows more than one or two kinds of lettuces at a time? As a 20-minute gardener, though, you want to grow something special, such as 'Trout Back', a red-flecked romaine that until *Cook's Garden* started carrying it, you would have seen at only a few fancy restaurants.

More important, you want a lettuce that's easy to grow. In springtime, you want one of *Cook's Garden*'s "spring lettuces," while for a summer planting you want one of its "summer lettuces." The point is that, often, the different varieties of the same vegetable have been developed to suit different conditions, and the broader selections you find in mail-order catalogs make your plantings more likely to succeed.

There's another reason to order your seeds from catalogs. The vitality of vegetable seeds depends largely on how they have been stored. A hardware store or garden center leaves their seeds out in a rack, or maybe in a back room or basement. There the seeds may be exposed to considerable changes in temperature, which reduces their vitality. Worse yet, they are likely to be exposed to high humidity. Over a period of weeks or months, this can kill many of the seeds in the packet, ensuring gardening disappointment for the customers.

At a good mail-order nursery, the seeds are stored in conditions engineered to keep the seeds healthy. At *Cook's Garden*, for example, as shipments arrive from growers, they are unpacked in a special room where the air is kept at 8 percent humidity and continually circulated by fans. This draws out any excess moisture that may have accumulated in the seeds prior to arrival.

After a few days of this treatment, the seeds are moved to the packaging area, the place where they are sorted and sealed into packets. The air in this room is kept at 12 to 14 percent humidity, and the temperature maintained at 40 to 50°F. There they stay until it's time to assemble shipments for the customers. Then the seeds are transferred to the picking rack in an environment of 50°F and 40 percent humidity. After each order is put together, it's sealed in a moisture-resistant plastic membrane before shipment.

All in all, Shepherd Ogden says, the biggest threat to the vitality of his seeds comes after arrival at the customer's house. Once the shipping package has been opened, there's no telling what humidity the seeds may be exposed to, and unless planted promptly, the vitality will decline. Though you can beat this problem, Shepherd points out, by saving the silica gel desiccant packs that come in the shipping boxes of electronic equipment such as computers, radios, cameras, etc. (*Cook's Garden* also sells desiccant packs by the dozen.) Leave the used packs in a 200° oven for eight hours to redry them. Then put one desiccant pack with twenty standard-sized seed packets in a quart canning jar, screw on the lid, and set the jar in the refrigerator. Stored this way, the seeds should stay safe and healthy for months.

Are there any mail-order suppliers Shepherd Ogden would avoid? Stay away, he says, from the bargain catalogs that offer collections of seed and plants at low, low prices. Too often, he says, the low price reflects poor quality.

Tom and Marty have their own criterion. They throw out any seed catalog that advertises the "tree tomato." This is not a tomato, nor is it a tree. It's a tropical shrub. If you keep it in a greenhouse for several years it will eventually produce acidic red fruits which are adequate only for jelly making.

don't plant them out the way they tell you on the seed packet—in the lonely, widely spaced rows. That's too inefficient for a 20-minute gardener.

Actually, you can plant the salad seeds two ways. You can segregate the crops, if you are fussy ("neat" is what Tom calls this). Or you can follow Marty's example and employ a bit of flair.

Both planting methods start in the same fashion. You break up the surface of the soil in your garden bed with an iron-toothed rake, carefully leveling the surface and removing any pebbles or twigs. Then, if you are Tom, you allot a block of space to each crop. The size of the block depends on the size of the harvest you want. Lettuce, the basic fabric of the salad, gets a large block, while radishes, which are a garnish, get a small one. After you've worked out the boundaries, you open the seed packets and sprinkle each one all over its allotted home. Then with a hand cultivator ("the claw thing," as Marty calls this tool) you lightly scratch the very surface of the soil to just bury the seeds. Water, and it's time to frustrate the birds again. If you are feeling lazy, you can just toss a sheet of plastic netting over the bed. Marty, of course, came out in favor of the netting, explaining that "lazy" translates as "smart" as far as he's concerned.

The seedlings, when they sprout from the ground, will be too close together. That's part of the plan, though. When germination has finished and the seedlings are starting to develop their first leaves, you comb the blocks with your hand cultivator; by pulling out every other seedling, this thins the bed. As the seedlings grow yet larger, you thin again, this time using your fingers to pull every other plant. These thinnings, by the way, once the roots have been pinched off, can go right into the salad bowl, where they provide the earliest and sweetest greens of the season. You continue thinning in this fashion as the plants expand until you reach the spacing recommended for that crop.

Marty was rummaging around in his kitchen drawers as Tom explained this process to him. Finally, with a mutter of "Eureka!" he pulled out a can that had once been filled with 2 pounds of choice espresso grounds. He set this on the counter and then, as Tom protested, he ripped the tops off of all the seed packets and dumped in their contents. He capped the can, shook it, and pronounced with satisfaction: "Mesclun." That, of course, is the chic mixture of greens that is universally served in Westport salad bowls (with, need we add, a raspberry vinaigrette).

Marty did allow Tom to rake flat the soil in his (Marty's) garden bed. Then, with a skewer, Marty punched a dozen holes in the coffee can's plastic cap. Upending this, he shook the mixed seeds out over the whole garden bed.

"How are you going to find anything in that mess," Tom demanded.

"That's the point. If I can't find anything, neither can the bugs." In fact, that was how it worked. The lettuce-eating pests got lost among the carrots and radishes, the spinach leaf miners laid their eggs on lettuce leaves, where the larvae starved to death, and the root maggots couldn't find their way to the radish roots. This planting remained virtually pest-free as it matured over the course of the next six weeks.

Marty thinned as Tom had recommended, filling and refilling his salad bowl as he did. He kept pulling so that the leaves of one plant just barely reached those of its neighbors. By keeping the bed always full, he left no opportunities for weeds, and so eliminated another boring chore. As the roots began to fatten, he got so he could recognize the radish and carrot plants; he pulled those as he needed them. For the rest, he did his harvesting with a pair of scissors, clipping back almost to the ground a different area each night. Unlike Tom's greens, Marty's mesclun was always premixed, "the natural way," as he continually pointed out.

Tom's Guide to Individual Salad Crops

Some of us like to keep our gardens neat and our plants discrete. Marty's note: Some of us also keep the various foods separate on our plates, and eat the peas first, then all the meat loaf, and save the mashed potatoes for last. But at least Tom doesn't pose any physical threat to society.) Growing the different crops separately is also handy if sometimes you like to make special salads. Say you want to make a spinach salad. If you've grown the greens in Marty's haphazard fashion, you'll spend an hour or more picking through the mess to harvest the stuff you want.

I find it easier to mix the greens *after* they have been harvested, just as I find it easier to locate vegetables in a store or a book if they have been arranged in some sort of rational order. That's why I am including thumbnail guides to growing ten of the essential salad crops, and I am arranging these guides in alphabetical order, by the name of the vegetable. You'll notice the lack of any references to lamb's quarters, leeks, legumes, rhubarb, rutabaga, and rape. Radicchio, Marty will deal with elsewhere.

1. **Arugula** (aka Rucola, Roquette). This plant is as easy to grow as it is good to eat. The seed is large enough to be easy to handle; scatter it thinly over a block or band of loose, smooth-raked soil and water well. Water again regularly whenever the soil dries out, and you'll be picking arugula leaves in less than a month. Don't wait, either, since arugula has the best flavor while still young. For this reason, you shouldn't sow a whole spring's worth of arugula all at once; instead, sow a small block every couple of weeks until late spring.

After the arugula is up and growing, thin the plants every few days—you can eat the thinnings. I start this process when the arugula seedlings have developed their first pair of real leaves (the ones that appear after the seedling leaves). I pull up alternate plants so that the remaining ones will have room to expand, but I make sure not to leave broad expanses of bare soil, which would serve as an opportunity for weeds.

Arugula sprouts in tufts—to harvest, snap off the older leaves from the outside, or take a pair of shears and decapitate the whole plant an inch or 2 above the ground. Either way, new leaves will sprout from the bud at the tuft's heart.

This green is great raw (my neighbor Ron says if he has another kid, he's definitely going to name it Arugula) but you can also toss a handful into a chicken soup a few minutes before you take the pot off the stove.

20-minute tip: Ordinary cultivated arugula doesn't do well in the long, hot days of summer; plants started at that season turn bitter and go to seed before they produce any substantial number of leaves. For summer plantings, sow Arugula selvatica. This is a wilder form of arugula that is smaller than its domesticated relative but which continues to yield harvests of leaves right through the hot weather.

2. Carrots. Carrots are so easy to grow that even if the home-grown type weren't so much sweeter than the store-bought roots, I'd still grow this crop. For the 20-minute gardener, the best types are the short and round varieties like 'Kundulus', or 'Thumbelina'. The regular long-stemmed carrots need a deep, sandy, stone-free soil, and preparing a bed for them is a lot of work. The short round types, in contrast, do fine in average garden soil.

For the sweetest carrots, sprinkle a thin layer of ashes from the fireplace over the soil before you plant. With a garden fork, work this into the top 4 inches of soil and then rake the area smooth. You can sow carrots from early spring until early summer. I usually sow carrots in bands or blocks, too, though I sometimes sow a row ll around the outside of a garden bed because the fernlike carrot greens make a nice edging. Sow the seeds about three to a square inch—a thin sprinkling—and work them into the soil with your hand cultivator. Carrot seeds like to rest about a quarter inch under the surface. When sowing in a row, make a furrow a quarter inch deep and drop a carrot seed every third of an inch, and then gently pull the soil over them.

If you are going to get any roots out of them, carrots must be thinned so that they stand about four inches apart. You can thin a small block of seedlings by waiting until they stand an inch high and then hand pulling the ones you don't want. Larger plantings are easier to thin if you start earlier, when the seedlings are a half inch or less tall. Just comb the block, band, or row of seedlings gently with a rake.

If you plant short or globe-rooted carrots, they will be ready to pick in five to six weeks. Again, a series of sowings rather than one planting extravaganza will give you a more gradual, easier-to-manage harvest. Only pull as many roots as you need at any one time—carrots keep better in the ground than in the refrigerator.

20-minute tip: After sowing carrot seeds in early spring, water and cover the planted area with a sheet of clear plastic. By trapping sunlight, this warms the soil and speeds up germination. When the sprouts begin to emerge from the soil, remove the plastic immediately.

3. Corn salad (aka Mâche, Miner's lettuce, Lamb's lettuce). Why this was ever named corn salad I can't figure out, as this plant is no relative of corn. Instead, it's like a little wild lettuce, which was how it was identified when seed was given to me. Actually, I had tried to raise corn salad in my salad bed several times, but the seeds had never sprouted—in retrospect, I think I planted them too late in spring.

So I gave up on corn salad. But I had to try the seeds a friend gave me very early one spring when he told me that they came from some "German lettuce" that had seeded itself all over his garden. I poured the tablespoon of seeds and dry flowers out of the sandwich bag into the palm of my hand and tossed them onto a patch of roughly dug, semi-shaded earth. Apparently, this plant really likes chilly, wet weather, for it soon sprouted and has been reappearing in early spring, and again in late fall, ever since. In fact, it has been spreading steadily, so that I would have to classify this as a weed if it didn't taste so good.

Corn salad makes little rosettes of spoon-shaped leaves that taste like a very tender lettuce anointed with a drop of lemon juice. Not only is this green delicious, it's the first to appear in the spring—my first picking comes in March.

20-minute tip: 'Gayla' is a variety of corn salad that is especially cold tolerant and resistant to the mildew which can attack the leaves. 'Piedmont' is a heat-resistant type better suited to Southern gardens.

4. Curly cress. This comes the closest to instant salad of any plant I know. Curly cress tastes like the more familiar watercress, but it thrives in an ordinary garden bed. Actually, "thrives" understates the case. Plant cress seed and the seedlings will be up and growing within ten days, and within four to five weeks you'll be picking the peppery, crunchy sprigs.

Although you'll more likely be cutting the cress sprigs, since barbering is an essential part of how I cultivate this plant. I sow the seeds thinly, maybe three to a square inch, on a smooth-raked, sunny or semi-shaded bed anytime from early to mid spring. Next, I work the seeds into the soil with my cultivator and water as usual. Then, when a salad needs some picking up, I just cut off the top of a small patch with an ordinary pair of scissors.

I also use the scissors to give my cress patch a haircut. This is essential for the ornamental patterns of cress I sow to decorate the garden for parties, barbecues, birthdays, etc. I described this technique at length in *The 20-Minute Gardener* (on pages 103–4). Really, though, all you have to do is draw a pattern onto a bed or flower border with lime some three to four weeks before your event, and then ink in the pattern with the cress seed. Grow it in the usual way. A message appearing in green ("Welcome Home, Suzanne!" "Clean Up Your Room, Matthew") never fails to amaze the recipient.

5. Lettuce. Marty to the contrary, I'm not too much of a snob to appreciate something simple like lettuce. Actually, with all the gourmet types of lettuces that have appeared in the more fashionable nursery catalogs in recent years, you can be a snob and still enjoy lettuce. The ability to complicate something simple is the heart of true connoisseurship.

I prefer the loose-leaf lettuces, the types that don't form heads. That's partly because I rarely need a whole head at any one time. With loose-leaf lettuces, I can pick a handful of leaves from a plant and yet leave the rest intact. That gives me a longer harvest—I pick lettuce for a couple of months from a single planting. Besides, I don't want to pull whole plants (as you do to harvest heading lettuces) because I use my lettuces as decorative plants. A pattern of frilly-leaved, red and green lettuces makes a beautiful formal display—but not if a hole appears every time you want a salad.

My favorite red lettuce is an Italian kind, 'Lollo Rossa', and my favorite green is its relative, 'Lollo Biondo'. Both are quite heat tolerant, and an early spring sowing will last until the end of June. I often sow the seeds into plastic cell packs indoors (see page 115 for directions on this) as early as eight weeks before the last spring frost because it's easier to create the precise patterns I like by transplanting seedlings. You'll find a description of this technique in the 20-minute projects at this chapter's end. If you are less concerned about aesthetics, you can make life even easier by sowing the seeds right into the garden as soon as the soil thaws and dries out enough to be forked up and raked smooth in the spring.

Block sow the lettuce sparingly. Drop the seeds about half an inch apart, and work them a quarter inch down into the soil. Water and thin as you would any other spring green.

20-minute tip: Lettuces turn bitter with the onset of hot weather.

You can temper this by refrigerating the leaves for two to four days
before serving them. Another way to beat the heat and extend your
harvest is to plant seed in late spring in a semi-shaded spot.

6. Malabar spinach (aka Indian spinach, Pasali, Pu-tin-choi). I
can seem deliberately cruel. Your garden addicts you to a nightly
fix of tender, just-picked, truly superb salads. Then comes the hot
weather, and suddenly, the greens of spring disappear.

Malabar spinach will stand by you. It's not really a spinach,
though the leaves taste like one. Actually, it's a perennial tropical
vine, which in its native southern India climbs to a height of thirty
feet. This plant can't stand our winters, however, so you will have
to grow it like an annual, and you can't expect it to reach its full
stature. Especially if you keep pinching off the tips of the stems—
and you will do this, once you discover how good the young leaves
taste in a salad or in a soup.

Outside of the Deep South and the mildest parts of the Southwest, you should start your Malabar spinach indoors. This plant
needs a long, warm growing season. In Middletown, Connecticut,
I sowed seed into 3-inch peat pots filled with a commercial seed
starting mix on April 11th, just about a week before the average
date of the last spring frost. Maybe because I soaked the large, hard
seeds overnight before planting them or maybe because I set the
seeds 6 inches under a fluorescent light, which kept them extra
warm, my Malabar spinach sprouted promptly, and shoots were
poking up out of the soil by the 19th (for the no-brainer guide to
starting seeds indoors, see page 115).

I kept the seedlings under those fluorescent lights until the end
of May, however, when I started moving them outside for increasing periods of time to harden them off (see page 71 for an explanation of this process), and I didn't plant them into the garden until
June 4th. I set them in a narrow strip of soil that runs between the
south side of the house and a blacktop driveway, so they got lots
of sun and heat. They liked that, though they needed deep and
regular draughts of water. Soon, however, the Malabar spinach

was finding its way up the stakes and strings, and just about the time that the last of my lettuce went to seed and I had to rip it out (on June 30th) the Malabar spinach kicked in with a daily double handful of shoot tips and leaves.

Like true spinach, Malabar is tasty either raw or gently steamed. It has a mucilaginous quality similar to that of okra, though less pronounced, and this makes it a great thickener for soups, gumbos, and vegetable stir-fries. Best of all, the local insects didn't recognize it as edible.

7. **Mizuna.** This is another warm-weather standby, a type of mustard commonly grown in China and Japan, but rarely seen in American gardens. That's a shame, because this plant is not only easy to grow, it's easy on the eyes, too. The long, feathered leaves sprout up in tufts about 12 inches tall and wide, and you may decide these are too pretty for the vegetable garden and instead stir them into a flower bed to lighten the texture of the flowers. Because it gets going early in the spring, mizuna also makes a good temporary cover to plant among your bulbs when their flowers have withered, and no other perennials have yet appeared to take over the display.

Mizuna greens are equally appealing in a salad bowl. The flavor is mild, but mizuna is apparently full of vitamins and minerals, and if picked young, the leaves have that homegrown tenderness you won't find in store-bought stuff. You can also add mizuna (at the last minute) to your stir-fries, or mix it into soups.

The best reason to grow mizuna, though, is that it's both cold and heat tolerant. Sow the seeds right into the garden in early spring, setting them 2 inches apart and half an inch deep. Gradually thin the seedlings so that the full-grown plants (mizuna takes about a month to mature) stand 10 inches apart.

In the Deep South, mizuna is a fall, winter, and spring crop, but north of there, this plant will keep its figure and flavor, too, right through the summer. On really hot days your mizuna clumps may wilt, but will revive in the cool of the night.

As with other greens, you shouldn't plant all your mizuna at once. Instead, plant a cluster of plants in early spring, another cluster two or three weeks later, and another two or three weeks after that. Et cetera. In this way, you'll always have a few plants reaching that wonderful stage of first, succulent picking—just pull out the tougher leaved older plants as the young ones come in to replace them.

20-minute tip: In a pinch you can renew an aging mizuna by gathering the leaves up into a bunch and slicing them off an inch or so above the ground. The new growth that emerges in a week or so will have the appearance and the taste of a youngster. This treatment will also help cleanse any insect pests from the plants.

8. Radishes. This is a fast-growing, no-brainer kind of vegetable, the one that all the authorities on gardening with children tell you to plant with your kids. That makes it just about ideal for a 20-minute gardener.

There are actually two classes of radishes, spring radishes and winter radishes (which you actually grow in the fall in most places). We deal with the fall radishes elsewhere (see Chapter 6, page 135), and will confine ourselves to the spring kind here, because the spring radishes, the familiar red-rooted ones, are the most fun.

Start planting your radishes in early spring, setting the seeds an inch apart and a half inch deep. The plants will be up in three to four days and ready to harvest in four to six weeks. Don't delay the harvest, either. Spring radishes are good only while the roots are young and crisp. That's why it's best to plant your radish seeds a pinch at a time. Plant a whole packet at once, and you are going to find yourself stuck with half a bushel of radishes at pulling time. If you do, try grating your radishes and mixing them with a little sesame oil to make a side dish, or slicing them very thin and marinating them for a few hours in sugar, water, and rice vinegar to make a Chinese pickle. Or peel the radishes, grate them, and stir fry them with scallions and shrimp.

There are all sorts of designer radishes: "French" radishes such s 'D'Avignon', which have long, cylindrical roots, and Chinese 'Shunkyo' radishes, which have a hot but sweet flavor. My favorite s 'Easter Egg', whose little globular roots may be red, purple, white, or lavender.

20-minute tip: There's a particularly unpleasant insect, the cabbage root maggot, that likes to burrow into radish roots and spoil your harvest. To discourage this pest, mix a sprinkling of ashes from the fireplace into the soil when you plant, and dust some more over the seedlings when they emerge.

9. Spinach. The only trick to growing spinach is being prompt. Sow the seeds right into the garden in early spring, as soon as the soil warms and dries enough that you can dig it safely. In general, four to six weeks before the last frost date is about the right time. If you are sowing the seed into an old garden bed, work in a half inch of composted manure first, because spinach likes a rich soil.

Sprinkle the seeds thinly over the planting area and work them in with your hand cultivator. Water regularly and thin the emerging seedlings to stand 4 inches apart. The leaves will be ready to pick in about a month and a half. I snap them off at the base of the stems, taking one here, one there, trying not to butcher any one plant. When a stem starts to shoot up from a spinach's center, I cut the whole plant back just above ground level. In this way, I keep the plants producing right into June, which is the end of the spinach season, even in Connecticut.

20-minute tip: The worst pest of spinach is the leaf miner, a type of fly whose larvae tunnel through the spinach leaves. You'll know you've got them when you see the twisting gray tracks. By that time, it's too late to do anything except cut off the infested leaves and get rid of them with your garbage. Don't put them in your compost heap, for that will help the leaf miners establish a permanent colony.

10. Swiss chard. Switzerland is not known for its adventurous cuisine, and Swiss chard *is* bland, if you steam it or boil it in the traditional fashion. So don't. Instead, pick the leaves while they are still young and tender, chop them up, and add them raw to salads. Most gardening guides and seed packet instructions will tell you to start planting Swiss chard two to three weeks before the last spring frost, so that you will harvest the leaves as early as possible. That strikes me as stupid. As a salad green, Swiss chard isn't in a league with loose-leaf lettuce, spinach, arugula, and the other spring greens. Save it for a summertime harvest, when its sheer persistence makes it a star—Swiss chard is both heat and cold tolerant. Plant again in late summer, and you can have a fall picking of chard that will last well into winter in the South.

So don't plant Swiss chard until midspring, say two weeks after the last frost date. Set the seeds 2 to 4 inches apart and a quarter inch deep. After the seedlings emerge, let them grow to eating size—3 to 4 inches tall—and then pull every other plant. The remaining plants should now stand 4 to 6 inches apart. You can start harvesting individual leaves from them when the plants reach a height of 6 to 8 inches. Cut the leaves off about 2 inches above ground level, and within a week or so, new growth will sprout to replace the casualties.

20-minute tip: To hide your Swiss chard away from vegetable-eating bugs and critters, buy seed of one of the 'Ruby' or 'Rhubarb' chards, and plant them in your flower bed. The brilliant red stems of the ruby chards make a vivid contrast to the deep green of the leaves, and the display puts your average petunia or salvia to shame.

11. 'Sugar Snap' peas. Quite likely, the sweet pods will never make it into a salad. But that's okay, because the pest in this case will be your children. This is a vegetable they'll eat without nagging, and as such you should treat it as one of the miracles of Nature. Of course, if you find out that your partner or spouse is the thief, then strong measures are indicated.

Saint Patrick's Day, my wife, Suzanne O'Connell, maintains, is the time to plant peas in southern New England, though I suspect this connection has more to do with the color of the vegetable than s horticultural needs. Still, it is true that peas need a quite early owing; they should go into the ground as soon as the soil thaws nd dries enough to be dug and raked. Make sure that the soil is well drained, however, for if it stays soggy as well as chilly, the pea eeds are liable to rot before they can germinate. The soil mix we reated for Marty's instant garden is excellent for peas. If your soil s sticky and dense, be sure to spread a couple of inches of compost nd an inch of "sharp" sand over the pea-growing area and dig this n with a garden fork before you plant.

Peas are one vegetable that I do sow in a row. Because I always lant climbing types, I line my peas up along the foot of a trellis, set-ing the seeds in 2 inches apart and an inch deep. There are *dwarf* edble podded peas, varieties that don't climb and so don't need upport, but a 20-minute gardener isn't so foolish as to plant them. hey need lots of horizontal space to spread over, and that means a igger bed, more digging, more weeding, etc. Climbing peas expand ertically, and so produce far more harvest per square foot of garden.

That's why I favor the original 'Sugar Snap' pea over its newer, 'improved" offspring. I plant it along the road side of the porch, nd it has climbed to 6 or 7 feet there, furnishing privacy as well as distraction for my eight-year-old son.

20-minute tip: One of the great advantages of peas and beans is hat their roots cooperate with a natural soil bacteria to extract nirogen, a major plant nutrient, directly from the air. Essentially, hese plants (which are known as legumes) manufacture their own ertilizer. However, if you grow peas in an area where they haven't rown for a number of years previously, the bacteria may not be resent in the soil. Without its help, the peas won't be able to ather nitrogen. To make sure this doesn't happen, dust your pea eeds before planting with a "legume innoculant," which is noth-ng more than a concentrated culture of the helpful bacteria. You an buy this at the local garden center and from most seed catalogs.

2⏰-MINUTE PROJECT:
Tom's Checkered Career

As we have mentioned before (someplace, sometime), one of the central skills of 20-minute gardening is getting double mileage out of a single plant. Like growing flowers you can also eat, as Marty does with his zucchinis (though, of course, it is really Judy who does that). Or growing salads that you can use to decorate the front yard. That's what Tom does with his lettuces.

This is a technique Tom developed out of necessity. As in most suburban yards, the only really sunny spot on Tom's property lies in front of the house. That's because his house, like most, was designed for the last generation's lifestyle. It has a separate dining room for those sit-down meals that the family would have enjoyed thirty years ago, back when people had time for such graces. Likewise, the yard has been entirely planted with shade trees, from which to sling hammocks, if one had time for that. But the area outside the front door (which nobody uses—visitors and family all go straight from their cars to the kitchen door) has been kept treeless and open. This is so that in the evenings, when Tom is sitting with his paper on the front stoop (which he would do, if he weren't still at work), he can call hello to his neighbors as they stroll by on the sidewalk (if they strolled, instead of rocketing by in their sport utility vehicles).

To get to the point: the broad field of vision that the builder thoughtfully and uselessly created in front of Tom's front door, and probably in front of yours, means that there is no canopy of foliage overhanging this spot and hence the sun actually reaches the ground there most of the day. This is precisely the situation that most vegetables prefer. Besides, Tom reasoned that his front yard was actually the most private spot in his yard for a vegetable garden. Those Land Rovers and Jeeps were moving by too fast, Tom figured, for the occupants to notice anything as small as a vegetable garden, let alone the animals that their bumper stickers claim they stop for.

Nevertheless, Tom wanted the front-yard vegetable garden to be attractive. (He still strolls along the sidewalks whenever he has time, even though that isn't often enough.) Tom trained under immigrant Sicilian gardeners, and from them he learned to love the beauty of well-grown vegetables. He sees no reason to grow hostas for foliage effects when there are so many colorful lettuces. The lettuces taste better, too.

To lay out a decorative lettuce garden, Tom first assembled his palette of colors. That means he ordered seeds of a red and a green leaf lettuce from *Cook's Garden:* 'Lollo Biondo' (green) and 'Lollo Rossa' (red). On March 27th, he moistened a 10-quart bag of commercial seed-starting mix by cutting off a corner and pouring in 2 quarts of hot water. Afterward, he used the mix to fill all thirty-six compartments in each of two plastic seed-starting flats he had bought at the garden center. Then into each compartment he dropped two lettuce seeds, reasoning that if one seed didn't germinate, the other was sure to do so. After covering the seeds with an eighth inch more of the seed-starting mix, he watered the flats and set them under the fluorescent lights he has hung up in the basement for this purpose (see page 115 for a description).

Four days later the seeds had germinated and wisps of green were poking up through the surface of the soil. When the little plants had started making leaves recognizable as lettuce, Tom snipped off any extra seedlings, reducing to just one the population of each of the trays' compartments. Once a week he fed the seedlings with ordinary houseplant fertilizer, the type that you dissolve in water and then apply with a watering can.

By the third week in April he was already hardening off the seedlings. (See "Tom Starts from Seed" on page 115 for details of this process.) This process is like sending your kid off to school for the first time—it's less traumatic for everyone if you ease into it. So Tom gave his lettuce seedlings a week to adjust to life outdoors. Then came the great day.

Tom had been contemplating a variety of designs for his lettuce garden, but had finally settled on a red-and-green plaid. That seemed festive. After forking up the raised bed nearest the road and digging in a half trash barrel of compost (lettuce prefers a rich, organic soil), he raked the soil smooth. This work absorbed all of Tom's twenty minutes, but he decided to splurge. He'd work another twenty minutes, and take off the next day. Then, taking a handful of lime, he began dribbling it onto the bed's surface, drawing a bold crisscross of perpendicular lines. When finished, these divided the bed into a series of squares, each one 2 feet by 2 feet.

Into each of the squares he planted lettuce seedlings of a single color, making sure to space the little plants about 8 inches apart (from center to center) so that they would have room to spread their roots and expand. One square he filled with red lettuces; the next one he filled with green. When the whole bed was planted, he watered with a half-strength solution of the water-soluble houseplant fertilizer. Then he stepped back to admire his work.

Within a couple of weeks the lettuces had covered every scrap of soil in the bed, creating a sort of golfing-pants tartan effect. This didn't stop traffic, but it did slow the passing cars. Tom wouldn't have thought that possible. Nor would he have thought it possible to find lettuce harvesting so fraught with decisions.

He had planted leaf lettuce because it is harvested leaf by leaf, rather than a whole head at a time, as are the more familiar heading types such as iceberg. To pluck a whole head would leave a gap in the lettuce garden's pattern. By planting the leaf lettuces, Tom planned to eat his garden and have it, too. But if his plaid was not to develop a moth-eaten appearance, Tom found that he had to pick his leaves judiciously, just one here and one there. Needless to say, he wouldn't let any other family members harvest the salads. They couldn't be trusted to take the job seriously.

By June, the longer days of summer had caused his lettuce to bolt. That is, the neat little leaf lettuces started sending up tall, unsightly flower stalks. There was nothing to do but uproot the whole plaid garden. But that is one of the great pleasures of this kind of display. It is what the artists call "ephemeral." That means you can do something different the next year. You can plant your lettuces in stripes. Or zigzags. Or chevrons. Personally, Tom liked the stripes. They were somehow more elegant than plaid.

2🕐-MINUTE PROJECT:
Less Is Less

Marty isn't sure who came up with the maxim about less being more, but he does know that they got it wrong. Or at least, they left out the important first part. Really, less is less: less garden (we're speaking spatially) is less work. Of course, the corollary of that is that less work is more fun, so maybe less *is* more, ultimately.

The best illustration of this notion, Asher's Second Law, is what Marty calls his open-air salad bar. This is a long, double-length window box that hangs outside the east-facing windows of Marty's sun porch. The morning sun strikes this window box, but after noon, the house protects it from the hot afternoon sun. The shade-tolerant greens Marty grows in the window box don't miss it, however, and they do appreciate the coolness.

Because the soil in a window box cannot draw moisture up from deep in the ground as garden soil does, window boxes tend to dry out quickly. You can compensate for this by watering more frequently, but dragging the hose over even once every couple of days is plenty of work for a 20-minute gardener. So instead, Marty has chosen to protect his aerial garden from drought by mixing a greater proportion of sphagnum peat into his window-box soil. His recipe for this is one part (by volume) bagged topsoil, one part perlite, and two parts peat. The perlite, a kind of volcanic rock, sounds exotic but it's sold at every garden center. It serves to loosen the soil, just like sand, but it weighs almost nothing and helps to keep the window box lighter. Finally, for every bucket of the soil mix, Marty adds a half cup of ground limestone.

Marty starts the window-box season with a quick crop of arugula. Mostly, he picks individual leaves from various plants, but as the arugula production starts to peak, he opens up planting spots by pulling whole plants and inserts a couple of lettuce seedlings (whatever kind he can find at Thee Plante Shoppe). The lettuces take hold by the time the arugula starts going to seed, so that pulling the arugula doesn't leave the window box empty. He fills in around the lettuces with whatever else strikes his fancy: perhaps some basil to chop into the dressing, or some 'Ruby' Swiss chard.

When summer weather put an end to the lettuce last year, he plugged that gap with a couple of seedlings of Malabar spinach that he begged off of Tom. The festoons, glossy green leaves, and red stems were striking, and not a single visitor, whatever his or her horticultural pretensions, identified the plant correctly.

Marty, who abhors confrontations with the local wildlife, appreciated the fact that his window-box salad bar didn't force him into conflicts with the resident rabbits and woodchucks. Of course, the box was too small to furnish more than a taste of anything. But what it produced tasted pretty good, and even better when the horticultural high flyers stood speechless before his edible display.

Chapter 5

Hot Tomatoes
(Not to Mention Eggplants and Peppers)

In spring a young man's thoughts may (as Alfred Tennyson claimed) turn to love, but by midsummer one thing is sure: this same Romeo will be thinking about tomatoes.

The fruit, we mean. Surprisingly, this is a food that until relatively recently, nobody much wanted. In its original Andean homeland, the natives didn't even think it worth cultivating, and when Europeans first encountered a golden-hued tomato in Aztec Mexico (the Mexicans, at least, knew a good thing), they decided that anything so awful-tasting must be medicinal. Promoted as a cure for skin diseases, glaucoma, and "the vapors" (a feminine ailment, apparently), the tomato was also suspected of serious side effects. For it was rumored that this "love apple" was really an aphrodisiac. No doubt that's why the English grew it for three hundred years as an ornamental plant without developing a single recipe. Even in the United States, tomatoes were, until the middle of the nineteenth century, invariably reduced to catsup before consumption.

Today, though, the tomato is first among vegetables. It's a national obsession. We can survive a baseball strike. We've done that before. But summer just wouldn't be summer without the rich burst of mingled sweet and sour you get when you bite into a dead ripe, fresh-picked tomato. Every expert we consulted (we don't just make this stuff up as we go along) emphasized the tomato is the best single argument for a vegetable garden. You just won't get that genuine flavor unless you raise the tomatoes yourself.

Of course there are other reasons to grow tomatoes. They are the most ego-bolstering experience that gardening has to offer. Virtually anybody can grow tomatoes—they are that undemanding—especially if you practice a couple of 20-minute tricks. In a period of just two months even Marty can turn a pinch of dry little seeds into lush vines hung with fruits better than those any farmstand can supply.

That's no exaggeration, either. Economics oblige commercial growers to cultivate types of tomatoes that lend themselves to mass handling, long-distance shipping, and days on the shelf. Flavor comes second, if it enters into the equation at all. Only home growers can afford to grow the cost-ineffective types of tomatoes that taste the best.

Tomato growing is also the closest thing to a competitive sport that vegetable gardening has to offer. If virtually anyone can grow tomatoes, well, virtually everyone with any kind of garden does. That means if you manage to ripen your first tomato of the summer a week before anyone else in your area, you'll have bragging rights over *all* your neighbors. Tell your brother-in-law about your triumph with the dahlias, and he'll roll his eyes and turn up the television. Tell him that *you* have been picking tomatoes for a month already, and that, oh, really, he still hasn't got any, it's prob-

Hot Tomatoes

9 5

ably the soil, not his fault, and the poor guy may pretend not to listen. But you will have scored a hit.

Or you can go for size. Raise up the biggest tomato in town, and you'll get your fifteen minutes of fame, plus an opportunity to condescend to all those less skilled. Sure, this is mean-spirited, but gardening is largely about this sort of ruthless competition. Anyone who thinks otherwise has probably never gotten his or her hands dirty.

Obviously, we are going to offer tips for how to win at both competitions, the one for precocity *and* the one for size.

Of course, for many people, tomato growing is a matter of family or ethnic tradition. Such individuals are both fortunate and cursed. They are fortunate because they usually have the best recipes for cooking the tomatoes into sauces, salsas, etc. As a rule, they won't share those recipes, either, or at least the version they do share lacks one or more essential ingredient.

Maybe the bad karma that they earn with that selfishness is the reason for their ultimate misfortune. It seems that most of these guardians of tradition not only preserve a recipe but also the seed of some special tomato that a grandfather brought from Naples, France, Russia, or wherever. Each year the descendants carefully save seed from their harvest so that they will have seed to plant again next year. Unlike most modern hybrid vegetables and fruits, whose seeds will not produce offspring like the parents, heirloom tomatoes generally do reproduce true to type from collected seed.

By growing the same strain of tomato year after year, though, the tomato traditionalists ensure that their gardens build up a permanent population of whatever pests and diseases to which their tomatoes are vulnerable. Almost certainly, the heirlooms will perform better in your garden. Point that out when you ask for seed (and offer to trade part of your harvest for the recipe—the complete recipe).

One more benefit of tomato growing: once you have this down, you can use the same skills to grow those tomato relatives, peppers and eggplants. Really, these three crops, with a jug of wine, loaf of

Are you tired of the annual spring pilgrimage to the woman down the street with the special tomato that has been in her family for umpteen generations? Have you thought about the fact that she's probably just as tired of handing over seedlings to you each spring, just to get you out the door? It's time you learned to do what she does: save a few seeds from this year's fruits to start the plants for next year's. In short, it's time to learn all those things your parents were continually promoting: independence, self-reliance, thrift, foresight. Fortunately, this is a lot easier than they made it out to be. It shouldn't take more than five minutes' study.

After all, this is something that until recently, everybody used to do. Everybody who grew their own food, anyway. Even a hundred years ago, most farmers and gardeners routinely saved seed for the spring planting. So it's got to be easy.

It is, except that modern science has complicated the process a bit. Many, or even most of the seeds you'll find in the mail-order catalogs are hybrids. That is, they were produced by crossing two dissimilar parents. Gardeners like hybrids because they have the reputation for being more vigorous and disease resistant (and often they are, though they may not taste as good). Nurserymen *love* hybrids because they are genetically unstable, and the seeds they bear won't produce plants anything like the parent. In gardener's lingo, they don't "come true." That means it's not worth saving those seeds.

So what seeds do you save? The older varieties, the ones that are classified as "standards" or "open pollinated." How do you identify tomatoes of this type? In part by what the catalog doesn't say. Seedsmen are required by law to label hybrids as such, and most catalogs observe this rule. So if a tomato isn't identified as a hybrid, it's probably a standard variety.

Another clue is if the tomato is advertised as an "heirloom." Heirlooms are survivors from the days when seed saving was the rule rather than the exception, so virtually all of them are of the standard type.

How do you save tomato seeds? Inspect all the plants of the type of tomato you want to preserve. Choose the best performer, the plant that has the most vigorous growth, and has produced a big crop of first-quality fruit. Then, on this plant find a large, well-shaped fruit. Leave it on the plant until it is dead ripe, still firm but fully colored, pick it, cut it open, and scoop out the seeds and pulp.

Put this goo in a jar with a little water and let it sit for two to four days. Then pour it into a sieve and run water through the seeds to clean them. Spread the seeds on a paper towel and set them out in an airy and warm, but not hot, place to dry. When the seeds have completely dried, scrape them off into an ordinary paper envelope on which you have written the type of tomato and the date. Seal the envelope and put it somewhere dry, airy, and cool, like a pigeonhole in your desk. Stored in this fashion, the seeds should remain healthy and viable for several years.

bread, and thou, are all you truly need. So, master tomatoes, declare yourself a gardener, and get on to something else.

Tomato Basics

What do tomatoes need?

- **Lots of sun, for starters.** For a tomato patch in a Northern garden, choose the spot that comes as close as possible to getting full sun all day. Six hours of full sun a day is the minimum requirement in the northern half of the country.
- **Some shade, too, in the South.** You can have too much of a good thing. In the South and Southwest, the intense summer sunlight can sunburn the fruits. It may also overheat the plants. Temperatures above 90°F can cause the tomato blossoms to abort, and without flowers, you get no fruit. In those extra-sunny regions,

you would do well to set the plants where they will be shaded in the early afternoon, the time of day when the sun is most intense.

- **Elbow room.** Tomatoes won't stand crowding. Most vegetables we recommend packing in shoulder to shoulder, to keep out weeds and increase the harvest. Tomatoes sulk when treated that way and bear fewer, smaller fruits. In average conditions, a tomato plant needs at least 4 square feet of a garden, and 6 square feet is better.

- **Good soil.** Tomatoes will grow in most soils, but perform dramatically better in good ones. A slightly acidic, well-drained soil that is rich in humus, such as Tom created for Marty's raised bed, is ideal. If your soil is sandy or a sticky clay, spread 3 inches of compost over your tomato plot and dig it in with a garden fork, turning the soil to a depth of a foot, before planting.

- **Fertilizer.** Tomatoes like fertilizers in which the last two numbers of the nutrient ratio (the string of numbers on the label) are highest. Accordingly, a week before you plant, sprinkle 5-10-10 fertilizer over your tomato-planting area at a rate of 1 pound per square foot (that's a third pound for our standard 4′ × 8′ bed). If you are an organic gardener, you can make your own tomato fertilizer by mixing equal parts of wood ashes and bonemeal, and applying this at the same rate.

- **Plant deep.** Before you set a tomato seedling into the soil, pinch off the bottom leaves, and dig a planting hole deep enough so that at least half the stem ends up below ground. If the tomato seedling is really tall, a garden-center leftover that you picked up cheap, maybe, plant it on its side. Bury the stem in a 6-inch-deep trench, bending the tip upward so that the topmost leaves stand above the soil. When you plant in this fashion, be sure to pinch off any leaves that would end up buried. Otherwise, they'll rot and create an entry point for soilborne diseases and parasites.

- **Protection from the cold.** Ideally, you shouldn't plant tomato seedlings in your garden until the soil has warmed up and you are reasonably certain that the temperature won't drop much below 50°F. If the weather gets much colder than that, the tomato seedlings may suffer a chill that will slow their growth. The plants will look okay, except that they won't thrive. So don't rush your tomatoes.

Of course, we all (even Marty) occasionally make mistakes and misjudge the season. Sometimes, like Tom, we make mistakes deliberately, because we have to have the earliest tomatoes in the neighborhood. If you do set out the tomato plants too early, however, there are a couple of easy ways to protect the plants from the cold. Covering the seedlings with a floating row cover (see page 258) will get them through a day or two of raw, chilly weather. If a serious frost is predicted, dump loose leaves or straw around the plants until they are completely covered. Then spread a plastic painter's drop cloth over the bed, pinning the plastic down at the corners with stones. As soon as the danger of frost has passed, exhume the tomatoes, taking care not to damage the little plants.

- **Conscientious irrigation.** Tomatoes need lots of moisture, but they won't tolerate waterlogged soils. They don't like drought, either, and letting the plants go thirsty for even a day or two is likely to ruin the fruit, for when you resume watering, the ripening tomatoes will split or rot at the bottom.

A drip irrigation system with an electronic timer that turns the water off after a preset interval offers one way to keep your tomato plot moist but not wet. Mulching the soil around the plants with straw or shredded leaves also helps keep the soil moisture even.

In general, you should water newly transplanted seedlings every day or so during rainless weather through the first few weeks of their outdoor life; then cut back to one deep watering every five to seven days as the plants become established.

To encourage self-sufficiency, use a trick advocated by Fred Dubose, a man who learned his tomato growing in the South Pacific kingdom of Tonga, and later went on to write *the* text, *The Total Tomato* (Harper & Row, 1985).

Fred suggests digging a planting hole for each seedling that is

3 feet wide and 2½ feet deep. Into this you first put a 6-inch layer of some vegetable waste such as rotting leaves or even corncobs and shucks. This will absorb water and serves as a reservoir to the tomato roots. Over the vegetable waste you spread a bucket of well-aged manure. Then you refill the hole with soil laced with compost, and you plant the tomato seedling into that.

- **Fertilize** again with the same formula at the same dose just as the tomato plants start to flower.
- **Rotate your planting.** Tomatoes are prone to a number of diseases (see "Tomato Terminology") and the pathogens that were a minor problem for this year's plants may persist in the soil to become a serious problem for next year's seedlings. So don't replant tomatoes in the same spot each spring. Instead, move the planting each spring and don't return to any previous planting area until an interval of three years has elapsed. By then, these pathogens will have died of old age.

Tomato Terminology

When shopping for tomato seeds, you'll find that, as always in gardening, there is a jargon of incomprehensible terminology. To help you with this process, we are including a brief glossary.

1. Indeterminate. An indeterminate tomato is one that continues to grow and bear fruits a few at a time throughout the summer. This is the type of tomato that most of us want.

2. Determinate. Tomatoes of this type make smaller, compact plants whose fruit ripen all at once. These are plants that have been bred for sauce making and canning. Unless you intend to do this with the fruits, avoid determinate tomatoes, as they will choke the kitchen with fruits for a week or two and then leave you dependent, Blanche Du Bois style, on the kindness of neighbors and strangers for the rest of the summer.

3. V or VF, or VFF, or VFN, or VNT, etc. You may find a string of initials right after the name of the tomato in the catalog listing. This is good. Each one of those letters indicates a disease to which the tomato is resistant. In general, the more letters the better, especially if you are gardening in the Southeast, where hot, humid summers create perfect conditions for a tomato epidemic, or in a cool, cloudy climate, where tomatoes may struggle to survive at all, let alone bear fruit.

4. Early season, main season, and late. These terms indicate the length of time the tomato plant will require to mature and then bear ripe fruit. Early-season varieties are fastest, usually producing ready-to-pick tomatoes in less than sixty-five days after you transplant the seedlings into the garden. As a rule, midseason varieties take sixty-five to seventy-nine days; late-season varieties typically take eighty or more days.

So plant just early varieties, right? Wrong—with a few exceptions, the fast-maturing tomatoes don't taste as good as the mid- and late-season types. Anyway, the early-season tomatoes may wear themselves out by mid to late summer. Usually, it is a better plan to grow some early-season tomatoes and some midseason. Late-season tomatoes should be reserved for southern areas, where the growing season is really long and warm. In the far north, of course, where the growing season is short, you may not have time to grow anything but the early-season tomatoes.

Keep in mind, too, that the number of days to harvest listed in catalogs and on seed packets are an average figure. If your summer proves to be a bit chillier or cloudier than most, then your tomatoes may take longer to bear than the days-to-harvest figure specifies.

Starting from Seed

Tomatoes are the best argument for investing in some plastic seedling trays, and starting a few plants from seed. This is a simple and virtually fail-safe process with tomatoes, and it fits right into a 20-minute gardener's schedule. Most gardening guides advise you to sow your tomato seeds six to eight weeks before the last frost date for your area. In fact, we find that using our certified 20-minute method for indoor seed starting, four weeks is plenty. Actually, to label this as 20-minute gardening is deceptive advertising, because never will your indoor tomato nursery demand more than five to ten minutes a day. For a complete guide, turn to the end of this chapter, page 115.

Of course, you don't have to start your own seedlings. You can wait until the last minute and then scour the local garden centers for whatever tomato seedlings they have on hand. This is a spring tradition with Marty. But whereas you will find hundreds of varieties of tomatoes in seed catalogs, at the local retailer you find maybe two or three. What's more, those two or three weren't chosen on the basis of their fruits' spectacular flavor. Instead, they are just whatever the wholesale nursery (the grower that supplies your local retailer) decided was easiest and most profitable for them to grow.

Not only do you sacrifice flavor in going with the off-the-shelf tomatoes, you'll probably find those mass-produced seedlings more difficult to grow. Tomatoes are regional. Each type prefers a different climate and a different soil, and the secret of trouble-free growing lies in choosing those that like your region.

Just as a for-instance: Tom's mother-in-law in the Berkshire Hills of western Massachusetts had never ripened a full-sized tomato in her yard. Ever. She had succeeded in annually harvesting a handful of red cherry tomatoes. But the larger-fruited, slicing types she planted every Memorial Day had never borne even one red tomato before the end-of-the-summer frost cut them down. The problem was not just that the growing season, the interval between the last spring frost and the first fall frost, is short in her region, but also that the Berkshire summers are cool and cloudy. As a plant from equatorial regions, tomatoes like their weather hot and bright.

Then Tom heard of a Czech tomato named 'Stupice' that was supposed to thrive in cool conditions. He ordered seeds, raised seedlings, and that year his mother-in-law harvested buckets of really good-tasting red fruits. She seemed slightly outraged by this break with tradition. Her neighbors, though, would take as many of the 'Stupice' seedlings as Tom could grow, and he was able to trade a dozen for a supply of really chic llama manure.

What are the best tomato selections for your region? We've listed a few regional favorites below. For truly local expertise, though, you should make your way to the garden of the retired gentleman down the street. Tomato growing seems to be a male preoccupation. In addition, it's a contemplative activity that we usually concentrate on with increasing age. Try the senior center in

Trading Up

For Tom, the tomato seedlings he started under fluorescent lights in his basement had always been a cherished symbol of self-sufficiency. Marty, though, soon taught him the real value of those little plants. They are, he explained, the bait.

Gardening may *seem* like an idyll, but only to outsiders. Anyone who has ever actually gotten dirt under his fingernails knows how relentlessly competitive gardening is. There's always someone in the neighborhood who has better sources for plants, and an obsessive focus a 20-minute gardener cannot match. That someone gets the 'Italian White' sunflowers that make your old 'Russian Mammoths' look as cheap as a Soviet suit. Your competitor orders early and gets the new daylily hybrid that's sold out when you finally call the nursery. And do you think that this plant miser will share? Absolutely—because he or she wants a cut of your tomato seedlings.

These are the ultimate bargaining chip because everybody grows tomatoes, so everybody wants tomato seedlings, and they are the most painless plants for you to grow. Tomatoes are so easy to start from seed that even Marty has considered trying it. He's the one who figured out that the real secret of horticultural success lies in identifying ahead of time what will be next year's hot tomato. Sow a good supply of that, and you can dictate terms to your gardening neighbors.

Three years ago, following Marty's advice, Tom focused on heirlooms. He started two trays of 'Brandywine' seedlings. A century-old Amish tomato, this bears medium-sized to large fruits with a flavor that experts (like Tom's neighbor Luciano) describe as "incredible." With those seedlings, Tom scored his first white sunflowers.

The next year, Tom shifted gears to Native American, sowing 'Cherokee Purple'. The color of this fruit is as intense as the name suggests, the flavor excellent, and the provenance is politically most correct. Tom traded these for seedlings of a lemon apple cucumber he just had to have, and his neighbor sweetened the deal with a pinch of seeds of a "perennial German lettuce." That proved to be a particularly sweet-flavored strain of mâche, and because Tom lets a few mâche plants go to seed each year, this green has returned spontaneously every succeeding spring and fall. He depends on this to provide free beds of greens on which to serve his tomatoes.

Last year, Marty recommended practical, so Tom sowed 'Stupice'. We've already detailed his experience with that, and will only add that though the neighbors scoffed at Tom's "designer manure," he knew that secretly they were envious. This year, though, Tom's going for tall. He's going to try 'Climbing Trip-L-Crop', otherwise known as the "Italian Tree Tomato." (It's okay—this is a true tomato, not some exotic counterfeit.) This is reputed to make vines 10 to 15 feet long that you can train up a trellis like a rose. It's supposed to bear large crops of big fruit, too.

Marty, meanwhile, has yet to sow his first tomato seed. But he's figured out how to get his bargaining chips ready to swap. He's found a nursery in California that will ship connoisseur tomato seedlings to him by air freight. The Santa Barbara Heirloom Nursery has an "Heirloom Collection" that Marty hopes will be good for whatever the people over the fence have got and he hasn't. Especially when he tells them how he rescued the seed for his tomato seedlings from a salad in that little bistro on the Left Bank.

town, or the Sons of Italy club, or the Polish Falcons, or any othe
ethnic club where older guys hang out together smoking truly fou
cigars, boasting and lying, and planning their next banquet. Failing
that, write to the National Council of State Garden Clubs, Inc.
401 Magnolia Ave., St. Louis, MO 63110, and ask for the neares
chapter of the Men's Garden Club of America.

Tomatoes for Areas with Cool, Short Summers

'Stupice' (indeterminate,* early) The Czech tomato that has immi
grated to the Berkshire Hills of western Massachusetts. Heavy
crops of small (1 to 2 ounces) red, very flavorful tomatoes.

'Valencia' (indeterminate, midseason) An heirloom variety from
Maine that produces dependably even in northern regions, bearing
large orange, good-tasting tomatoes.

Tomatoes for the Damp, Cool Pacific Northwest

'San Francisco Fog' (indeterminate, midseason) "The coldest winter I ever experienced," wrote Mark Twain, "was the summer I
spent in San Francisco." Though most tomatoes crave hot, sunny
weather, this variety thrives in the chilly, foggy conditions of the
coastal Northwest.

'Nepal' (indeterminate, late) A Himalayan tomato adapted to cold
weather, this variety is the best beefsteak-type tomato for this region.

Tomatoes for the Mid-Atlantic States

'Druzba' (indeterminate, late) A Bulgarian heirloom that bears
large, exceptionally flavorful tomatoes on plants that are resistant
to disease and that cope well with environmental stress.

'Tropic' (indeterminate, midseason or late) An exceptionally disease-resistant variety that performs well in this region's hot, humid
summers.

---

* For an explanation of this and other terms, please see the glossary on pages
101–2.

Tomatoes for the Deep South

'**Manalucie**' (indeterminate, late) Exceptionally disease resistant, with upright vines that keep the large fruits shaded and so protected from sun scald.

'**Porter**' (indeterminate, midseason) A Texas heirloom that sets even at high temperatures, bearing small, egg-shaped fruits with an outstanding flavor.

'**Southern Night**' (determinate, late) A Russian heirloom that bears small to midsized tomatoes with a rich, sweet flavor and mahogany, almost black skins.

'**Sun Leaper**' (determinate, midseason) This variety sets fruit even when nighttime temperatures are high, a condition that causes crop failure in most other varieties. Large (9 ounce), good-tasting fruits.

'**Tropic**' (indeterminate, midseason or late) In addition to its disease resistance, this variety bears the fruit up under the leaves so that they are shaded and less liable to suffer scalding from the intense Southern sun.

Tomatoes for the Southwest

'**Chiapas Wild Tomato**' (indeterminate) Sprawling vines that bear cherry-sized fruits throughout the summer.

'**Punta Banda Tomato**' (indeterminate) These plants cope well with heat, water stress, and poor soil, still bearing lots of meaty, cherry-sized tomatoes.

'**Rio Grande**' (determinate, late) Disease-resistant plants that withstand this region's combination of hot days and cold nights especially well. This tomato bears 4-inch, pear-shaped, meaty fruits ideal for sauce making and canning.

A Personal Trainer

Every town has at least one: the gardener who turns his tomato plants into a type of bonsai. This obsessive type manages every inch of the plants' growth, pinching off extra shoots and shaping the others with a corset of stakes and strings. Ask the tomato trainer why he or she bothers with this, and you will be told that this is the *only* way to grow really satisfactory tomatoes.

The proper response to this statement is, of course, a rude noise. Tomato training of this sort is all about the gardener's insecurity and need for control, and has very little to do with the needs of the tomato. You can, if you choose, let your tomato vines sprawl. The plants actually produce a larger crop of fruit when grown in this way. Unfortunately, as Marty has found, you lose quite a number of these fruits, as the tomatoes are liable to rot where they rest on the soil.

For this reason, we recommend caging your tomatoes at planting time. Get a 5-foot-tall roll of wire fencing. You want a coarse mesh whose wires are far enough apart that you can slip your hand through them. Cut the fencing into 6½-foot lengths. Roll these into cylinders 2 feet in diameter, and twist the cut ends of the wires around the other end of the sheet of fencing to fasten the rolls together. Slip one of these homemade cages down over each of your tomato seedlings, driving a stake into the soil on either side to anchor it.

As the seedlings grow, the cages will contain the sprawl of the vines and channel it upward. That will keep the fruits safely elevated above the soil, and by keeping the tomato leaves clean and dry, it will also help protect the plants against disease. As for the pinching and pruning, forget them, unless you are in a competitive mode. By reducing the number of tomatoes a plant bears, pruning the vines tends to increase the size of the remaining fruits. So if big is your goal, prune. But if all you seek is good flavor, don't bother.

Winning at Tomatoes

As we mentioned earlier, tomatoes are the subject for the most intense gardener-to-gardener competition. Forget winning the blue ribbon at the rose show—that's nice, but who besides a few other rose fanatics will care? Forget winning the award for your town's most welcoming yard." If you want to impress the other men and women in the gardener club, if you want to leave them sick with envy, you have to win at tomatoes.

Winning at tomatoes depends on two things, and two things only. None of your rivals will care if your tomatoes are the best tasting in town. That's a subjective judgment, and they can dispute your success on that score. No, this is competition on the most primitive, childish level. The only criteria that really count are size and speed. You can win by producing the biggest tomato, or you can win by picking your first tomato before any of the neighbors. That's all that matters.

The secret of producing big tomatoes, real monsters, is to start with the right strain of seed. 'Giant Belgium' is the best bet. This is not, in fact, a Belgian tomato. It comes from Ohio. But it is a giant. Or, at least, the fruits are. They average 2 pounds and may reach a full 5 pounds. In sheer, gross bulk, such a cantaloupe-sized fruit is guaranteed to shame any neighbor's 'Burpee Big Boy'.

To get the maximum size out of your 'Giant Belgiums', plant the seedlings in an area of soil in which you have not grown tomatoes or tomato relatives such as eggplants or peppers for several years previously. Otherwise, there may be diseases lurking in the soil that will sap your contender's strength. Give your plants the usual treatment of sun, compost-enriched soil, fertilizer, and consistent watering, but add one secret ingredient: mix a teaspoon of Epsom salts into each hole at planting time. Mulch around the plants with a couple of inches of shredded leaves or straw when the hot weather sets in. Feed the plants weekly by watering them with a solution of kelp extract (available from organic gardening suppliers).

Training and pruning are important when you are striving for jumbo fruits. Erect a tripod of sturdy, 6-foot-tall stakes over each tomato seedling at planting time, and tie the vines up with a soft cotton twine. Pinch off the "suckers," the little shoots that emerge at the base of the vines' main branches, as they appear. There's one more thing you must do, too: to raise the biggest fruits, you have to limit the size of the crop. Tomato plants bear their flowers and fruits in "trusses"—little branching bunches. As soon as the first couple of trusses of flowers have turned into little green fruits, you should make a habit of pinching off all additional flowers as they appear. That will help your plant concentrate all its resources into a few prizewinners, rather than a bushel of measly two-pounders. Incidentally, you'll find that your 'Giant Belgium' tomatoes are quite tasty.

Speed Matters

That may not be true of the tomatoes you'll grow if your goal is the earliest harvest. The earliest tomatoes tend to be fairly tasteless, little better than their supermarket relatives. This, of course, is irrelevant to the really dedicated competitor. For those halfhearted souls who wonder why precocious tomatoes can't taste good, we should explain that in breeding for early picking, other characteristics are more important. You want a fast-growing plant, naturally, but you also want one that is cold tolerant. Why? Cold tolerance lets you move your transplants out into the garden while your competitors are still nursing theirs along on a windowsill, thus providing you with a crucial head start.

'Siletz' is actually a pretty good compromise. On average, this plant bears fruit within fifty-two days of the date when the seed is sown. This variety also flowers and sets fruit even in cool weather, something that most tomatoes won't do. Set a 'Big Boy' or a 'Brandywine' out extra early and you won't get fruit any sooner, because the plants will simply mark time until warm weather arrives.

To help your 'Siletz' tomatoes along, plant them in a sheltered warm nook—a sunny spot against the south side of your house is ideal. Dig a 2-foot-deep, 2-foot-wide hole, and fill the bottom 18 inches with fresh horse manure (check the Yellow Pages for the nearest riding academy). Top off the hole with soil mixed half and half with compost, and cover this with a sheet of black plastic. Pin down the black plastic with a rock at each corner, cut an X-shaped pair of slits at the center, and plant through that. The fresh manure will heat the soil from the bottom up as it decomposes, and the black plastic will collect solar energy to heat from the top down. The combination should be enough to make you the most precocious tomato grower your town has ever seen. Your harvest won't taste like much, but that's beside the point.

Tomato Relatives

As we mentioned in the early pages of this chapter, success with tomatoes brings dividends. If you can grow tomatoes, you can also grow the tomato's close relatives, the eggplant and the pepper. They like the same kinds of site and soil, and the same kinds of fertilizers and watering. In fact, tomatoes, eggplants, and peppers are so closely related that they suffer from many of the same diseases and insect pests. For this reason, you should treat these plants as virtual tomatoes and rotate them to new planting areas each spring on the same three-year cycle (for a complete explanation of this process, see Chapter 11, page 256).

There is an important difference in how you raise the seedlings of these plants. Eggplants are slower growing than tomatoes and should be started six weeks before the last spring frost. Peppers are slower growing yet, and should be started eight weeks before the last spring frost.

One word of warning about eggplants: this is not the most versatile of vegetables. An occasional dish of eggplant is a pleasure, but as daily fare it soon palls. How much eggplant parmigiana can you eat? And there doesn't seem to be any easy way to preserve eggplant other than freezing. So don't set out more than one eggplant seedling per family member. But if you do get too ambitious, here's a recipe that can help.

Eggplant Caponata

2 pounds eggplant
1 large onion
¼ cup olive oil
1 cup homemade tomato
   sauce
1 stalk celery, chopped

¾ cup green olives, pitted
   and roughly chopped
4 tablespoons capers, rinsed
   and patted dry
Salt and pepper to taste

Peel and slice the eggplant into ½-inch cubes. Salt the cubes and set them aside on paper towels to drain.

Chop one large onion and sauté in ¼ cup olive oil (the good stuff, the first virgin cold press). When the onion bits turn golden, add the tomato sauce. Simmer this uncovered for 5 to 10 minutes, until it starts to thicken. Add the celery, the olives, and the capers. Salt and pepper this mixture to taste and simmer for an additional twenty minutes. Then remove it from the heat and set it aside to cool.

While the sauce is cooling, dry the eggplant chunks with a paper towel and fry them in hot olive oil until lightly browned. Drain the chunks on newspapers covered with paper towels. Stir the cooked eggplant into the sauce and season to taste. Serve at room temperature.

Peppers for That Natural High

It may be easy to achieve a surplus of eggplants, but peppers—hot peppers—are another matter. The more you eat, the more you want. Just like any other drug, you build up a tolerance to peppers. Besides, peppers are easy to preserve. You can dry the big chilies such as the *poblano* by stringing them together through the bases of the stems with a needle and heavy thread and then hanging them up in the kitchen. It's even easier to turn the small-fruited, fiercer kinds such as 'Scotch Bonnets', 'Tabascos', and 'Thai' peppers into your own homemade pepper sauce from hell. Just fill a jar with the fruits and top it up with white vinegar or vodka. Let this steep for a couple of months and it will be pure jet fuel.

Such a sauce is more than a condiment. A spoonful of pepper juice, Tom was assured by Texan folklorist and former cowhand Bill Brett, is a sure remedy for a sore throat. And the vinegar-based kind is the only sure cure for alcoholism. Every time you get the urge for a drink, Bill explained, you take a sip of the pepper juice. In a matter of weeks, the mere thought of demon rum will arouse an intolerable disgust.

Mind you, Bill told Tom this as he was pouring clear liquid from an unlabeled mason jar. Tom had arrived at Bill's ranch house in the Big Thicket with his fiancée, Suzanne, whose career had temporarily relocated to central Texas. Tom had brought a shopping bag full of hot peppers that he had grown in his Northern garden, and transported to Texas as hand luggage. Tom, Suzanne, and Bill were waiting for the arrival of Bill's son, John Brett, so that they could have a pepper tasting. "John Brett's real macho," Bill had assured the visiting Yankees, "he'll eat anything." Which distinguished him from the other three, who had the good sense to fear that bag's contents.

John Brett, when he arrived at the ranch complete with a pickup truck and rifle in hand, did indeed eat peppers like candy. After slowly chewing each one, he'd make a sorrowful face. "That wudn't real hot," he would explain and reach for another cayenne—or tabasco, or jalapeño, whatever. The problem, John Brett insisted, was that the peppers came from the North, where things were, well, weaker.

"If you weren't here," Bill whispered, "he'd be jumping around the room screaming."

Perhaps it began with a desire to uphold the honor of the North. Surely, though, it was the clear liquid that finally persuaded Tom and Suzanne to match John Brett pepper for pepper. No one remembers how the night ended, or how Tom and Suzanne got home.

But Tom will never forget the phone call that woke him the next morning. Suzanne was gone, she had made her way in to work, and Tom was experiencing a blinding headache as he struggled to find the receiver. There was no identification, only a solemn voice. "I want you to know that I just went to the bathroom," the anonymous caller said. "And I am in agony."

Which goes to prove that peppers have more than one method of teaching sobriety.

Wild Peppers

Bill Brett's most intriguing instruction about pepper growing concerned the *chiltepin,* or "bird peppers," that grow wild across the Southern and Southwestern United States. These are called bird peppers, he said, because birds relish the pea-sized red fruits. In particular, Texans always plant them around the barnyard so that the chickens will eat them. This diet, Bill insisted, leaves the chickens' flesh intrinsically spiced, so that there is no need to season them when they are cooked.

Tom knows from personal experience that chiltepin peppers grow with the vigor of a weed (which is what they are), making small rounded bushes that cover themselves first with small white flowers and later the red fruits. These have a fierce bite, but one whose heat fades quickly. The bushes are naturally drought resistant and Tom has never seen them seriously troubled by insects or disease.

In frost-free regions, these peppers are perennials, but throughout most of the United States they must be grown as annuals. Tom dries and saves a fruit or two in the fall so that he'll have seeds to start indoors the next spring. The rest of the fruits he pours into a bottle to make his own pepper sauce.

In Texas, the fruits serve as a proof of nativity. There, the fruits are dried and used to keep a small silver pillbox filled. This is carried in the pocket, to be casually brought out at power lunches. A chiltepin is extracted and crumbled over the dish, proof that the bearer is a *real* Texan, a person to be reckoned with.

2⊙-MINUTE PROJECT:
Tom Starts from Seed

Raising your own tomato seedlings is more than a matter of practicality. It's therapeutic. For a very modest investment of time, far less than you would spend on a couch spilling your guts out to a therapist, and for a tiny fraction of what the therapist charges, you can achieve the same results. You can delude yourself that you are in control and in charge. The difference is that raising tomato seedlings is a project you finish in four weeks, unlike the years and years you would spend in therapy.

So take your choice. And if you opt for tomatoes, be sure to order your seeds early—in January, ideally—before the types you want sell out. Then, because an emotionally healthy individual like you would never procrastinate, start right in on assembling your underground seed-starting complex. Actually, this is just a shelf in the basement or utility room, but Marty says that sounds dull. Hang a couple of no-frills fluorescent fixtures over the shelf. You want fixtures that accept two four-foot-long fluorescent tubes; you'll find these at the local hardware store, where they sell them as "shop lights." Equip each fixture with one cool white tube and one warm white one.

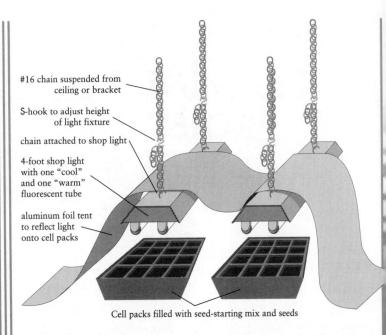

#16 chain suspended from ceiling or bracket

S-hook to adjust height of light fixture

chain attached to shop light

4-foot shop light with one "cool" and one "warm" fluorescent tube

aluminum foil tent to reflect light onto cell packs

Cell packs filled with seed-starting mix and seeds

The best containers for starting seedlings are "cell packs," the divided plastic trays that you find at every garden center in springtime. Buy a couple of these and a bag of packaged seed-starting mix, and stop off at the supermarket on your way home and get a roll of aluminum foil. Then, four weeks before the last spring frost, open the bag of seed-starting mix and pour in a cup or two of hot water to moisten its contents. Fill the cell packs with the moistened seed-starting mix and sow two tomato seeds in each "cell" or compartment, planting the seeds a quarter inch deep. You sow two seeds as insurance—if one doesn't germinate, the other will.

After you've planted all the compartments, water the cell packs (a spray bottle filled with tap water works well for this) and set them under the fluorescent lights. Adjust the cords or chains on which the light fixtures are hung so that the fluorescent tubes are suspended about 8 inches over the surface of the seed-starting mix. Take sheets of aluminum foil and drape them over the light fixtures so that they make a tent over the cell packs. Then turn on the lights.

Leave the lights on round the clock initially. The heat they generate will warm the seed-starting mix and speed the germination of the tomato seeds. As soon as the seedlings pop into view, however (this should happen in eight to ten days), cut the lighting back to fourteen hours a day, and adjust the chains so that the fluorescent tubes hang 10 to 12 inches above the seed-starting mix.

Make sure the seed-starting mix stays evenly moist. A week after the seedlings first emerge, take a pair of nail scissors and snip off extra seedlings so that only one remains in each compartment; plucking out the extras might injure the seedlings you want to keep. Feed the seedlings once a week with water-soluble houseplant fertilizer.

After four weeks of this coddling, your tomato seedlings should have reached the proper size to make the transition to the great out-of-doors. So you give them a proper hardening off (see page 71). And you? By this point, you'll be hardened off, too. You'll be ready to write that self-help book, *Tomatoes Are from Seed and Therapy Is from Hunger,* and go on *Oprah.* Tell her all about how you are saving your own seed. Growing your own antiques.

2🕐-MINUTE PROJECT:
Tomatoes by the Bale and Bucket

"The world is full of wonders, is it not?" Nancy Patenaude says this with a laugh, but also genuine delight. Eight years ago she took a Master Gardener's course from the University of Connecticut's Cooperative Extension program, and ever since she's been spreading the word. "I'm not retired," she explains, "I'm a professional volunteer." Master Gardeners pay for their training with volunteer work, and Nancy has chosen to donate her time as a speaker. She speaks to 4-H clubs, senior centers, Cub Scout troops, garden clubs, and professional women's organizations, spreading the word about the quirky but effective tricks she has collected for making gardening fun.

Today, Nancy is teaching Tom about growing tomatoes. She takes him out to the backyard to see the bales of alfalfa hay she laid out in a sunny spot back toward the end of March. She instructs her student to push his hand into the center of one bale, and he finds it hot, uncomfortably so. Nancy explains that she soaked the bales with water as soon as she had positioned them, and that the nitrogen-rich alfalfa is composting now. It's the beginning of May; in a few more weeks the centers of the bales will be soft with rot and Nancy will punch a 5-inch-deep rectangular depression into each bale's top. She'll fill these with sterilized potting-soil mix and then plant two tomato seedlings in each, a seedling at either end.

She waters the seedlings how often? "Stick your finger in," she advises. When the soil around the seedlings feels dry, you irrigate. A couple of waterings a week should be plenty, for the seedlings soon root into the bales themselves, and the rotting hay acts as a reservoir to hold extra moisture. It also provides most of the nutrients the tomato plants need. Nancy feeds the tomatoes "whenever I think about it," which translates into three or four times a summer. She adds a reduced dose of soluble fertilizer to the water she pours onto the hay. This helps the tomato plants push out a new flush of blossoms (Nancy plants only indeterminate plants in her hay-bale garden).

Otherwise the principal upkeep consists of shoring up the bales with stakes and wire fencing as the decay robs them of their structural stability. With the tomato cages screwed into the bales' tops, the various braces and attachments give them a Rube Goldberg look, a suggestion that with the right tuning these gardens might receive on the shortwave band or perhaps take flight.

In a series of slides she projects onto the wall, Nancy shows off last summer's results: a bale draped with clusters of cherry tomatoes and another draped with cucumbers. But then it's time to look at another project, a hanging garden of tomatoes fashioned from a four-gallon bucket in which frosting was shipped to a local bakery. To make this, she cut a 3-inch-wide hole in the bucket's base. She then lined the bucket's bottom with a piece of fiberglass screen.

By cutting a slit in the screen, she was able to slip the roots of a tomato seedling up through the hole and liner into the bucket itself from underneath. She buried the roots with potting soil until the bucket was about a third full and then hung the garden in a sunny spot. The tomato stem soon righted itself, crawling out and up the bucket's outside, while the roots burrowed through the soil inside. As roots began appearing on the soil's surface, Nancy poured in more, eventually filling the bucket to the brim—filling the bucket in stages in this fashion encourages more extensive root growth. With regular watering and twice-monthly feedings, the bucket was providing a good harvest by midsummer.

How do adults react to these schemes? The older folks tend to raise an eyebrow, Nancy admits. But the younger generation, Tom's generation, are appreciative. They haven't got time, or often the space, to garden in a traditional way, but "they've got the itch."

And kids?

"Oh, they eat it up." To interest them, she adds, your gardening has to be quick, it has to be easy, "and it has to be different." Has Tom, she wants to know, ever tried making a tepee out of poles and then planting it with scarlet runner beans? The kid sits inside and the hummingbird comes to feed. Or has Tom ever made a tunnel trellis? You roll chicken wire into a tube just big enough that a kid can slither in, then you lay it out into the garden and train cucumber or zucchini vines over it. "Line the tunnel with hay and you've got the coziest little spot." And only the child can get in to pick the harvest hanging from the vines.

"Start telling someone else about all the things I get excited about—that's the whole idea." Tom had to go. He had to get to those bales of alfalfa hay. And then stop by the bakery.

Chapter 6

Roots

Foreign visitors, social commentators, and various other busybodies are always characterizing America as a rootless society. Tom and Marty are determined to prove them wrong. We have returned to our roots, and now we are going to show you how you can return to yours. Or to someone else's, if you prefer. The great thing about 20-minute gardening is that their roots are your roots. And vice versa.

Of course, once upon a time, America was a land with lots of roots. Indeed, as near as we can tell, roots were about the only thing our ancestors ate, aside from bacon and biscuits. Why was this? For one thing, roots grow underground. This may seem an obvious point (although it was news to Marty).

However, this behavior is what makes root crops so close to perfect for a 20-minute garden. To begin with, their subterranean growth makes most root crops masters of self-preservation. If you grow cabbages or apples, you store the harvest by picking it and then stashing it in the root cellar. Root crops do this to themselves. In many cases, you can just leave the roots in place once they mature and dig them as you need them. Turnips and parsnips are two root crops that will stay fresh all winter if simply ignored in this fashion.

Even if the root crop you have chosen to grow won't tolerate such casual treatment, even if you must gather the roots and bring them indoors to store them, chances are they'll still last longer and with less loss of flavor and texture than practically any other kind of vegetable. That's because root crops were designed to last by nature. This is their purpose. The plant banks carbohydrates, proteins, and sugars in the root or tuber (which is, technically, an underground stem, but never mind) so that it can withdraw them as it needs them, most likely in the spring of the following year when it is recovering from winter dormancy. The stored nutrients do the plant no good, though, if they have perished in the meantime. So root crops have to be durable.

Hiding their most attractive part below ground also protects root crops against most pests. The rabbit or deer who forces its way through the garden fence may eat the leaves and stems of your sweet potatoes, but it won't get the good part. There are some insect larvae that specialize in attacking root crops, but they are far fewer and less varied than those that focus on aboveground crops. In general, the subterranean pests are less mobile—tunneling is a lot slower than flying—and so easier to control.

Irish Potatoes

Purists may grumble when ignoramuses like Tom stick a European ethnic label on what is a South American plant. As usual, they are missing the big picture. True enough, the cultivated potato did originate in the Andes, and that region remains the area of greatest potato diversity. Hundreds of distinct types of potatoes are still grown in the uplands of Peru, Colombia, Ecuador, Chile, and Bolivia, and you'll find more types of potatoes in a rural market square there than you will in the fanciest *norteamericano* gourmet grocery.

That's impressive. But in Tom's opinion, this achievement pales in comparison with those of his Irish ancestors. Certainly, no one has ever adopted the potato with their enthusiasm. Except maybe his wife's Irish ancestors. Be that as it may, Tom's mother raised him on stories of how in the old country (a place inhabited principally by relatives she didn't want to meet) the entire diet of the people was a sort of cottage cheese called "clabbered milk," and potatoes.

Tom has since found historical accounts substantiating his mother's claims. According to observers of the period, back in the heyday of Irish roots, before the potato famine of the mid-nineteenth century, the average daily potato consumption was approximately 8 pounds per capita per day—and that figure rose to 10 to 12 pounds in the case of an active working man.

It was also the Irish, with their "lazy bed" method of cultivation, who turned potato growing from hard labor into an art form. The Irish farmers would first mark out a strip 2 to 4 feet wide on some untilled field and spread on it the manure from their animals. Then they'd lay out, right on the turf, their seed potatoes. They'd spread the tuber pieces so that they rested a foot apart and at least a foot in from the edge of the planting strip.

Afterward, the farmers would cut clumps of turf from the areas immediately adjacent to the planting strip and, turning these over, would lay them facedown, right over the seed potatoes. Then they'd shovel more soil out from the excavated area on either side and heap that on the planting strip until the seed potatoes were buried 4 inches deep. The buried grass, kept moist by the Irish rains, would promptly decompose to provide humus for the potatoes.

Later, a couple of weeks after the potato shoots had emerged

When Is a Seed Not a Seed?

When it's a potato, of course. Seed potatoes are really just small potato tubers that have been grown for planting rather than eating. Often, the seed potato will be no bigger than a hen's egg, in which case you should plant it as is. If the seed potato is much larger than this, you can cut it up. Make sure that each piece is about the size of a large ice cube and that it has at least two buds, or "eyes." After cutting up seed potatoes, spread the pieces on newspaper somewhere out of direct sunlight and let them dry overnight before planting.

One thing to keep in mind, though, is that although you may stretch your seed potatoes to plant a larger area by cutting them up, you may actually reduce your total harvest. As a rule, larger seed potatoes yield larger potatoes at harvesttime. So unless a seed potato is really huge, it's probably better not to cut it up.

from the surface of the lazy bed, they were "hilled up": another few inches of soil was shoveled on. The truly ambitious might hill up the potatoes a second time a few weeks later. That was all. The only other work was the hunt for the new spuds at summer's end, after the potato leaves and vines had withered. This left lots of time for Tom's ancestors to practice their other traditional crafts: bickering with the relatives, hosting whiskey tastings, and emigration.

Inevitably, though, when Tom recommended the lazy-bed method of potato culture, Marty insisted that any activity that involved busting sod wasn't lazy enough for him. So he encouraged Tom to further refine the method, offering his own garden, once again, as a test plot.

From their joint efforts (Tom planted, Marty harvested—"turn about," Marty called this), the two 20-minute gardeners developed the following principles.

Potato Basics

• **In the garden, plant only "certified" seed potatoes.** Seed potatoes are small tubers that have been raised for planting and eating; the "certified" ones are tubers that have tested as free of disease. You can grow a potato crop from leftover, sprouting supermarket potatoes (see page 28) but such potatoes are likely to carry in them viruses that will not only stunt their own offspring but also infest your soil so that any other potatoes planted in that spot subsequently will become infected.

Undoubtedly, such viruses are already entrenched in your compost heap, carried there by potato peelings. So don't hesitate to plant potato pantry discards there—you've got nothing to lose.

• **Plant early or plant late.** Potatoes prefer cool, moist weather. This means that they should be planted in early spring from the upper South (Tennessee, Kentucky) on north. Plant your potatoes soon after the soil has thawed and dried enough so that you can dig it without stirring it into mud. Farther south, where summers set in fast and hard, plant your potatoes in late summer so that the plants can enjoy the long, temperate fall. In Florida, along the Gulf Coast, and in the mildest parts of the Southwest, plant potatoes in January for a winter crop.

• **Don't add lime or wood ashes to the soil in your potato patch.** They make the soil more alkaline, and alkaline soil encourages potato scab, a disease that will cover the tubers with rough, corky blemishes. Alkaline soil may also stunt the tubers.

• **Tuck them in with pine needles.** An easy way to ensure a slightly acidic soil is to line the bottom of the planting hole with half an inch of old pine needles before you drop in the seed potato.

• **Don't fertilize with fresh manures.** These are rich in nitrogen, a nutrient that will encourage your spuds to make more leaves and fewer tubers.

• **Do add compost.** Spread a 3-inch layer over the surface of your potato patch and mix this in thoroughly before planting.

• **In the trenches.** To encourage the potato to make more tubers you plant them deep. Scoop out a pit about 8 inches wide and deep. Set one seed potato in the bottom and cover it with 3 to 4 inches of soil. Space the seed potatoes 12 to 18 inches apart; 12 inches apart if the potatoes are a small type, 18 inches if they are big bakers.

• **Keep 'em covered.** When the shoots from the seed potatoes reach a height of six inches, push in soil from the sides to fill the planting pits and cover all but the topmost leaves and tip of each shoot. Three weeks later, drag up more dirt from around the planting pits to cover the new growth of the stems.

• **Water faithfully in dry weather.** No water translates into no tubers; your potato plants may survive a drought, but they won't make a crop. So water the patch well at least twice a week during hot, dry weather. Mulching the potato patch with an inch of straw or shredded leaves as summer weather sets in will also help to keep the soil evenly moist.

• **Steal some new potatoes.** A week or so after the potato plants start flowering, probe around their bases with your fingers. Carefully pluck a few of the little tubers you find there. Go ahead. If you replace the soil and mulch afterward, the plant won't know the difference.

• **Harvest the rest a couple of weeks after the potato vines wither.** Dig carefully, taking care not to bruise the tubers, working from the outside of the patch inward. Don't wash the potatoes until you are ready to cook them. Instead, spread them out on the ground and leave them a couple of hours to dry. Then store them in paper grocery bags in a cool, dry place.

Potato Favorites

Typically, both Tom and Marty soon developed potato preferences. Tom opted for quiet good taste. Marty didn't.

He had become absorbed in a scheme for making a patriotic red, white, and blue potato salad for the family's Labor Day picnic. For this he planted:

'Red Thumb'—A small-tubered or "fingerling"-type potato that has bright red skin and pink flesh.

'Butterfinger'—A light, yellow-fleshed fingerling, one that is supposed to hold its shape when boiled and then chopped into a salad or cooked up as home fries.

'Peruvian Purple'—A South American potato that produces small and knobby dark, blue-purple-fleshed tubers.

(Okay, so Marty's color scheme was a little off, but it's the patriotic thought that counts.)

Tom, meanwhile, has returned to his roots. He has come to prefer:

'Kerr's Pink'—A pink-skinned potato that is a traditional Irish favorite. When boiled, its flesh is floury but still so tender that it has the texture of mashed even when it isn't.

To sample another tradition he also grew:

'German Butterball'—A golden-skinned, golden-fleshed potato with a flavor that tastes buttery even when it isn't.

And lest you should think that these distinctions are evident only to 20-minute gardeners, Tom invited an expert panel to sample the patriotic potatoes, boiled. His mother pronounced 'Peruvian Purple' to be "fundamental." The two six-year-olds, Tom's son Matthew and his friend Gita, said that they also preferred the 'Peruvian Purple' because "it goes better with butter," while expressing the opinion that 'Red Thumb' and 'Butterfinger' were "too sugary, too sweet," a criticism that Tom had never heard his son express about any food before. However, Katchen Coley (née Smith), an umpteenth-generation Connecticut Yankee whom Tom had invited as a spokesperson for this "land of steady thinking," dismissed the purple potatoes as having an aftertaste, and said that while 'Red Thumb' was "delightful," the more conventionally colored 'Butterfinger' was best.

Anyway, everybody cleaned his plate.

Marty's Patriotic Potato Salad

6 to 8 medium potatoes of mixed colors—include some pink- or red-fleshed, some blue- or purple-fleshed, and some white-fleshed types. Double total number of potatoes when using smaller, fingerling types.

½ cup mayonnaise
2 teaspoons fresh lemon juice
1 teaspoon dry mustard (wet mustard may be used if dry is not available)
½ teaspoon salt
½ teaspoon fresh ground pepper

¼ teaspoon paprika
½–1 teaspoon horseradish (or Japanese wasabi)
¼ cup capers, minced
Heavy cream
Garnish with sprouts or sliced tomatoes

Boil potatoes gently until just soft (peeling optional). Remove potatoes from water and set out to cool.

Mix other ingredients in a large stainless-steel or ceramic bowl. Reduce or increase the amount of horseradish to taste (keep in mind that the potatoes have a tempering effect and that the dressing will taste less spicy in the completed salad). Add heavy cream to thin dressing to desired consistency. Dressing may be prepared 1 to 2 days ahead and stored in refrigerator.

Cut potatoes into pieces of a size and shape that suits you. Mix in salad dressing. Store for several hours in refrigerator to let flavors blend.

Sweet Potatoes

Marty persists in calling these roots "yams," which they are not. Yams are a tropical root crop that belongs to an entirely different family of plants than the sweet potato. Still, Tom would forgive Marty far more than this botanical lapse. He owes Marty for the half dozen truly memorable sweet potato pies he has made with Marty's misnamed harvest.

Tom spent four years of his gardening and gustatory career in central Texas, after his pepper-loving fiancée became his wife. As a result he understands that sweet potatoes are to the true Southerner what the Irish potato is to the Yankee. Only more so. Sweet potatoes are a totem down South, sort of like vegetable possum. This is why Tom had always assumed that sweet potatoes are a Southern crop.

Tom would never try growing a Southern crop in his Northern garden. But Marty, who can't remember what sort of crop sweet potatoes are or even what to call them, didn't know any better. He ordered a dozen "slips" from a Southern nursery, and when they arrived in late May, he planted them in his backyard. They flourished. Marty had discovered by chance what Tom should have known. Sweet potatoes often grow even better in the North than in the South.

These Southern plants flourish in the North, at least as far north as southern New England and the Great Lake states, because when taken there they leave behind the pests and diseases that commonly afflict them in the South. Nematodes, for example, the nearly microscopic worms that attack sweet potato roots, are endemic in many Southern soils but relatively rare in Northern ones.

The great advantage that Southern gardeners have is that their climate does produce the long, warm growing season that sweet potatoes demand. Sweet potato roots stop growing when the soil temperature drops below 60°F, and if it drops below 50° for very long, the plants catch a cold from which they may not recover even when the heat comes back on. Eighty days of warm weather, and warm soil, too, are essential to raise a crop of sweet potatoes. The summers of all except the most northerly states offer that much warm weather. And a couple of 20-minute gardening tricks ensure warm soil.

Do like Marty did and plant your sweet potatoes in a raised bed. By elevating the soil within them, raised beds expose it more fully to the warmth of the sun. As a result, the soil in raised beds thaws more quickly in the spring and warms up more quickly with the

The Un-Freudian Slip

What is it with potatoes, that they can't do anything the normal way? Is this why they have such a special appeal for Marty? Alas, we don't have the answers to those questions. But we do know how to start a crop of sweet potatoes, which is probably more than you do. And if you said, "Plant seeds, right?" you are wrong. You start your sweet potatoes from slips.

Slips are the shoots that sprout from sweet potatoes when they have been kept in storage too long. They ease out from the root, looking uncomfortably like worms. Eventually, though, the slips grow leaves at their tips and roots around their bases. Cut from the potato and transplanted to the garden bed, these are what give rise to the new generation.

You can start your own slips, but not even Tom is willing to go to all that trouble. Besides, the slips you order from a seed catalog should be certified as disease free, which means that by planting them in your garden you won't inadvertently infest the soil with horrible diseases such as "scurf" and "black rot." The slips you raise from the sweet potato you forgot to bake at Thanksgiving, on the other hand, may look okay, but who knows whether they are healthy?

When your bundle of sweet potato slips arrives from the nursery, they may be a sorry-looking lot: wilted, seemingly dead. Don't worry. It's hard to kill a sweet potato. Immerse the roots of the slips in a jar of water, slip a plastic bag over the top, and set them in a brightly lit spot, but one that is out of direct sunlight. In a day or two, the slips will have perked up and started to make new growth. They are ready, then, to transplant into the garden.

onset of summer. In Marty's raised bed, the sweet potato roots found all the heat they needed, even in Connecticut.

If you want to help the sweet potatoes along even more, you can enhance the warming effect of the raised bed by covering it with a sheet of black plastic a couple of weeks before you plant. You can buy this by the roll at hardware stores or garden centers. Spread the plastic over the top of the raised bed and tuck its edges into the soil just inside the wooden frame. This dark skin will absorb extra sunlight and act as a solar collector to heat the bed. Later, you plant right through the cover, cutting slits in the plastic to set the sweet potatoes into the soil. These slits also act as irrigation devices, since the rainwater that collects on the plastic will run in through them right around the bases of the plants.

Sweet Potato Basics

• **Location, location, location . . .** Sweet potatoes need at least six hours of sunlight a day if the plants are to make a good crop of roots. In the North, you should, if possible, locate the patch so that it gets the hotter, afternoon sun.

• **Bush-type sweet potatoes,** varieties such as 'Vineless Porto Rico' that produce short stems just 1 to 3 feet long, are best for the compact 20-minute garden. The older types of sweet potatoes run to vines and can spread 20 feet in every direction. Plant these sprawlers and the sweet potato patch may swallow up your whole garden.

• **Compost!** As with Irish potatoes, the best soil preparation for sweet potatoes is to cover the planting area with 3 inches of compost and then dig that in thoroughly with a garden fork, turning the soil to a depth of 10 inches.

• **Dig well.** Make sure that when you finish turning the soil with your fork or spade the soil in your sweet potato patch is loose and airy. If you make it hard for the roots to grow and expand, they won't.

• **Elevation.** Sweet potatoes do better when planted at the peak of little hills—the elevation ensures good drainage and allows the sun to warm the earth around them. So with a hoe (or your hands, if you are Marty), scrape the soil into broad mounds about 10 inches high, leaving a distance of about 2 feet from center to center.

• **In the North,** forget about the mounds; just dig the soil well and stretch a sheet of black plastic over the whole bed about two weeks before planting time. Then plant right through the black plastic bedspread. With a sharp knife, cut an X into the sheet at the appropriate spot and plant the slip right through this.

• **Plant by the thermometer.** The usual advice with sweet potatoes is to plant two weeks after the average date of the last spring frost. But before you do set out the slips, make sure the soil has warmed to 60°F, and that nighttime temperatures aren't dropping below 55°.

• **Set the slips deep.** Plant them so that only their top leaves emerge from the soil.

• **Water the slips well** immediately after planting and often and generously for two weeks thereafter. Then back off. Sweet potatoes are drought tolerant, though a deep watering once a week or so during dry weather will increase your harvest of roots.

• **To mulch.** Conventional organic mulches such as shredded leaves or straw help keep the soil cool—which means that in Northern gardens, they are bad for the sweet potato crop. In the South, where heat is not in short supply, a summertime mulch helps sweet potatoes by keeping weeds in check.

• **Harvest.** In the South, start checking into the mounds about one hundred days after planting. When the sweet potato roots have swollen to what you feel is an acceptable size, dig 'em up. First pull all the vines, then turn the soil in the patch with a garden fork, starting from the outside and carefully working in. Any roots you bruise or cut, you should eat promptly, since injured roots spoil in storage.

In the North, you should delay the harvest as far into the fall as possible, but you must dig the roots before the soil cools, for that will damage the roots. As a rule, the best time to harvest is about the time of the first fall frost. Otherwise, follow the procedure outlined above.

Sweet Potato Favorites

One of the most exciting parts of gardening for Marty is his horticultural amnesia. By picking time, he rarely remembers what it was exactly that he planted. This makes his raised beds a source of continual wonderment.

Consider, for example, the early fall afternoon when he turned up at Tom's door with a sackful of roots. He had found them, he said, lurking in one of his beds and they looked like something cool. Could Tom help him? Tom assured Marty that he could, and took the sack into the kitchen.

As soon as he had shooed Marty out the door, Tom turned the oven up to 425° and sorted the roots into two piles. He remembered the afternoon when he had helped Marty plant the sweet potatoes, so he knew which was which instantly:

'Vineless Porto Rico' (aka 'Bush Porto Rico', 'Bunch Porto Rico', 'Porto Rican'). These were the copper-skinned roots with the deep-orange flesh. This variety produces a cluster of short, 12- to 30-inch vines, and requires 110 to 150 warm days to mature.

'Vardaman'. Also a "vineless" or "bush" variety, 'Vardaman' makes a compact cluster of short stems well suited to small gardens. This actually makes an attractive ground cover—the leaves are purple when they emerge and mature to an attractive dark green. Needing just 100 to 110 days from planting to harvest, 'Vardaman' is a bit better adapted to Northern gardens than 'Porto Rico', and it bears golden-skinned roots with dark, red-orange flesh.

Preliminary tests of roots (baked for one hour) revealed that there was no comparison. The copper-colored 'Porto Rico' roots had been advertised as possessing "old-fashioned flavor." Maybe, but only if the old-timer preferred mealy, bland sweet potatoes. The 'Vardaman' roots (which were smaller) were firmer fleshed and sweeter.

The critical test of any sweet potato, however, is its success as a pie filling. You can, of course, just bake and butter the roots. You can even bake and mash them and, God help you, melt marshmallows onto the mess. But sweet potato pie, topped with real whipped cream, is the best use for this vegetable and the real test.

Tom's initial assessment of the two sweet potatoes was born out by this process. He found that while a 'Porto Rico' pie was superb, the 'Vardaman' was unforgettable. It was good enough to inspire guilt; Tom saved a piece to share with Marty. What's more, he's decided to share the recipe with you.

'Vardaman' Pie

'Vardaman' sweet potatoes	*½ teaspoon salt*
Pastry for a 10-inch pie shell	*¾ teaspoon cinnamon*
2 eggs	*½ teaspoon ground ginger*
½ cup sugar	*½ teaspoon ground nutmeg*
1 cup light cream	*⅛ teaspoon ground cloves*
2 tablespoons melted butter	*Whipped cream*

Preheat oven to 400°.

Bake sweet potatoes under tender. Peel and mash. You should have 2 cups.

Line a 10-inch pie pan with the pastry (how you make that is your concern—no two cooks agree on a pie pastry recipe, and, anyway, Tom won't share his).

Beat the eggs in a large bowl. Beat in the mashed sweet potato, and then blend in the sugar, cream, butter, and spices.

Pour this mixture into the pastry shell and bake for 40 to 50 minutes, or until a knife slipped into the pie's center comes back out of the filling clean.

Serve the pie warm or cool, topped with slightly sweetened whipped cream.

(Some add pecan halves to the pie filling before baking; others insist that no sweet potato pie is authentic without bourbon, and they reduce the light cream by ¼ cup and add ¼ cup whiskey. Personally, Tom doesn't drink bourbon and finds nuts a distraction when savoring the smooth perfection of sweet potato pie.)

And so, on to more roots.

Asian Radishes

Radishes, the familiar red-skinned, spring-planted kind, we have already covered in a previous chapter as a 20-minute winner (see page 49). They are well worth growing but not very versatile in a culinary sense. You can slice them into a salad, or dip them in salt and eat them whole. That's about it. But Asian radishes, that's another matter.

There's diversity here. The Asian radishes can be white rooted, rose pink, purple, or black; the roots may be long and cylindrical or rounded, and some varieties grow to enormous size, so that a single root may weigh 65 pounds. That's a lot of radish.

Fortunately there are a lot of ways to eat these radishes. You can slice them and toss them into stir-fries or soups. You can shave them thin and marinate them in sugar, water, and rice vinegar to make an instant pickle. Or you can grate them and mix them with soy sauce to make a condiment to serve with the meal, or add a little sesame oil and serve them before the meal as an appetizer.

Marty treasures these roots because they suit his hypochondria. They are supposed to dispel melancholy, which is a terrible problem for sensitive guys like him. Tom has no problem with sensitivity. He loves Asian radishes because they're easy to grow, practically pest free, and because they supply fresh vegetables right into the heart of winter, that time of year when every other vegetable is coming up from the far south and has left its flavor behind.

A quarter of Japan's vegetable crop each year is devoted to radishes. Try them, at the table and in the garden, and you'll know why.

Asian Radish Basics

• **Plant in late summer or fall.** Some varieties of Asian radishes have been bred for spring planting, but you'll value the harvest more if it comes in late fall or early winter, when other pickings are slim. Most Asian radishes need about two months to grow from seed to maturity, so in general, you count backward two months from the average date of the first fall frost in your area to determine the right planting date. If, for example, your first fall frost falls, on average, on October 19th (as Marty's does), then you plant around August 19th.

• **Lighten up.** Like most root crops, Asian radishes prefer a loose, well-drained soil. If your soil is sticky and dense, cover the radish patch with 3 to 4 inches of compost and an inch of coarse "sharp" sand (see page 23 for a definition of this), then turn the soil with a fork, mixing well to a depth of 10 inches. This will do for most types of radishes, though for the really long-rooted kinds (and there are Asian radishes whose roots reach a length of 4 feet), you'll have to double or even triple the amount of compost and sand and dig twice or even three times as deep. Sow the seeds an inch apart and a ¼ inch deep. In such a close-set planting, the radish seedlings will soon spread their leaves to create a weedproof canopy over the whole bed. You keep thinning through the first month of growth, removing every other plant to give the survivors room to expand. The thinning also provides an additional harvest.

• **Mulch,** tucking the radish plants in with an inch or 2 of straw. This blanket will keep the soil moister and enhance the radish's growth. In northern regions, the mulch will also help to keep the soil from freezing and make it possible to dig a root whenever you need it, well into winter.

• **Store your harvest outside.** Leave the roots in the ground, even after the onset of cold weather seems to put a halt to plant growth. Actually, the roots will continue to bulk up and develop an ever-sweeter flavor until the soil temperature drops to around 40°. At this point, you should bury the radish patch under a foot of hay or straw and then cover that with a sheet of plastic (a painter's cheap plastic drop cloth works well). Weight the plastic's sides and corners down with rocks, bricks, old boards, whatever.

Alternatively, you can dig the radishes, gently brush the roots clean, and then cut off the leaves, leaving half-inch stubs. Seal the roots in plastic bags and stash them in the crisper drawer of the refrigerator and they will keep for months.

Asian Radish Favorites

'China Rose' (aka 'Rose of China', 'Scarlet China', 'China Rose Winter', 'China Red Winter', 'Winter Rose'). Rose-colored skin, up to 8 inches long and 2 inches in diameter. Sow late summer or early fall, allowing a month or so between the planting date and the expected date of the first fall frost. (Brought back to the West by Jesuit missionaries prior to 1850.)

'China White' (aka 'China White Winter'). Mature roots up to 8 inches long, 2½ inches in diameter. Sow two months before the expected date of the first fall frost. Mild flavor, stores well, stays crisp all winter.

'Green Skin and Red Flesh'. Just what it sounds like. Mature roots are 4 to 5 inches long, up to 4 inches in diameter, with deep pink hearts. If sliced crosswise with a sharp knife, a good specimen falls into a series of crisp white disks marked with pink sunbursts. These are beautiful tossed raw over a salad, or pickled. Sow two months before expected date of first fall frost.

'Shogoin' (aka 'Shogoin Round Giant', 'Shogoin Large Round', 'Shogoin Giant Fall'). Turnip-shaped roots, mild and sweet in flavor, up to 6 inches in diameter. A Japanese variety that is particularly productive, and performs better than most other root crops on heavy clay soils. Sow fifty to eighty days before the expected date of the first fall frost.

Marty's Recipe for Japanese Radish Pickle

2½ tablespoons sugar
½ cup rice vinegar
½ cup dashi stock (available in a dried, packaged form at Asian food stores) or ½ cup diluted canned chicken broth

Carrots
Asian radishes
Salt
Kombu (Japanese dried kelp), cut into a 1½-inch square

In a pot, dissolve the sugar in the rice vinegar, and add the *dashi* or the chicken broth. Heat the mixture to a boil, remove from heat immediately, and let cool.

Peel the carrots and the Asian radishes, then slice lengthwise into wafer-thin pieces about 1½ inches long and ½ inch wide (an easy size for picking up with chopsticks). In a mixing bowl, combine 4 cups radish slices and 2 cups carrot slices, spinkle with salt, and set aside for 5 minutes.

Massage the sliced vegetables with your fingers until the radish slices become translucent. Then gently squeeze them, and pour off any liquid. Move the slices to a clean bowl and douse them with ½ cup of the vinegar-*dashi* mixture. Work this through the slices carefully with your fingers, then squeeze out and discard the liquid once again. Add the remaining vinegar-*dashi* mixture. Toss in the *kombu*, cover the bowl, and set it in the refrigerator to marinate overnight.

Serve as an appetizer or as a side dish.

2🕐-MINUTE PROJECT:
Tom's White-Trash Potato Patch

This is how the neighbor described Tom's front garden last year. Nor did Tom's friend Katchen like this planting. She was trying to ease him by the admissions committee of the local garden club, and complained that Tom was going out of his way to make that difficult. Tom, though—well, Tom thought this garden was a triumph.

After all, imagine harvesting almost half a bushel of potatoes from stacks of old tires.

Tom resorted to this expedient because he had no soil in which to plant his crop. He doesn't have much sunny space in his garden, and what he has was already consumed by arugula, lettuce, tomatoes, and asparagus. The only sunny spot left in the whole yard was the driveway. Who would have thought you could grow anything on asphalt?

But Tom had heard that you didn't need a garden to grow potatoes as long as you had a sufficient supply of discarded automobile tires. The manager at the local tire shop confirmed that this was possible, but then made ominous reference to the potato blight. "I heard it's coming back. You know about that potato famine they had in Ireland?" Tom had a momentary vision of Connecticut highways choked with fleeing Volvo station wagons. Then he tossed the eight treadless tires into the back of his station wagon and went home.

That was on April 1st. Two blizzards later, April 14th arrived, bringing warmer weather and the UPS truck with the box of seed potatoes. Tom laid out four tires in a row along the sunniest part of the driveway. Fortunately, this lay back toward the garage, so that Tom still had somewhere to park the family cars. Then he filled each tire to the top with a mixture of two parts topsoil (purchased in bags from the local garden center), one part sand, and one part sphagnum peat. Next, with his son Matthew's help, he dropped three little seed potatoes on top of each tire planter. They planted a different type of potato in each tire, four in all: 'Butterfinger', 'Red Thumb', 'Anna Cheeka's Ozette', and 'Purple Peruvian'. All of these are "fingerlings," potatoes that make small, elongated, especially flavorful tubers.

As soon as the seed potatoes were in place, Tom topped each of the four tires with another. He dumped a couple more inches of soil/sand/peat mix into each stack to bury the seed potatoes. Then he watered each white-trash planter well.

Two weeks later, all the potatoes were sending shoots up out of the soil. When these reached a height of 6 inches, Tom dumped in more soil/sand/peat mix to fill each stack of tires, then flopped a third tire onto each. By now, Tom was stopping on the highway whenever he found a discarded spare, and bringing it home to build up his potato patch. He filled the third tire in each stack and added a fourth, and on May 24th, he filled those, too, and then mulched around the potato shoots with straw.

Maybe that was a mistake; more likely it was the heat. The black tire stacks absorbed a lot of sunlight, as did the surrounding black-topped surface of the driveway. Potatoes do not like heat and drought, and Tom had to compensate by increasing the frequency of his watering. This created a zone of tropical humidity around the potatoes, additional stress for plants that prefer their weather Irish.

The potato vines continued to expand, they had even begun to sprout little white flowers, when brown spots popped out on the leaves of 'Anna Cheeka's Ozette'. It was the "early blight," the fungus *Alternaria solani*. The guy at the tire shop had been right after all. Within a week or two, Tom was holding a wake for 'Anna Cheeka's Ozette'. By quickly clearing out the remains and disposing of them with the trash, however, Tom managed to preserve his other potato plants. (Rule of thumb: never add diseased plant material to the compost heap—that's going to perpetuate and spread the infection.)

The extra heat did bring in an early crop, however. By late July, the potato vines had yellowed and withered, sign that it was time for the harvest. One evening, Tom, Matthew, and Suzanne pushed over the stacks of tires and scrabbled about in the resulting mess. Within a few minutes, they had filled several big bowls with red, white, and blue tubers.

Tom's planning another trial of 'Anna Cheeka's Ozette'. In deference to Katchen, though, and to the neighbors, this time he'll grow them in 2½-foot-wide cylinders of chicken wire. He's going to move them off the driveway to someplace cooler, too. There's a flower bed he's going to sacrifice. Roots are much more beautiful.

2🕐-MINUTE PROJECT:
Goobers

Potatoes and radish pickles are fine, but Marty insists that, really, his roots are peanuts. According to family tradition, he says, the Ashers never ate daikon, and indulged in sweet potato pie only rarely. They might eat the odd potato pancake. What they ate by the sack, though, was peanuts, every time they went to Ebbets Field to watch the Dodgers play.

In his usual tiresome fashion, Tom points out that peanuts, which are not really nuts, are not roots either (they are actually subterranean seeds). To which Marty replies that you find them underground, and that's close enough for him. He knows what he's talking about, too. Last fall he harvested quite a crop.

Of course, the Ashers didn't grow their own peanuts when Marty was a boy. Few in Brooklyn did. But then, they didn't have the kind of acreage Marty enjoys now. So it was that Marty experienced a strong sense of having arrived in the world last spring when he sowed his first peanut crop.

This helped to comfort him when he had to compromise his principles. Marty *never* starts seedlings indoors, but peanuts had to be an exception. Peanuts are planted directly into the garden down South. That could be risky in Connecticut, though. Peanut plants need 100 to 110 days of warm weather and warm soil to set a crop of the nuts (which aren't nuts). Because the soil can be slow to warm up after a New England winter, a spring planting of peanuts is likely to rot rather than germinate, and waiting until the soil has warmed may leave too short an interval before the fall chill sets in.

So Marty made an exception and on May 2nd planted his 'Spanish-type' peanut seeds indoors. These seeds look just like the peanuts you get in a sack at the stadium, except that they haven't been roasted. Marty cracked the shells carefully and extracted the seeds without damaging the red paperlike coat—ripping the coat exposes the seeds to rots and diseases and reduces the chance that the seed will germinate and grow. Then he filled a half dozen 4-inch peat pots full of off-the-shelf seed-starting mix. Poking a finger into each pot, he dropped in a seed, burying it an inch deep. After setting the pots in a shallow pan of water to soak for ten minutes, he transferred them to a warm, sunny windowsill.

Within a week, little cloverlike shoots emerged from the surface of the seed-starting mix, and by May 22, when the soil in Marty's garden felt warm to the touch, the peanuts had made neat little bushes. After digging up the soil along a sunny edge of the herb garden, Marty set out the peanuts in a row along a winding path. Peanuts like the same kind of sandy soil that pleases herbs, and the little, clover-leaved bushes were, honestly, quite cute.

There isn't much else to tell. Peanuts feed themselves. Like other members of the pea family, they host beneficial bacteria in their roots; these convert nitrogen from the atmosphere into fertilizer. Although drought tolerant, peanut plants appreciate a weekly watering during dry weather. Keep the patch clear of weeds, and when the plants start flowering, take a hoe or cultivator and loosen the surrounding soil. Then get down on your knees for the vegetable garden's strangest show:

The peanut's flowers start to appear about six weeks after the plants first sprout from the soil. Initially, the blossoms seem unremarkable. They are small, and look like a scrawnier version of a sweet pea. But after the pollen (the floral equivalent of sperm) makes its way into the ovary, the stem that holds up the blossoms bends, so that the flowers hang down toward the ground. As the flowers wither, a slender stalk, the "peg," emerges and stretches down to bury its nose in the earth. It is at the tip of this peg that the peanuts grow. Essentially, what the peanut plant is doing is planting its own seeds for the next year's crop.

Don't mulch around your peanut plants. That may protect them against drought, but it also makes it harder for the pegs to reach the soil. Mulch, and you're likely to get larger, healthier, peanutless plants. Actually, peanuts are generally no-fuss plants. As with sweet potatoes, Northerners will find them to be virtually pest free. That's an advantage of planting things where they don't normally grow. Southerners may have to contend with thrips, leaf spot, and stem rot, but these problems aren't likely to be serious unless you live among peanut farms. If you do, there'll be big-time peanut predators wandering in from next door, and you should consider growing some Northern root like Jerusalem artichoke (see *The 20-Minute Gardener,* page 102, for the lowdown on that). This will frustrate the pests, which should please you.

In the South, you wait until the peanut plants yellow before you dig your harvest. Chances are a frost is going to kill Northern peanut plants before they reach that stage. In either case, you loosen the soil around each plant with a garden fork, then you grab its stem and pull, gently but with determination. Shake the plant free of soil and you should find it spangled with the familiar, brown-shelled nuts.

Marty spread his unshelled nuts out on newspaper and set them in a shaded corner of his sun porch to dry. When the shells turned brittle, he shelled the nuts and spread them on a well-oiled cookie sheet. He slipped this into a 350° oven for fifteen minutes. Then he salted the nuts, dumped them into a paper sack, and headed for the television. He was just in time for the "world serious" (as they used to call it in Brooklyn). It was only the Yankees. At least the peanuts were authentic.

Chapter 7

Cooked Down

"Comfort food" is a too-cozy phrase, but we know of no other way to describe the vegetables we're recommending next. These are the basis for those formative childhood dishes. Not the TV dinners we ate during our sanitized, middle-class upbringings, but the dishes we would have eaten had we been raised someplace with soul like Yoknapatawpha County or Little Italy or Koreatown. What we are talking about here is greens. The really cool people, from Sojourner Truth to Sophia Loren and the Dalai Lama, have always eaten greens.

Are these healthy foods? That depends how you cook

hem. You can steam them lightly and dress them with a dab of sesame oil or something, if that's your inclination. Ask Marty about that. Tom, however, is coming out in favor of tradition. As he points out, the people who built this country ate their greens cooked down.

To prepare your vegetables this way couldn't be simpler. To "cook down" you put the greens in a pot with water and a hunk of salt pork, and then you boil them until there can be no mistake: those greens are cooked. Tom learned this recipe from an elderly Texan friend who had grown up a sharecropper's son. He had worked fourteen hours a day in the fields, gone to a one-room schoolhouse between the harvest and planting seasons only, and had no money to buy textbooks and so did without. Yet he had gone on to become a dean at Columbia University. Would this man have traveled so far on a diet of steamed vegetarian greens? No way—if he'd eaten that low on the food chain, he would have stayed low on the food chain himself.

Will our greens make you smart and successful? And cool? Tom's willing to bet Marty's life on it. But there's another advantage to greens, as well. The salt of the earth grew these crops because they were easy and foolproof. Sharecroppers didn't have time to fuss with Belgian endive. They wanted good-tasting stuff, lots of it, and in a hurry. You get exactly that with authentic greens.

Collards

Botanically speaking (which is something Tom does and Marty doesn't), this green is just a variant of cabbage. But while cabbage is gaseous and bland, collards have a bite to them that wakes you up at the dinner table. As plants, collards also tolerate heat and drought better than cabbage, which is another reason why they are more popular among Southern gardeners. We believe that Yankees would grow collards, too, if they just knew what they are missing. After reading this, you'll have no excuse.

Collard Basics

• **Plant early and late.** Collards may tolerate heat and drought, but that doesn't mean they like those conditions. Actually, it is in cool moist weather that they thrive. So plant them in early spring, four to five weeks before your last spring frost. Plant again for a fall harvest; for that, sow seed in early to mid-August in the North, and in the South, as soon as the heat breaks and you feel a hint of the return of cool weather.

• **Note to Easterners, and gardeners in the Northwest:** You've most likely got acidic soil, and that makes collards susceptible to a disease called clubroot, which is as unpleasant as it sounds. You really ought to get your soil pH tested (see page 42) and follow the recommendations that will come back with the test results. But if you are like Marty, you'll just scatter a cup of limestone over every 10 square feet of bed, dig it in, and hope for the best.

• **Prepare for planting.** Fork up the soil in the planting area, breaking up the clods, and mix in four bucketfuls of compost for a standard 4′ × 8′ raised bed. Or fertilize with 5-10-5 (what the garden center sells as its standard "all-purpose" fertilizer) at a rate of 3 to 4 pounds per 100 square feet.

• **Plant shallow.** Just scatter the collard seed lightly over the surface of the bed and scratch it in with a hand cultivator or rake. Sprinkle the bed to moisten it, and keep it moist until the seedlings appear.

• **Note to Southerners:** Don't buy the ready-to-plant seedlings. Yeah, they'll grow, but they cost more than seeds and they don't really offer any advantage, as collards are so easy to start from seed sown directly into the garden.

• **Thin the seedlings.** You've got two goals here. You want to keep the soil covered with greenery as much as possible, so that you don't create opportunities for weeds; but you also want to give the collards the room they need to grow. So let the collard seedlings read their leaves until one plant is almost touching another, then pull every second plant. Repeat this process periodically until the plants stand about 2 feet apart.

Incidentally, these thinnings provide some of the tastiest and tenderest messes of greens you'll get all season.

Fertilize. Collards are what Tom calls "a heavy feeder" (and he should know). About a month after planting, sprinkle composted manure (you can buy this already hygienically bagged, if you wish) over the seedlings at a rate of two bucketfuls per raised bed.

Pick selectively for a longer, sweeter harvest. Wait until the plants stand a foot tall, then snap off the largest, outer leaves, leaving the smaller inner ones to grow. Fall harvests provide the best-tasting collards—the first light frost sweetens the leaves.

Collard Favorites

'Georgia' (aka 'Georgia Southern', 'True Southern', 'Southern', 'True Georgia', and 'Creole'). It's a good sign when a vegetable has so many names. That's a clue that lots of people have grown it and liked it over the years. (Equally, it's a bad sign when a particular weed has lots of names.) This variety of collard dates back to the nineteenth century, and offers, as the name suggests, the true collard flavor. Eat a heap of this with a square of cornbread, and maybe you'll finally understand all that verbiage in *The Sound and the Fury*. It's worth a shot.

Kale

Another cabbage relative with flavor. Treat this like a cold-hardier version of collards. Kale is so tolerant of cold, in fact, that if you tuck the plants in with 6 inches of mulch in late fall, they will survive even most Northern winters to furnish early pickings in spring.

For the most part, kale is grown like collards. It does have its idiosyncrasies, however.

Kale Basics

• **Plant late.** Take advantage of this plant's cold tolerance, and use it to provide a harvest when frost has wiped out most of your other plants. Sow kale seeds in mid to late August in the North, in early fall in the South.

• **Watch the lime.** Unlike collards, kale prefers a neutral to modestly acid soil. If you are gardening by guess rather than soil test, be careful. Unlike collards, kale doesn't like limy (alkaline) soil.

Kale Favorites

'Vates' (aka 'Dwarf Blue Vates', 'Dwarf Blue Scotch', 'Dwarf Curled Scotch', 'Dwarf Blue Curled'). Compact, with handsome blue-green leaves. This variety is outstandingly cold hardy, even for kale, and one of the best at wintering-over for a spring crop.

Mustard Greens

Yet another cabbage relative, mustard greens are less cold tolerant than kale or collards, but mature more quickly—some varieties are ready to pick in little more than a month. The American types, which are a staple in the Southern states, have a pungent, peppery flavor that may become too strong in warm weather. Usually, the American mustard greens are tempered by cooking. The Chinese mustards typically have a more delicate flavor, and may be used as a spinach substitute either cooked or raw.

Like kale, mustard greens thrive on the same basic routine as the one laid out for collards above. You'll need to make the following adjustments, though.

Mustard Green Basics

• **Careful with the lime.** Like kale, mustard greens thrive in a neutral to mildly acid soil, so hold back on the lime when preparing the bed, unless you live in an area with strongly acidic soil.

• **Plant early or late.** Sow seed three weeks before the last spring frost, and five to six weeks before the first fall frost.

Authentic Flavors

Treasured American dishes such as cooked-down collards don't taste the way they used to, and that's because the ingredients have been changed. When you buy collards, or tomatoes or potatoes or even beans, you aren't getting the same vegetables that your grandparents did. You are, in almost every instance, getting a new hybrid "cultivar" of the vegetable.

Often, these hybrids have been bred for practicality rather than flavor—a modern tomato may set fruit in less time than the old-fashioned cultivars, but chances are the new, faster fruit doesn't taste as good. Even if the modern version of the vegetable is delicious, still, it is almost certainly different. If you want to taste the flavors that made baked beans a treasured New England tradition, and sweet potato pie a Southern obsession, then you have to make these dishes from the original vegetables. And to do that, in most cases you have to grow the vegetables yourself.

Does this kind of authenticity matter? That depends on you. Fans of early music insist that Bach concerti should be played on the instruments for which they were written. In fact, the sound of a harpsichord is very different from that of a Steinway grand piano, and, obviously, substituting one for the other is going to change a performance dramatically. Similarly, if you want a salsa like your grandmother used to make, you need not only her recipe, but also a basket of the same peppers and the same tomatoes.

Fortunately, it's easy to obtain seed of period vegetables. There are many mail-order nurseries that specialize in such heirlooms, and you will find them listed in "Sources for Plants and Seeds" at the end of this book. If you really get serious about this sort of culinary authenticity, however, then you will certainly want to join the Seed Savers Exchange. Based in Decorah, Iowa, this organization maintains a 170-acre farm on which grow eighteen thousand different varieties of heirloom vegetables; the collection of tomatoes alone runs to four thousand distinct cultivars.

The exchange sells selections of different types of heirloom-vegetable seeds, as well as ethnic smorgasbords, such as the "Polish Collection," which provides the basis for authentic Old Country harvests. In addition, the exchange publishes garden-seed inventories that direct readers to mail-order sources for virtually any vegetable seed or fruit plants for sale in North America.

But the exchange's most important function is as a clearing-house for the thousands of rare and historic vegetable seeds collected and preserved by the organization's nine hundred members. The annual *Seed Savers Yearbook* puts members in touch with one another, and serves as a directory of who has what. From other members, you can obtain not only seed but also gardening tips—they may be just about the only living gardeners to have grown a particular heirloom vegetable—and, maybe, recipes. If, that is, a member should be so generous as to share not only seeds of that tomato his ancestors brought from Naples, but also the secret of his *nonna*'s sauce.

Annual dues for a basic membership is $25. Send your check or money order to: Seed Savers Exchange, 3076 North Winn Road, Decorah, IA 52101.

· **Thin the seedlings** as outlined for collards; mustard greens, however, should stand a foot apart at maturity.

· **Fall plantings have a milder flavor.** That's because the weather is cooling as they mature. You may like your greens pungent; if so, plant in spring.

Mustard Green Favorites

'**Green in Snow**' (aka 'Hsueh Li Hung'). A mild-flavored, Chinese type that is also the best mustard for very early or very late sowings.

'**Savanna Hybrid**' A more pungent-flavored American mustard, one of the fastest-maturing kinds, ready for picking in thirty-five days from sowing.

Two-fers

A 20-minute gardener is always looking for a better deal. In fact, if you don't care about that, you should get out your hoe and go back to traditional gardening. If you do like a bargain, though, read on.

There are a pair of plants that we like to grow because they take no more work than others (actually, less than most), and yet produce two harvests. Typically, Tom and Marty can't agree about which harvest is better. Marty likes the roots that you get from beets and turnips, while Tom prefers the greens. Cook 'em down (you know how), Tom says, and there's no contest. Truer words were never spoken, says Marty.

Turnip Basics

• **Fall crops are tastier and easier.** You can plant turnips in early spring for a spring harvest, but the greens and roots will be tenderer and sweeter on a fall crop. Sow seed in late summer in the North and in early fall in the South. By fall, many of the insects that attack spring plantings of turnips have given up or wandered off, so that fall crops also tend to suffer less damage from bugs.

• **Well-aged manure** is good for turnips; spread it a couple of inches thick over the bed and then dig it in with a garden fork before planting. Fresh manure is *not* good for turnips (nor, for that matter, for other root crops). It can make the roots fork and split. If you are squeamish, like Marty, you can buy precomposted manure by the bag.

• **Work wood ashes into the soil surface before planting.** This discourages the turnip's main insect enemy, root maggots. These tunnel into the roots, ruining one harvest, and often leave the plant so sickly that you don't get much in the way of greens, either.

• **Scatter plant.** Sow the seeds thinly over the bed, then rake the bed lightly to cover the seeds with a half inch of soil.

Companion Planting

Beets like onions and turnips, but they don't like pole beans, and onions like beets, strawberries, tomatoes, and lettuce, but they don't like peas and beans. Basil *hates* rue, and all the vegetables dislike fennel, so you should plant it by itself.

Change the names a bit, and it could be high school. Actually, though, what we have been describing is companion planting, a system of matching plants by their likes and dislikes to decide what gets planted next to what. It's sort of like computer dating for vegetables. Many gardeners swear by companion planting, insisting that the right partnerships not only improve the growth of the plants but also enhance the flavors of the harvest.

Ask the companion planters, though, where this lore came from, and they'll probably be stuck for an answer. They may claim that it's traditional, a kind of folk wisdom. They are wrong.

In fact, the first reports about companion planting appeared in the late 1920s and early 1930s and they were written by a German chemist, Dr. Ehrenfried Pfeiffer. Pfeiffer was an imaginative fellow, to say the least, and he got the idea of applying a chemical analytical technique called sensitive crystallization to garden plants. What he did was mash and extract the sap from a variety of common garden plants, and then mix each extract with a 5 percent solution of copper chloride. He'd pour these liquids out into separate flat-bottomed, round glass dishes. When the liquids had evaporated, patterns of crystals were left behind.

If a pattern was "beautiful, harmonious, and clearly formed," that was evidence, according to Dr. Pfeiffer, that the plant which was the source of the extract had been strong and healthy. If, however, a pattern was lopsided or indistinct, that was evidence the plant had been sickly. By mixing extracts of two different plants with the copper chloride and applying the same criteria to the resulting crystals, Pfeiffer decided that he could also tell if the two plants were compatible or incompatible. In addition, if the characteristic pattern of one plant predominated, then Pfeiffer decided that was a sign the partnership helped that plant more than the other; the bean might be exploiting the cucumber, for example. Eventually, Pfeiffer developed an intricate social system in this fashion.

Marty likes to keep an open mind, but Tom can't be bothered. He really enjoyed, though, reading through old gardening magazines and tracking the developments that sprang from this crackpot research. The first English-language reports, monographs printed by other crackpots, were quite honest in describing the source of this "data." But the writers that adapted this material for various semi-crackpot magazines usually alluded only in passing to Pfeiffer. And the journalists who stole material from the semi-crackpot journals to write articles for mainline gardening magazines never indicated the source at all. They relied on the journalist's favorite cop-out: "Recent research has indicated . . ." In this way, companion planting went from fantasy to scripture by the mid-1960s.

Does this mean that one plant never benefits from the presence of another? No. French marigolds release a chemical from their roots that repels root knot nematodes, parasitic worms that can stunt or kill okra, carrots, tomatoes, celery, beans, spinach, and other plants. So by all means plant marigolds among those vegetables, especially if you live in the South, where nematodes are particularly common. Likewise, there is some evidence that strongly scented herbs such as mint may protect nearby plants by masking their smells and so making it more difficult for pests to find them.

You can also use extra-susceptible plants as a trap. Nasturtiums, for example, are very attractive to aphids, so if you plant them near the vegetable garden, you'll probably divert any passing aphids from your food crops to the hapless flowers. The nasturtiums will serve as an early warning system, for the aphids will probably turn up on them first. Treat them with insecticide, and you'll kill the aphids without putting poisons on your food. Beans may not "like" nasturtiums, but they do grow better when they are aphid free.

• **Thin seedlings** when they reach a height of about 4 inches, so that the remaining plants stand 4 inches apart. The thinnings provide a first taste of greens.

• **Water weekly during dry weather.** Otherwise, the roots are likely to get stringy and bitter. A blanket of shredded leaves or some other organic mulch is also good for turnips if spread after the seedlings have been thinned.

• **Harvest** the turnips when the roots have reached eating size, anywhere from the size of a golf ball to slightly smaller than what you whack with your tennis racket. First harvest the roots by cutting them off 3 inches above the ground. If you've mulched the turnip patch as we advise, the roots can stay in the ground until winter threatens to freeze the bed, or until you need them, whichever comes first.

Turnip Favorites

'**Purple Top White Globe**' (aka 'Red Top White Globe', 'Early Purple Top White Globe', 'Mammoth Purple Top White Globe'). A nineteenth-century variety with old-fashioned flavor. Generations of more or less great Southern novelists—William Faulkner, Erskine Caldwell, Eudora Welty—were raised on these turnips. Truman Capote wouldn't eat his, which explains a lot.
   Plant these two months before the first fall frost and pick when the roots are 3 to 4 inches in diameter.
'**Shogoin**' (aka 'Japanese Foliage', 'Foliage', 'Shogoin Round'). Start picking the greens thirty days after planting; the mild-flavored, tender roots mature in seventy days. This turnip is unusually tolerant of hot, dry weather, and resistant to insects, which makes it a good choice for spring as well as fall plantings.

Beet Basics

• **Beets like manure, too,** as long as it is well aged. Or you can substitute ordinary garden compost for the manure and add a sprinkling of bonemeal—half of a standard 5-pound bag for our standard 4′ × 8′ bed.

• **Beets like lime.** Actually, what they like is a neutral to slightly alkaline pH, so if your soil is acidic, as it tends to be in the Northeast, Northwest, and much of the Southeast, either have your soil tested and follow the instructions that come back with the test results, or use Marty's KISS method (Keep It Simple, Stupid) and dig in a cup of ground limestone per 10 square feet of bed. Or forget the lime and scatter wood ashes over the bed (at the rate of 1½ cups per 100 square feet)—this will make the soil more alkaline and also discourage root maggots.

• **Northerners: plant in spring.** Beets are less heat and drought tolerant than turnips and also less cold hardy. For that reason, a spring planting works best in Northern climates. Sow the seed two to three weeks before the last spring frost.

• **Southerners: plant in late summer.** You can raise a spring crop of beets below the Mason-Dixon line, but because springs tend to be short there, the cool, moist weather soon giving way to summer heat and drought, you'll do better with a fall crop. Sow the beet seeds three months before the first fall frost.

• **Wash the seeds.** Beet seeds are naturally coated with a germination-inhibiting chemical. You'll find that your beets sprout faster if you wash the seeds in a mild solution of dishwashing detergent and then pat them dry between two paper towels before you plant—wet seeds stick together and so are hard to distribute evenly.

• **Scatter the seeds 1 to 2 inches apart.** Then rake or scratch them in.

• **Thin the seedlings when just half an inch tall** so that they stand 2 inches apart. You can do this most easily by combing out excess seedlings with an iron rake. A month later, thin the beets again so that the remaining plants stand 4 inches apart.

• **Water weekly** during dry weather; otherwise, the roots may become stringy and tough. You'll get a better-tasting harvest, especially in the South, if you also mulch your beets with an inch or two of shredded leaves or some other organic mulch.

• **Harvest the greens** by snapping off a few of the older leaves as the plants mature. For the best-tasting roots, pull the whole plant when the roots reach golf ball size.

Beet Favorites

'**Chioggia**' (aka 'Dolce di Chioggia', 'di Chioggia', 'Candystripe Beet'). Slice across the scarlet-skinned root of this Italian heirloom beet and you'll reveal a bull's-eye of alternating white and pink rings. The flavor of the root is sweet, and the greens are mild.

'**Golden Beet**'. Rich yellow-orange roots with mild flavor and tender texture. Great for what Marty calls "crudités" and what the rest of us call raw. Makes a pretty pickle. The leaves are golden stemmed, too, and good for brightening up any planting.

'**MacGregor's Favorite**' (aka 'Dracena Beet', 'MacGregor's Red Bedding'). An old Scottish variety that is grown for its spear-shaped, metallic purple leaves. Tuck this into the flower garden as a foliage plant. The greens not only look good, they taste good. Don't expect much root, though, as they are small and slow to form on these plants.

'**Red Ace**'. The traditional beet look, with roots that mature early (about fifty days after planting, on average), but keep a sweet flavor and tender texture for a longer harvest.

Kitchen Notes

You don't *have* to eat your beets à la Harvard, though that can be a remarkable experience, the closest thing to time travel Tom has ever come across. One bite of those sweet-and-sour, clammy crimson slices and you are eight years old again, being told to clean your plate by a lunchroom monitor whom you know is going to give you detention when the slop on your plate makes you sick, just like you said it would.

So maybe you're not up for that. You could try Marty's vegetarian borscht, which tastes far better than anything they served in the cafeteria. Or you can keep things simple, as Tom does. Slice the beet roots and steam them together with the greens and a bit of ginger root.

Gramma's Original Borscht

Decades after Marty's grandmother left Brighton Beach for that bingo game in the sky, people in that community are still talking about her borscht (they are still talking about her grandson, too, but that's another story). After countless reminders, Marty located a copy of the original recipe and transcribed it onto the back of an old envelope, which he then passed along to his editor. She, in turn, translated the text to English, corrected the spelling, and eliminated Marty's marginal comments and tedious footnotes. Here's the result: a classic, Brighton Beach borscht.

2 pounds raw beets	Lemon
Salt	6 peeled, boiled potatoes
Sugar	1 cup sour cream

Cut beets in strips, cover with water, cook until tender. Add salt and sugar to taste. Chill in refrigerator. Add lemon and sugar to taste. Just before serving, place a hot boiled potato in each dish. Top with sour cream. Eat fast—life is short.

2🕐-MINUTE PROJECT:
Gourmet Cabbage

In the wretched depths of his ignorance, Tom had thought that there was only one kind of Chinese cabbage, the crispy but bland cylindrical heads that he had always bought at suburban outlets. Why didn't it ever occur to him that a people who have been gardening expertly for five thousand years and more might have gotten bored with that?

Sometimes, though, you have to be told. That's what happened one day when a catalog arrived that Tom had sent away for on a whim. This was Sunrise Enterprises' *Oriental Seed and Flower Catalog*. This offered a text full of exclamation points: "With the new year comes our new 1997 Sunrise Enterprises catalog! . . . It's a wondrous new year and life is good (especially if you're a gardener!)!" It was also stuffed with vegetables that Tom had never dreamt of, such as fuzzy gourd, edible loofahs, asparagus peas, water spinach, and Oriental pickling melons. Resolving to try all of them someday, Tom first buckled down to explore thoroughly the cabbages, starting with the basics.

Eventually, he settled on three types: 'Celery Chinese Long Cabbage', 'Winter Giant', and 'Shantung'. A handy if somewhat cryptic chart in the catalog recommended these varieties for fall plantings. Because Tom had already planned salad plantings for his three vegetable beds, there would be no space in spring. But when the lettuces gave out in summertime, that would open up a bed, and Tom intended to take advantage.

The catalog chart recommended very specific planting times based on the number of frostless weeks that each type of cabbage required to grow to maturity. Tom has trouble keeping things straight, though (ah, the wisdom that comes with age), so he started all the cabbages at the same time. He sowed the seed indoors on August first, under fluorescent lights (see page 115) in segmented plastic trays, cell packs filled with ordinary, over-the-counter seed-starting mix.

In retrospect, Tom decided that he had made both a good move and a bad one. The good move was selecting the fall as his growing season. Chinese cabbages need cool weather but if exposed to temperatures below 50°F when still young, the plants will bolt. That is, they will switch into seed-making mode, send up a tall flower stalk, and never make edible heads of leaves. Spring planting is perilous, unless you live in a genuinely mild area such as the coastal Pacific Northwest, or unless you plant special bolt-resistant varieties such as 'Spring Triumph'.

Tom's mistake was sowing the seeds into the plastic containers. He later learned that Chinese cabbages have sensitive roots which are easily injured during transplanting. He should have sown the seeds directly into the garden, planting the seeds one half to 1 inch deep and setting them out 2 inches apart. Or else he should have started the seeds in peat pots, which could be planted intact. As it was, Tom's cabbage seedlings survived his treatment, but the plants never fully attained the sizes they were supposed to, and this early trauma may have been the reason.

Chinese cabbages prefer deep, loose, organic-rich, and slightly acidic soils, which is exactly what they got in Tom's raised beds. If your garden soil tends toward sandy or toward a sticky clay, you should dig in several inches of compost before planting. This will also help satisfy the Chinese cabbages' healthy appetite for nutrients—they are heavy feeders and you should enrich the soil with a couple of bucketfuls of composted manure (four 2-gallon pailfuls for a standard 4′ × 8′ bed) or with 3 to 4 pounds of 5-10-10 fertilizer per 100 square feet of planting area.

Tom hardened off his cabbage seedlings toward the end of August and transplanted them into the garden on September 4th. He set them out in a staggered pattern, 18 inches apart, measuring from center of plant to center of plant, filling the whole bed. Then he watered the seedlings in well. Chinese cabbages need evenly moist soil and that means deep waterings once or twice a week during dry weather.

Because they were planted so late in the growing season, the Chinese cabbages escaped the usual onslaughts of cutworms, caterpillars, and flea beetles. Slugs, however, were waiting in the wings. From the gusto with which they attacked the cabbage seedlings, Tom had to assume that they had been working up an appetite for cabbage all summer. Since slugs are nocturnal, Tom counterattacked at night, venturing out with a flashlight and a bucket of soapy water. When he'd spot a slug on the cabbages, he'd pick it off with a plastic spoon and flick it into the bath to drown. Still the slugs came on in nightly waves until Tom spread poisoned slug bait in the adjoining flower bed, where Tom figured the headquarters to be. The slug bait is nothing you want to use in the vegetable garden, but applied sparingly to a flower bed, it should do no harm to family or wildlife. It stopped the slugs cold.

By October 14, 'Celery Chinese Long Cabbage' had expanded into a tall, pale head of leaves 3 to 4 inches in diameter and a foot or more tall. Tom picked one and chopped it; the long, thin stems did look rather celerylike. Then in his don't-care, ethnically inaccurate way, Tom stir-fried the cabbage in hot olive oil, with sliced onions and portobello mushrooms and a couple of links of a lamb sausage seasoned with rosemary and mint. The dish might have puzzled a true Chinese cook, but it pleased the family. The flavor of the cabbage, in particular, was much sweeter than that of the supermarket product.

About a week later, on October 19th, Tom picked heads of both 'Winter Giant' and 'Shantung'. These had survived a light frost without harm. 'Winter Giant' had formed a barrel-shaped head that wasn't the 10-pounder promised by the catalog, but which was still substantial. 'Shantung' was rounder, the leaves less densely packed. Both of these Tom chopped and stir-fried, once again in olive oil, with slices of ordinary mushrooms, onions, and chicken cutlet marinated in teriyaki sauce. It was easy to distinguish the two cabbages in the finished dish. 'Shantung' had paler leaves, but the real difference lay in the taste: 'Winter Giant' had an intriguing, slightly smoky flavor, while 'Shantung' was milder, more cabbagey, though it was crisper and sweeter than the Chinese cabbage you would find in a store.

As usual, Tom has plans. After experimenting with the head-forming cabbages, he now wants to dip into what the Chinese call "no head cabbages." These look more like loose-leaf lettuces, and are faster growing and more bolt resistant, and so better adapted to spring planting in the North, though they perform better in Southern climates. Tom's got his eye on 'Minato Santo'.

He's also looking at the mustard cabbages, which make long-stemmed leaves sort of like a Swiss chard. '*Hung Chin*', or 'Four Seasons', has a nice, exotic sound, and it matures in about half as much time (thirty days) as the head-forming cabbages require. Tom might even get some cookbooks out of the library and try an authentic recipe. Though he's found that Chinese cabbage is quite good poached in broth with bay scallops and shiitake mushrooms. Maybe that's the real value of homegrown vegetables, that they provoke the gardener to this sort of culinary excess.

2🕐-MINUTE PROJECT:
Marty Takes a Tropical Vacation

For Marty, gardening is a spectator sport. That's why when Marty agreed to invent 20-minute vegetable gardening, he did so with a proviso: that Tom should be responsible for all the work. Well, not all the work, because Marty's wife, Judy, would no doubt contribute some labor and Marty could hit up his son for heavy lifting. Maybe Tom's wife, Suzanne, would like to help, too. Actually, if she were in the neighborhood on Saturday, Marty suggested, his car needed washing.

Marty made a fatal error, though. The first task he shirked was that of planning all the projects by which the principles of 20-minute vegetable gardening would be tested and refined. "Why don't you do that?" Marty told Tom as he turned back to the latest *Publishers Weekly*. "You have lots of catalogs and stuff." So Tom did. He asked Marty if he had any objection to fruit growing. Then he pulled out his Pacific Tree Farms catalog and sent in an order with Marty's name and shipping address on it.

This is how Marty came to possess the largest banana grove in southern New England.

In fact, the shipping carton (which arrived in early May)

Cooked Down

held only three trees. Still, as Tom explained in response to Marty's panicked telephone call, that was three more banana trees than his neighbor Martha Stewart owns. Maybe he could write an article for *Martha Stewart Living* about how he gilded his banana trees, and made a Yuletide banana mousse flambé. Then Tom relented and agreed to help Marty plant the grove.

Marty did more than watch this time. He complained. What was he going to do with a personal rain forest? Where were the monkeys? If he had to maintain this jungle, he wanted monkeys. He *demanded* monkeys.

Meanwhile, Tom had unloaded from the back of his station wagon three half whiskey barrels. Banana trees, even the dwarf varieties Tom had ordered, need lots of root space. The people at Pacific Tree Farm had suggested a tub 18 to 24 inches in diameter, and the bisected barrels were the least expensive alternative Tom had found at the local yard and garden supply.

For soil, Tom mixed one part bagged topsoil with one part "sharp" builder's sand, one-half part sphagnum peat, and one-half part bagged, composted manure. After lining the bottom of each tub with a sheet of newspaper, so that the contents would not wash out through the drainage holes, he dumped in a couple inches of the soil mix. Then he unpacked the bananas.

These were all dwarf types: 'Dwarf Cavendish', 'Dwarf Jamaican Red', and 'Dwarf Lady Finger'. They had all arrived as semidormant corms: swollen bases from which sprouted thick, snaggled roots, and at the top of each, a pointed leaf bud. Tom washed these in lukewarm water and then set one corm in each tub, root side down. He sifted in the potting mix, repositioning the corms so that their tops stood even with the lips of the tubs. Finally, he dumped in more soil, firming it in with his fingertips as it rose, adding more and more until just the top fifth of the corm still remained in view. He carried the tubs into Marty's sun porch, where the bananas would be protected against any late-spring chill. Then he watered them well.

Bananas hate cold weather. 'Dwarf Cavendish' doesn't mind a brief spell as cool as 50°F, but most other varieties do not thrive at temperatures below 60°. So Marty kept his grove in the sunroom until the first of June, when he had his son, Dan, move the tubs outdoors, and set them on a sun-drenched patch of gravel between house and driveway. Following Tom's instructions, Marty watered the tubs whenever the soil was dry. After the corms had awakened from dormancy and each had sprouted a couple of leaves, he added more potting mix to fill the tubs to a level with the corm's tops. Once a month, Marty fed his bananas with an ordinary water-soluble houseplant fertilizer.

Tom chuckled nastily whenever he thought of Marty's predicament. He should have known better. One afternoon when he dropped by Marty's house, he found Marty hard at work, editing a manuscript. Marty had pulled a deck chair over into the shade of his bananas, which now stood four to five feet tall.

The leaves were huge: three to four feet long, broad and lustrous green. Except for those of the 'Dwarf Jamaican Red'; these, as the name suggests, had a distinctly reddish cast, so that the blushing leaves were set off by a crimson trunk and stems. The driveway looked like a set for *South Pacific,* with Marty as director. Stretched out on the chair with pencil in hand, Marty was an object of splendor himself in baggy swim trunks and a truly tasteless, toucan-adorned shirt. Close at hand, within easy reach, stood his glass of iced tea and cell phone. Tom was struck dumb with banana envy.

When fall brought cold weather, Marty asked Tom and Suzanne to carry the tubs into his sun porch. And when nights grew chilly even there, he supervised the winter storage. Lifting together, Tom and Suzanne slipped the bananas' root balls out of the tubs and into plastic trash bags. These Marty had them set in a cool (but not cold) area of the basement. Once a month or so he opened up the bags and poured a cup or two of water over the banana roots. In this fashion, he kept the trees alive until April, when it was time for Tom and Suzanne to carry them back up to the sun porch and repot them. Within a month, the little grove was back in full leaf.

Marty never has harvested any fruit from his banana trees—his growing season is just too short. The leaves, though, have provided him with delicious meals. These, he learned, are used as wrappers in Southeast Asian and South American cuisines; various ingredients are bundled up in banana leaves, tied up with string, and set to steam in pots of boiling water. His favorite recipe of this sort is for seafood tamales. He has promised to make this for Tom and Suzanne. Or maybe, he's suggested, they could make it for him.

Seafood Tamale

1 pound dry white hominy
4 large banana leaves
1 pound mussels
8 jumbo shrimp
½ pound swordfish
2 rashers of bacon
½ cup olive oil
4 cloves of garlic

3-inch piece fresh ginger root
2 small dried chilies
2 cups chopped onion
½ teaspoon ground cumin
1 tablespoon plus
    1 teaspoon salt
5 tablespoons dry vermouth
16 bay scallops

Add to hominy 6 cups hot water and bring to a boil. Boil for 2 minutes, then set aside to soak for one hour.

To prepare the banana leaves for cooking, split the thickened central vein of each leaf at the base with a sharp knife or shears. Then grasping the split ends of the vein, rip the leaf into two long pieces. Cut these into lengths 15 inches long with the shears; you should have at least 16. Then pass the pieces through the flame of a burner on a gas stove or a barbecue grill to bring out the flavor and make the leaf pliable.

Steam mussels until shells just begin to open; remove meat and discard shells. Peel, devein, and rinse shrimp. Chop the shrimp shells and cook them over a low heat for 10 to 15 minutes in a cup of water; strain and set aside the resulting stock. Skin the swordfish and cut into 1-inch squares. Mince the bacon and cook it in the olive oil over medium heat until slightly golden. Then add peeled and minced garlic and ginger root, crumble in the chilies, and sauté briefly before adding the onion, cumin, 1 tablespoon of the salt, and the vermouth. Cook for 5 minutes or so, then add the shrimp stock and continue cooking until the water has boiled off. Then scrape contents of the pan into a Pyrex measuring cup. Let the oil rise, pour it off, and save it; save also the sauce remaining in the bottom of the measuring cup.

In a food processor grind the hominy to a coarse paste. Transfer it to a mixing bowl and knead in the remaining 1 teaspoon of the salt and the oil you have flavored with bacon, garlic, etc.

Divide this dough into 16 equal portions. Flatten one portion onto the center of a prepared piece of banana leaf, making a broad bed a half inch thick or so, and arrange on top of it a shrimp, 2 scallops, a mussel or two (if they are small and you've got enough), and a square of swordfish. Dribble over this a tablespoon of the sauce from the measuring cup, then cover the whole with another flattened portion of dough. Fold up the sides of the banana leaf, and lay another piece on top, folding the edges of this down and under. Then tie the package up with plain cotton string, and set it aside.

Make 7 more tamales in this fashion, then stack them on a rack in a large pot so that they rest over, not in, boiling water. Cook tightly covered for 20 to 30 minutes, replacing the water in the bottom of the pot as necessary. Serve in the wrappers—for company, use banana leaves from your 'Dwarf Jamaican Red'. Even Martha couldn't make a prettier tamale.

Chapter 8
Perennial Pleasures

A couple of summers ago, Tom went on a canoe trip in northern Maine. (Just listen, Marty, okay?) A floatplane dropped him and his friends at an old logging dam, back in an area where the moose and bald eagles considerably outnumbered the human residents. (Will you be quiet?) And after two days of paddling, they set up their tents by a farm that the guidebook said had been abandoned since the 1930s. (I'm getting to the point, all right?) A wilderness-school party sharing the campsite invited Tom and his friends over for dessert: fresh rhubarb pie. The farmhouse was gone, all the outbuildings, too, as well as the farm animals and people. But the rhubarb some farm wife had planted maybe a century ago was still

ourishing, still offering up its stalks for anyone inclined to make
pie. Now *that's* gardening. (See?)

Rhubarb

o what about rhubarb? Is it actually a kind of strawberry, as
Marty maintains? Of course not. It's an Asian relative of the
knotweeds (*Polygonum* spp.), which are some of the most perni-
ious lawn and garden weeds. Frankly, rhubarb shows a family re-
emblance. It has big, coarse leaves, and in midsummer rhubarb
prouts a tall, really weedy-looking stalk of little off-white flowers.
But, for a 20-minute gardener, weedy is okay. In fact, it's good, as
ong as the weed is on your side.

Rhubarb definitely is on your side, if you treat it right. Never eat
he blades of the leaves, the broad, spreading part. This is full of
alcium oxalate, which in sufficient doses can cause kidney failure.
What you want are the leaf stems, which are free of the harmful
ubstance and which, if stewed or baked, have a tart flavor subtly
mixed with sweet in the better cultivars. A few hardy souls like
heir rhubarb straight. Most of us, though, prefer to temper it with
 sweetener: sugar, maple syrup, and maybe some sweet fruit, too,
ike the strawberries you traditionally mix with rhubarb in a pie.

If the toxicity of the leaves concerns you, consider this: one of
he secrets of the rhubarb's longevity is that even the deer won't eat
t. Once established in your garden, a good clump of rhubarb will
provide you with pies and sauce for years and demand nothing in
eturn.

Rhubarb Basics

• **Rhubarb needs cold.** This plant grows best where winter temperatures drop below 40°F—where they don't, show some sense and
ave that spot for bananas, or passion fruits or kiwis or something
uitably exotic. If you grow rhubarb in the South, you should plant
t in an especially chilly spot, such as a north-facing slope, or in a
hollow at the foot of a hill where the cold air collects in wintertime.

• **Rhubarb needs sun.** In the North where the sun is less intense rhubarb should be planted out in the open, away from trees. In the South, where the sunlight may be too intense, set your rhubarb where it will get full sun in the morning but some shade in the middle of the afternoon.

• **Start your rhubarb off with a good feed.** Remember that you only get one shot at improving the soil around perennials; you won't be replanting every year. So spend a little extra time (maybe a second twenty minutes—you can take tomorrow off) and dig a planting hole a foot deep and a couple of feet across. Then mix in a bucketful of compost and a bucketful of old, rotted-down manure, or, if you are squeamish (Marty?), a full bag of precomposted manure from the garden center. Dig in a bucketful of coarse sand, too.

All of these natural additives will bulk up the soil in the planting area so that what you end up with is a mound of organic-rich soil that will absorb and hold water, but also drain well so that it doesn't waterlog.

• **The final frontier.** That's space, in case you slept through twenty years of *Star Trek*. Space your plants 2 feet apart at planting time. Three to five rhubarb plants should be plenty for a hungry family. How many pies can you eat?

• **Start with roots.** You can buy rhubarb seed, but starting plants this way is slow and produces an inferior crop. Instead, buy roots of a superior strain (see below for the best choices). These are shipped while still dormant in early spring, and should be planted so that the big buds at the top rest an inch or two below the soil surface.

• **Mulch the plants** with old horse manure, if you can get it, or with a mixture of bagged manure and straw or shredded leaves if you don't live near a riding stable. This mulch will keep the rhubarb roots cool and moist and will feed them, too, as it decomposes.

• **Begin harvesting** the spring after planting. Leaves will spring up from the base of the plant with the leaf blades pleated; as the blade spreads and smooths out, the leaf stem is at peak condition. Gently twist and pull on the leaf stem to snap it off—cutting it off with a knife risks a slip and an accidental amputation of the bud at the center of the plant's base.

You can keep harvesting throughout the summer, but don't overdo it. Make sure to leave two leaves intact at all times so that you don't starve the plant. If the plant start sending up thinner stalks, quit picking—that's a sign it needs a rest.

And always, always, always cut off the blade of the leaf and dump it on the compost heap before you bring the stems into the kitchen.

• **Water weekly** in dry weather.

Rhubarb Favorites

'**Canada Red**'. Sounds like some illicit substance, but in fact this is safe, legal, and also tastes good. The tender stalks need no peeling, and keep their cherry-red color even after cooking. Actually, this rhubarb is pretty enough that you should be able to find a use for it as a foliage plant in the flower garden.

'**Crimson Red**' (aka 'Crimson Cherry Red'). This variety boasts exceptional flavor, a good balance of sweet and tart, and is also unusually productive. Vivid red stems make this a handsome choice, and its tolerance for extreme cold and drought make it a practical one for the upper Midwest, the plains states, and the Western mountains.

Asparagus

We've already laid out why we think asparagus is a garden winner (see page 42) and how durable it is. We've heard stories of asparagus beds that continued to make pickings eighty years after they were planted, and twenty years is standard if you start them right.

Asparagus is also an ornamental plant and we prefer to plant it as a hedge rather than in the traditional bed. After all, asparagus tolerates a wide variety of soils, as long as they are well drained, and thrives in partial shade as well as full sun. Its tall thicket of lacy foliage looks delicate and fresh and vaguely Oriental. An asparagus hedge can make a good backdrop for a strip of flowers, or a clever means of hiding the compost heap, dog house, or whatever. An edible hedge: what a concept. Instead of trimming it, you dine.

One word of warning: asparagus doesn't thrive in the heat and humidity of the Southeast. But, given regular watering, it does flourish in the drier heat of the West, especially at higher altitudes.

Asparagus Basics

• **First, cook the weeds.** The worst enemy of asparagus is creeping perennial weeds. Once they get in among the asparagus roots, you'll never get rid of them, because to pull the weeds you'll also have to uproot the asparagus. So begin an asparagus bed by "solarizing" the soil (see page 242 for detailed directions). That is, rototill the asparagus-patch-to-be the summer before you plant it, and then water it and cover it with a sheet of clear plastic. This will collect solar energy to steam cook all the weeds and weed seeds in the soil there.

• **In the trenches.** To plant asparagus dig a trench a foot wide and 15 inches deep. Then line the bottom of the trench with 4 inches of compost or old, rotted-down manure. Add 2 inches of the soil that came out of the trench, then scatter bonemeal at a rate of 1 pound for every 20 running feet of trench. Cover with another couple inches of soil and then mix all the layers up with a garden fork. Now you're ready to plant.

• **Buy "crowns" by mail order.** No one in their right mind starts asparagus from seed—that's a slow process that produces inferior plants. Instead, a sensible gardener buys dormant asparagus plants—

"crowns"—in early spring. You'll find plants for sale at the local garden center, but our experience is that these have been left out to dry on a shelf and are usually half dead by the time you get them. Plants ordered by mail from a reputable nursery usually arrive in far better condition.

• **Buy "all-male" asparagus plants.** We don't want to get bogged down in sexual matters (actually, our editors won't let us), so we'll keep this brief. Some species of plants are hermaphroditic, while others divide up the work of reproduction by producing both male and female individuals.

Asparagus follow the second lifestyle, and the cold, hard fact is that the male asparagus are more productive (why can't that be true of gardeners? Suzanne and Judy want to know). In recent years, a number of all-male strains of asparagus have appeared on the market. These produce *only* male plants (virtually—even asparagus make the occasional mistake) and a bed of these males is twice as productive as the old-fashioned kinds of asparagus.

Twenty-five plants are plenty for a family without some kind of asparagus fixation.

• **Store the crowns in the refrigerator** if you can't plant them as soon as they arrive.

• **Soak the crowns** in lukewarm water for an hour or two before planting.

• **Mound the soil at the bottom of the planting trench.** Scrape the loose manure or compost-and-bonemeal-enriched soil into a long ridge. Then drape the asparagus crowns over this, setting them down at intervals of 18 inches from center of plant to center of plant. Mix more compost or manure with the remaining soil outside the trench, the stuff you dug out to excavate it. Aim for a mix of a third manure or compost and two thirds soil. Toss this into the trench until you have buried the crowns 2 inches deep. The remaining soil and compost or manure mix you'll push into the trench later, after the asparagus shoots have emerged and grown up out of it.

• **Mulch.** Once the trench is completely refilled, and the asparagus shoots are nicely up, mulch the bed with a thick, 4-inch-deep layer of some organic mulch. Autumn leaves that you have shredded with your lawn mower are excellent for this purpose, and cheap too.

• **Fertilize every fall.** Rake the mulch to one side, then scatter on some balanced fertilizer such as 10-10-10, at the rate recommended for vegetable gardens on the package label. Or do it organically by covering the top of the bed with a thin blanket of old, rotted manure (a bucketful per 10 square feet). Then rake the mulch back into place.

• **Water once a week** during dry weather.

• **Cut down and get rid of the old brown stems** as soon as winter kills your asparagus back to the ground. Asparagus beetles and other bad guys hide in the old stems over the winter and reemerge to resume their life of crime in the spring. So *really* get rid of the old stems. Don't just drag them over to the compost heap. Tie them up into a bundle and set them out on the curb to be hauled away with the trash.

• **Harvest in early spring** by slicing off young shoots—the asparagus "spears"—while they are still short—6 to 8 inches tall—and before their tips start to open. Take only spears that are thicker than a pencil. Slice the spears off at an angle at or slightly below ground level.

Harvest just a few spears the first spring after planting; this actually encourages bigger harvests in future years. But limit your first harvest to a week or two of cutting. By the second or third spring, you can harvest more heavily, taking all the fat young spears that appear for the first 4 to 6 weeks after the asparagus breaks dormancy. When the shoots start to dwindle, so that they emerge from the ground thinner than a pencil, back off.

Asparagus Favorites

Jersey Knight'. That's "Joy-zee" to you. An all-male (or virtually all-male) strain that is highly resistant to the various diseases that afflict asparagus, and which performs well in cold-winter areas.

UC 157'. This may sound like an interstate, but it's actually the best asparagus for mild winter areas. Good flavor and disease resistant, too.

Horseradish

This vegetable would be classified as an incurable disease, if it didn't taste so good. Once you plant horseradish, you will always have it. In fact, you should either locate this plant in a sunny but out-of-the-way spot, where its colonial tendencies won't matter, or else you should confine the roots. Marty favors the first approach as effortless, though sloppy. Tom maintains that confinement makes it easier to find the roots (which are the part of the horseradish you eat). Marty says he likes the thrill of the hunt.

Either way you grow it, horseradish is close to foolproof. It's also a great investment: just a little has a big impact on your diet. And there's no comparison between the punch of homegrown, fresh-grated horseradish and some tired paste out of a jar.

Horseradish Basics

• **Choose a sunny spot.** About the only thing that can knock out horseradish is shade.

• **In early spring, buy roots.** You can order these from mail-order seed catalogs or pick them up at the local garden center. Either source is fine with this rugged plant.

• **To grow horseradish Marty's way** (unconfined roots): In early spring, prepare your horseradish patch. Layer on 4 inches of compost and 2 inches of coarse sand on an area 3 feet by 3 feet. Then dig the patch with a garden fork or spade, turning the soil to a depth of 18 inches. Plant the horseradish roots with small end down (duh) and the thick ends 2 to 4 inches below the soil surface. Set the roots 15 inches apart; five or six should fill your little patch.

• **To grow horseradish Tom's way** (confined roots): Cut the bottom off a 30-gallon plastic garbage pail. Set the pail (upright) in a sunny spot, burying the bottom foot of it. Fill it with a mix of part coarse sand, 1 part ordinary garden soil, and 1 part compost. Plant the roots in early spring as described above; two or three will fill the pail.

• **Water whenever the soil dries out.** Elevating the soil in a pail makes Tom's horseradish patch prone to drought. Watering is especially important in the late summer and fall, when the roots should be bulking up, getting ready for winter dormancy.

• **Harvest as you need the roots.** After the first couple of fall frosts, you can start digging up roots with a garden fork whenever you feel the need for some zest. Uncollected roots will store right in place in the soil for several months—be sure to cover the patch with a thick blanket of leaves or straw as winter sets in to keep the soil from freezing.

• **Let your horseradish replant itself.** If you grow your horseradish Marty's way, you can count on the bits of roots you missed harvesting to sprout next spring and provide next year's crop. Roots left in Tom's trash-can beds don't usually survive the winter. So Tom has to save a root or two from his harvest and bury it in a corner of the garden until the time for replanting in the spring. Or he has to go beg a few starts off of Marty, which is what he usually does because that's easier. After all, what are friends for?

Horseradish Favorites

'New Bohemia' and 'Maliner Kren' are two old Eastern European varieties, and cooks from that tradition may insist on them. Most of our sources sell generic horseradish, and it's fine with us.

Suzanne's Basic Horseradish Sauce

Scrub and peel roots, then take outside to grate (this is high-test stuff and the fumes are overpowering in a confined space). Mix grated root thoroughly with white vinegar to make a slurry and store in the refrigerator in a tightly capped jar.

Grapes

Why doesn't everyone grow grapes is what we want to know. No other fruit or vegetable gives so much pleasure. You watch the vine leaf out in spring, the buds opening and the foliage emerging so tentatively, a pale and waxy green. Then you spend the summer sitting in the shade of your arbor, eating cheese (a caciocavallo, maybe) and prosciutto on good bread and watching your grapes mature. You talk knowledgeably with oenophile friends about harvesting the "berries" at the peak of sweetness. When, shears in hand, you climb the stepladder to fill bowls with fruit, you are no longer some harried suburban wage slave. You are the *padrone* bringing in the harvest, celebrating the *vendemmia*. If you have been smart and planted a wine grape, you can turn your pickings into a truly remarkable jelly, and have most of your Christmas shopping done by early September.

If, besides planting a wine grape, you have also selected a type of grape adapted to your climate and soil (and there's one at least of those for virtually every region of the country), grapes more or less grow themselves. The only considerable task, aside from harvesting, is pruning. If you want your vine to keep bearing fruit, you have to cut it back each year while it is dormant—that is, in the wintertime. Horticultural fussbudgets have tried to turn this into an intimidating process, developing elaborate instructions for "umbrella Kniffen" systems, and the "Geneva double curtain."

Let them worry about that. All you have to know is that grapes don't stay healthy if they snarl in tangles, and that they bear fruit most heavily on new shoots off older vines. So as your vine grows up the trellis, keep the main branches apart from each other by tying them to the supports in parallels a couple of feet apart. Then, in late winter, you cut back the side shoots that have shot out from the main branches during the previous year. You cut these side shoots back to stubs with just a couple of big fat buds on each of them. After this, you go back inside, to sample again the truly inferior wine for which, in a misguided moment, you sacrificed last year's harvest.

Grape Basics

• **Choosing the right grape.** Success in grape growing depends on selecting a type that likes your climate and soil. Check out "Grape Favorites" (page 182) for tips.

• **Find a sheltered spot with full sun.** A south- or southwest-facing slope is ideal. The more sun, the more flavor the grapes will have.

• **Good drainage.** Marty thinks this is something you call the plumber about. In fact, good drainage means the soil absorbs water easily but lets any excess pass through so that it doesn't stay waterlogged after a rainstorm or session with the sprinkler. Planting on a slope helps ensure good drainage.

• **Support.** Grapevines need something to climb. They are worse than kids in this respect. Anyhow, you can save yourself lots of trouble if you think about this before your plant. Maybe you can plant the grapevine at the foot of a rail fence. Or maybe you can plant it beside the porch and tie it up to the railing. An old-fashioned, umbrella-type clothesline is great. Use your imagination, and bring the grape to the support, if possible, rather than vice versa.

• **Dig deep.** With luck, your grape will be growing in the same spot for years, even decades. And you'll have to plant only once. So give it an extra good start. Get your son or daughter or the kid down the street to dig a really big hole. Mark out an area 3′ × 3′ for each grape, and dig out the soil to a depth of 2 feet. That's right, *two feet*. Then mix into the soil from the hole a bushel of compost and, if the soil seems sticky, a bucketful of coarse sand. Finally, dump the improved soil back into the hole.

• **Plant in early spring.** Usually, grapes arrive from the nursery bare root; that is, they have been dug from the nursery field while they were still dormant and they are shipped to you without any soil around the roots. This is fine, as long as you plant them quickly.

To do this, dig a hole in the prepared planting area, which should be deep and wide enough so that you can spread out the roots of your new plant. Otherwise, it's like jamming your foot into a shoe that is just too small. Then look for the dark soil stain on the stem. That tells you how deep the grape was planted at the nursery, and your goal is to plant it at the same level.

Spread the roots out in the hole, hold the stem up to the right height, and sift soil back into the hole. Poke the soil gently down among the roots with your fingertips. When you have entirely re-filled the hole, push any extra soil into a low dam around the grape. Make a shallow saucer a couple of feet across that will catch and hold rain. Fill this with water, let it drain, and then fill it again.

• **Protect from birds.** If you want to harvest any grapes, you are going to have to ward off those winged lowlifes. When the color in-dicates that the grapes are ripening, cover your arbor with the same fine black plastic netting you used to keep birds away from your seeds (see page 70). You don't have to run the net all the way to the ground—if you do, how will you get in to lounge in the shade with your glass of cheap red wine? Just drape the netting over the grapevines and let it hang down a couple of feet below the foliage and fruit. Then tie strips of tinsel or bits of aluminum foil to the edge of the net. Whether this scares the birds, or merely repulses them with its tacky appearance, the silvery trash does keep them away.

Grape Favorites

Tom refuses to advise Californians or Pacific Northwesterners about grapes, as these people have so many good options and are so obnoxiously knowledgeable already. If you live in either of those regions, call your local Cooperative Extension for advice; you'll find the number under your county or state listings in the telephone book.

For hot, humid regions
'Carlos'. Good for wine and jelly making and eating fresh. Disease resistant.
'Noble'. Small to medium blue-black fruits good for wine, preserves, and eating fresh.

For cold, Northern regions and high-altitude gardens
'Edelweiss'. A disease-resistant white grape that is sweet yet mild, good for eating fresh or wine making.

For the desert Southwest
'French Colombard'. A white wine grape that bears big crops of highly flavored fruit.
'Petite Sirah'. A red with small to medium clusters of small but intense berries.

For areas with cold winters and hot, humid summers
'Foch' (alias 'Maréchal Foch'). Small blue-black grapes that make a spectacular jelly and a good Burgundy-type wine.
'Seyval Blanc' (alias 'Seyve-Villard 5-276'). Disease resistant and cold-hardy white grape that makes a nice, dry wine and a memorable jelly.

Other Pleasures

1. Alpine strawberries. We described why we think these are a winner in Chapter 3 (see page 47). We'll content ourselves with adding here that since these berries are small, you'll want a lot of these plants, and because these plants don't spread like regular garlen strawberries, you'll have to plant more of them. The cheapest way to do that is to sow a packet of Alpine strawberry seed indoors in early spring, and grow your own. That's a task you'll have to do only once, since alpine strawberries are long-lived as well as delicious.

2. Bamboo. This is a plant that Tom has grown only for its decorative value, but he's going to change that.

The Chinese and Japanese grow special varieties of bamboo for culinary use, but you can eat the young shoots from virtually any kind if you cut them in spring when they are about 6 inches high, and then boil them for ten minutes, drain, and boil again (in new water) for another ten. After that, you can slice them and use them in your stir-fries. Shoots are edible only when young, so harvest them all as soon as they reach an acceptable height and, after boiling, freeze any extras.

A warning about bamboos: there are two groups. One group is clump forming; it makes a compact cluster of stems that expands slowly outward at the edge. The other group consists of "running bamboos," which send out long, underground runners that pop out of the ground at the tip to start new colonies. These running types are aggressive spreaders, especially in warm climates, and can be hard to control.

All in all, Southerners are probably wisest to grow their bamboos in tubs. Use a container of at least 5-gallon capacity, and fill it with ordinary potting soil.

3. Jerusalem artichoke. We promoted this plant in our previous books, so if you haven't already planted it, shame on you. Tom likes it because it justifies his prejudice against the use of common names: this plant is actually a perennial sunflower and has nothing to do with Jerusalem or artichokes. Marty likes this plant because

A) it is unkillable (an important consideration for him).
B) it requires no care.
C) it's pretty—flowers are a great bonus if they cost you nothing.

The part of the Jerusalem artichoke that you eat is the crunchy tuberous roots. This is also what you plant—choose any sunny spot in spring or fall, and set the dormant tubers 18 inches apart burying them a couple of inches below the soil surface.

The plant sprouts, quickly grows to a height of 5 feet or more and bears its yellow flowers. As soon as frost cuts it down, you take a garden fork and start digging up the roots. Start by working around the periphery of your patch to control its spread, then dig here and there within, leaving some plants untouched to provide next year's crop.

In truth, though, you'd have trouble totally eliminating this plant even if you tried, because in your digging, you are almost certain to miss a root or two, and this overlooked piece will promptly establish a new patch. Of course, the irrepressible nature of the Jerusalem artichoke means that you should not plant it among other, less expansive plants. Find a spot at the edge of the lawn or by a meadow where it can spread its toes without aggravating any neighbors.

How do you eat the roots? Peel them and slice them into salads or boil them up like potatoes. Incidentally, because Jerusalem artichokes contain the sugar inulin rather than the starches and sucrose sugars found in most other root crops, doctors recommend them as a better food for those with diabetes.

2⊙-MINUTE PROJECT:
Tom and Marty Grow Up

Growing up was never something that particularly interested either Tom or Marty. Last summer, though, they discovered how useful this process can be.

It was Marty who pointed out the inherent problem with earthbound plants. By this, he meant any plant whose spread is primarily horizontal and along the ground, like strawberries or lettuces or turnips. Such plants can occupy a lot of square footage, and the only way you can have more of them is to plant even more square footage. That means expanding the garden and, he noted (harking back to his space-time Einsteinian equation), the bigger the garden, the more the work.

Just compare these earth huggers, Marty said, with the grape that Tom had planted. This grape had one stem and occupied a negligible amount of garden bed. Its spread was all *vertical*. You don't have to dig or weed or mulch air space. Not only that, but by elevating itself, the grape had left behind earthbound pests, too. Marty figured this was a nonviolent way that he could frustrate the rabbit and woodchuck who between them rule Marty's backyard like a four-legged Mafia.

From now on, Marty announced, all his gardening would be vertical.

So he gave up those modern bush beans and bush peas to plant old-fashioned climbing types: "pole" beans such as 'Kentucky Wonder' and long-stemmed climbing peas such as 'Tall Telephone'. To support these, he drove sturdy tomato stakes into the ground at 3-foot intervals, then stretched a 5-foot-high curtain of plastic bird netting from stake to stake, fastening it in place with staples.

He planted cucumbers, too, a type called 'Sweet Success' whose flowers don't need pollination to set fruit. This meant that Marty's cucumber vines (unlike those of neighbors like *Martha*) continued to make cucumbers even when bad weather kept the bees and other pollinating insects from doing their job. (Actually, Martha's vines kept bearing, too, but only because she made the rounds with a camel hair brush, pollinating her flowers by hand.) To support his cucumbers, Marty used a 6-foot-high trellis made of 2″ × 3″ lumber and chicken wire.

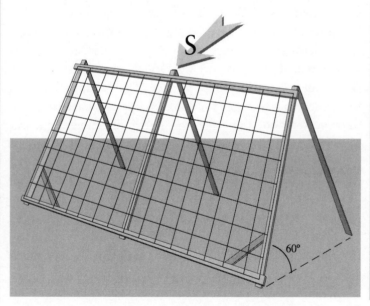

Orientation of the trellis proved crucial. So that each leaf would get full benefit of the sunlight, Marty borrowed Tom's compass and ran the trellises from east to west. For heat-loving plants such as the cucumbers, he actually tipped the top of the trellis back toward the north about thirty degrees. Because the sun comes from the south in the northern hemisphere (which includes the United States, as Marty informed Tom), a trellis leaned back like that gets the most sunlight. Marty had learned this trick while erecting solar panels at his old commune.

To support his leaning panels of cucumbers, Marty ran legs from their tops back down to the ground (see the sketch below). This made the trellis so strong that it could even support the weight of Marty's French 'Charentais' melons.

These he had purchased over the Internet as ready-to-plant seedlings from a nursery in Santa Barbara that grows a variety of heirloom and gourmet vegetables and fruits. For a price, the nursery will dispatch seedlings to you via overnight air freight. Marty had tried to persuade Tom to start melons from seed indoors in early May. Three-inch peat pots filled with seed-starting mix and a spot under the fluorescent lights would have done the trick. But Tom told Marty that tomatoes were occupying all of his space and time. So Marty had the melons shipped on June first.

By that date, Marty's garden had warmed up enough to plant the melon seedlings. After hardening off the new arrivals for a couple of days (for the basics on this important process, see page 71), he planted them right at the foot of his sunniest trellis. This ran the whole length of the north side of one of Marty's garden beds; and so the trellis was 8 feet wide and 6 feet tall. Marty had covered this trellis with welded wire fencing left over from enclosing the garden, because he figured that melons would need a sturdier support. Marty set three melon seedlings along the base of this structure: one about a foot in from either end and one in the middle. Before setting each of the seedlings into the ground, he mixed a couple of shovelfuls of composted manure (bought in a bag—Marty doesn't handle this himself) and a handful of bonemeal into the soil around the planting spot.

By midsummer, Marty had long since eaten all his 'Tall Telephone' peas and was deep into the 'Kentucky Wonder' and 'Sweet Success' harvest. His melons, however, were just setting fruit. He had been directing the vines up the trellis, tying the growing tips into place with bits of yarn. Now, looking at the little melons hanging from the vines, Marty realized that the fruits' slender stems would never be able to support the mature fruits. These weren't going to be Christmas tree ornaments, after all.

Fortunately, Marty had learned first aid in the Boy Scouts and he was able to rig a sling for each melon. He "borrowed" a pair of Judy's panty hose and cut them up into strips 4 inches wide and 10 inches long. Taking one of these strips, he tied the ends to the wire mesh so that the stretchy nylon cradled the little fruit. As the melons swelled, the sling expanded to accommodate them.

By the end of August Marty's melons were ripening. Their skins were turning tan beneath the netting of white that ran over its surface, and when he poked his nose into a sling, he could smell the sweet odor of the fruit. The harvest wasn't huge—Marty wasn't ready to open a farmstand—but it was . . . effective. Marty took to bringing a melon with him when he went out to dinner with friends. After everyone else had ordered their desserts, he'd ask the waiter to also bring bowls and spoons for the whole table. Then he'd take the melon out of the discreet paper sack in which it had been lurking, and he'd divide it up, distributing slices to all. It was an impressive moment.

More impressive, though, was the moment that his companions tasted the first pieces of truly vine-ripened melon they had ever eaten. The perfume was rich enough to make you truly understand the name "muskmelon," and the flesh was almost buttery soft, yet still fresh and very sweet. Marty's reputation as a connoisseur was confirmed, reinforced, and permanently enshrined.

Tom heard about this (repeatedly), and eventually he was even given one fruit, which he enjoyed at home. He doesn't have Marty's panache and he didn't think he could pull off the restaurant scene. But every time *his* wife gets a run in her panty hose, Tom asks if he can have the discard. He's thinking about growing up, too.

2🕐-MINUTE PROJECT:
Tom and Marty Promote Graft

Did you know that one sixth of the adult male population suffers from Attention Deficit Disorder? And that the other five sixths can't concentrate? Of course, women do better. At least, they would if they weren't too busy.

The sad fact is that the attention span of the American adult has dropped to near zero. This threatens to change the national lifestyle in some major ways. Take the ultimate American fruit (and the ultimate garden perennial)—the apple. Planting a tree and nurturing it to the point that it actually bears fruit, that takes *years*. Almost certainly, by the time your tree comes across with the first apple, you have moved to another time zone, or at least forgotten where you planted the damn thing.

So are we suggesting that the nation just give up, and make its pies from the generic red spheres you'll find at the supermarket? No way. We want pies made from homegrown apples, delicious, mouth-awakening classics such as 'Gravenstein' and 'Rhode Island Greening'. These are apples with real flavor, ones that make pies like ambrosia. And, as usual, we have a cunning trick for getting what we want the easy way.

Don't plant your own apple trees, is our advice. Instead, move in on someone else's planting. Find a neglected apple tree, one at the edge of the school parking lot or in the hedgerow growing at the edge of the state property across the street. Take over that tree and make it *your* tree. This is easily done in just twenty minutes with equipment no more sophisticated than a sharp knife and a roll of vinyl electrician's tape. Or, if you just aren't the aggressive type, you can use the same technique to turn that crab apple in your own front yard, the one the developer plunked down before rolling out the sod, into something genuinely useful.

The technique you use to achieve all these feats is grafting: you take a piece of a tree you wish you had, such as 'Gravenstein', and insert it into the top of a tree you don't like—such as the crab apple. Your insertion and the old tree fuse, and your addition goes on to become the part of the tree that flowers and fruits, while the old tree selflessly provides support.

Timing is critical in making this work. In late winter you order "scions," shoots of really good pie-apple trees, from one of the suppliers listed below. Marty's favorites are the aforementioned 'Gravenstein' (in case you were wondering), a centuries-old Italian apple that has a sweet and tart flavor and a winy aroma, while Tom prefers 'Baldwin', an eighteenth-century apple from Massachusetts whose fruits are best described as spicy. They both agree that 'Rhode Island Greening', a sour, green-skinned apple that dates back to the seventeenth century, makes remarkable pies, especially if you add a bit of ground ginger.

When the UPS truck brings the scions—and this should happen in early spring—you take the bundle of shoots out of their shipping box and stand them up in a pitcher of water in the refrigerator. If stored in this way, the scions will keep without harm for a couple of weeks. They'll stay dormant, with the leaf buds unopened, and this is what you want. For grafting to work, you must insert a dormant scion into the branch of a tree that is just coming out of dormancy, whose sap is just starting to flow. So wait to do your grafting until you see the pussy willows bloom.

Then you assemble your tools, the roll of tape and the sharp knife. You can spend a lot of money to buy a grafting knife, or you can stop in at the local art supply store and for a dollar or two pick up a disposable artist's snap-blade knife. A surgeon friend tells us that scalpels work well, too.

Choose several healthy, straight branches evenly spaced around the periphery of your victim—the apple or crab apple tree. Ideally, these branches shouldn't be too big, no more than two or three times as thick as your scions. Avoid those vertical branches that are rising up off the tree's limbs, to soar upward like utility poles through the center of its crown. Those are water sprouts, and they aren't ever going to amount to much. Instead, look for branches that are reaching out to the light and that you can imagine turning into main limbs of the tree. Your ultimate goal, after all, is a complete takeover.

Having selected branches on the host tree, you cut off their ends with a pair of pruning shears, and then with your snap-blade knife, you shave the tips into something like you'll find in the diagram below. Then you shave the end of a scion into the mirror image. With your knife, you next split each of the shaved ends across the middle (see diagram). Then you fit the branch and scion ends together, making sure that the bark of the scion lines up exactly with the bark of the branch on at least one side. You push the branch and scion together, so that their central splits open up a bit, and a tongue of the branch slips into the end of the scion, and a tongue of the scion slips into the branch. (Marty always gets excited at this point.) Finally, you wrap the point of union between branch and scion tightly with the electrician's tape, taking care to cover entirely the cut parts. That's it.

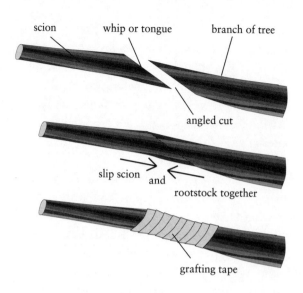

scion whip or tongue branch of tree

angled cut

slip scion and rootstock together

grafting tape

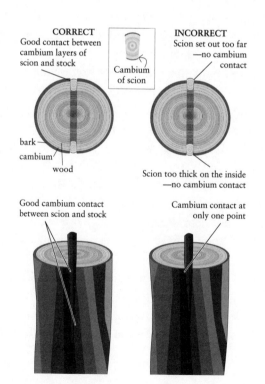

CORRECT
Good contact between
cambium layers of
scion and stock

Cambium
of scion

INCORRECT
Scion set out too far
—no cambium
contact

bark
cambium
wood

Scion too thick on the inside
—no cambium contact

Good cambium contact
between scion and stock

Cambium contact at
only one point

Actually, this grafting process goes better if you spend a few minutes first practicing your cuts on extra shoots clipped from the tree. Also, if you choose to graft a scion onto a branch of considerably larger diameter, you should whittle up an extra scion and then slip two scions into the branch end, one scion along each side. Again, it's essential that the bark on the outer edges of the scions line up with the bark on the outer edges of the host branch.

Graft scions onto the host tree at three or four points around its periphery; if you like, you can graft scions of different sorts onto the same tree. In that way, if your partner likes 'Gravensteins' and you prefer 'Rhode Island Greenings', each can bake pies that pleases him or her.

You'll know if the grafts have "taken" if, after a couple of weeks, the buds on the scions open and leaves appear. Leave the grafts alone until the next year, when you should remove the tape wrapping. This is easier done during warm weather, which softens the vinyl tape and its adhesive. Tie a bit of bright yarn around the branch after removing the tape, so that you'll recognize instantly which ones support grafts.

This is important because during the following winter you will need to start pruning off the nongrafted branches. Don't cut them *all* off that first winter. Just begin a policy of discouragement. You want to give the grafted branches an advantage, so that they'll outgrow all competitors.

You won't get apples the first fall after grafting, but you are likely to get them the next. At any rate, you'll get a crop of fruit years sooner by converting a tree than by planting one.

One word of caution: you can only graft like to like. In other words, you can't use this technique to turn an oak tree into an apple, or a birch into a peach. (Who would try that, Marty?) Leave that Frankenstein stuff to the science-fiction writers.

Chapter 9

Understudies

You've probably seen the movie, late at night on television. There's a Broadway hit, a great dramatic vehicle, with a glamorous but essentially amoral star. Every night after the performance, he or she goes out dissipating him or herself in the fleshpots, eating corned beef sandwiches at the Carnegie Deli, swilling down champagne cocktails at the Café des Artistes, making clever, amoral remarks at the Algonquin, that sort of thing. And that sort of thing catches up with you. So one evening, laid low by dyspepsia, the star cannot perform. The faithful understudy, who really is quite good-looking, though not in a hot and sexy way, steps in. Having spent his/her late

Understudies

195

nights getting healthful exercise by waiting on tables, he/she is in great shape and scores a smash success.

You can fill in the rest. And if *you* have ever waited tables in the hope of a career in theater, you know that the chances of this happy ending are less than slim. Unless you turn to gardening.

For the fact is that by midsummer every year, understudies take over the starring roles in the vegetable garden, and they are always a popular success. Who's going to turn down fresh vegetables, after all? But the best part is this: the understudies aren't second-best players. They are every bit as good as the original stars. Just different.

Why is there a need for gardening understudies? Because everywhere in the United States except for maybe Santa Barbara or Palm Springs or some other place where no one normal can afford to live, the climate changes with the end of spring. Spring throughout most of our country is a cool and moist season. So, if you are smart, you begin the gardening year by planting crops that like cool, moist weather. Then comes summer, which is hot and typically drier. Often *very* dry. Pretty soon the moist- and cool-loving crops fail. That's when you need to move in with the heat-loving understudies.

Who are these understudies? We happen to have a list. We are going to share it, too, together with some insightful comments by Tom and a few of Marty's unique perspectives.

But first a note: the vegetables on this list thrive in heat, but they aren't woven from asbestos. In the lower altitudes of the Southwest and in the Deep South, summer may be so hot that you should do the obvious thing and spend that season relaxing in the shade. There are a few vegetables that flourish even in the intense heat if given enough irrigation. But for the most part, where summers are truly incandescent, you should take a break and plant what are described here as summer understudies at summer's end. They'll still serve to fill a gap, because in the hot-weather regions, another crop of cool-loving plants should not go in until mid to late fall.

Whether you plant in summer or fall, though, you'll find the unlerstudies to be, typically, less work and more fruitful than spring plantings of the same vegetables. Why is this so? In Nature, seeds would sprout and the seedlings appear just as soon as the soil warmed to a temperature acceptable to that type of plant. Nature is a spring planter. So, too, are most of your neighbors. Most gardeners strive to start all their plants as early as possible.

This emphasis on early, both by gardeners and by Nature, is something that the insects have come to expect. Most insects are fairly specific in what they will eat—they like a particular plant or family of plants—and they time their appearance to coincide with the time that their food normally appears. Delay your planting until summertime, delay the appearance of the plants and their meal, and the corresponding insect pests will quite likely give up on your garden and move on. This is the reason why understudy plantings are usually far less troubled by insect damage.

Beans

Why bother? That was Marty's first reaction to this suggestion. He was quick to dismiss beans, whether homegrown or store bought, as generic and interchangeable. Harvest them already canned was his suggestion.

Then, with a little prodding (actually, more than a little), he took a look at the Vermont Bean Seed Company catalog. There he found more than one hundred different types of beans: string and snap beans, French flageolet beans, blue-striped pole beans from Switzerland, and all sorts of beautiful spotted and stained beans for shelling and drying.

What really made Marty a believer, though, was a taste of Tom's homemade, real New England baked beans. Tom served Marty two batches: one made from 'Steuben Yellow Eye Beans', and the other from a mix of 'Soldier Beans' and 'Jacob's Cattle Beans'. These both had a richness of flavor that Marty could not attribute entirely to the salt pork that Tom had surreptitiously slipped into the pot. But the uncooked beans themselves were so colorful that, later, when Marty had grown his own, he declined to bake them. Immediately after shelling them, he boiled them lightly and then served the spotted, colorful morsels with just a touch of butter. He billed them as tabletop art.

The standard recommendation for beans is to plant them as soon as the soil warms in the spring. This works, but if your garden is small, why hurry? Wait until the lettuce comes out and then plant beans into that bed. Beans are an especially good understudy to salad greens. Nitrogen is the nutrient that plants use most heavily for leaf making, and as a result, leafy greens such as lettuce or spinach tend to strip the soil of this element. Beans, though, those thrifty Yankee plants, have developed a means of making their own nitrogen fertilizer. They host bacteria in their roots that "fix" atmospheric nitrogen, manufacturing nitrogen fertilizer from the gaseous nitrogen in the air.

There is one last point to consider, before you plant. Tom insists that pole beans, the types that make long, climbing stems, are the best type to plant because they produce more beans per square foot of garden and so return more harvest per input of effort. (*Don't you hate that bogus organizational lingo?*—M.A.) Marty prefers bush beans, the types of beans that make short stems and so need no supports. Getting poles and trellises together takes more organization than he is willing to give to his garden. (*Or anything else*—T. C.)

Bean Basics

• **Avoid "treated" seeds.** For your own health and that of your beans, make sure that the seed you buy hasn't been coated with fungicides. This is a common practice, because it protects from decay early plantings of beans, the ones that go into the wet, cool soils of spring. Summer plantings don't face that risk, but the fungicides are toxic to far more than decay organisms. They will kill the nitrogen-fixing bacteria and won't do you any good either. Avoid them.

• **Dust your beans** with a "bacterial inoculant" when you plant. Available through seed catalogs and garden centers, this is a concentrated culture of the bacteria that help the bean plants make their own fertilizer.

• **Grow fast-maturing bush-type beans** in Northern gardens. These take less than two months to grow from planting to harvest. Where summers are short, there may not be enough warm days to ripen an early summer planting of slower-maturing pole beans. See "Bean Favorites" (below) for specific recommendations.

• **Erect trellises for pole beans** before you plant (see pages 185–88 for a discussion of the advantages of this). The easiest kind of support is a length of plastic bird netting stretched between 5-foot-tall stakes. A more scenic approach is to erect tepees of 6-foot bamboo stakes. Lash these together at the top with twine and set the tepees 2 feet apart.

• **Plant beans** as late as early July in the North, throughout the summer in the upper South, and in the fall in the Deep South and hotter regions of the Southwest. Plant the seed 1½ inches deep. Bush-bean seeds should be planted 8 to 10 inches apart in an even pattern throughout the bed. Plant pole-bean seeds 3 to 6 inches apart along the foot of the trellis or tepee.

• **Mulch** around the young plants to keep the soil moist and cool. An inch or two of shredded leaves or straw works well.

• **Stay out of the bean patch** when the plants are wet. By brushing up against the leaves then, you may spread diseases from plant to plant.

• **Harvest snap beans** (the type you eat pod and all) while pods are still crisp and firm and while the seeds inside are still very small.

• **Harvest shell beans** (types of which you eat only the seeds) just after the pods change color.

• **For dried beans,** leave the pods on the plants until they have dried. Be sure to pick the dried pods, though, before cold weather hits. Shell the beans, spread them out on paper towels, and leave them to dry for another week. Then store the beans in sealed jars in a cool, dry place.

Bean Favorites

'Contender Bush'. A green snap bean that starts to bear just forty days after planting. The best bean for cold regions with short summers.

'Jacob's Cattle Bean' (aka 'Trout', 'Dalmatian'). A very old strain of unknown origin; a longtime favorite in New England. 'Jacob's Cattle' is a bush drying bean that takes eighty to one hundred days from sowing to harvest, but it's worth the wait: the seeds shell out a bone white flecked with maroon, and have an ability to absorb flavors without losing their integrity.

'Kentucky Wonder' (aka 'Old Homestead', 'Texas Pole', 'Egg Harbour'). An old-time, fast-growing climber that will bear 9-inch pods ready for picking within sixty-four days. You can do that, and cook them up as snap beans, or you can leave the pods on the vines, and shell out the dried beans for soups the next winter.

'Soldier Bean'. A bush drying bean that has been the mainstay of New England baked bean suppers for generations. Flourishing in cool climate areas and drought resistant, this bean is ready for harvest eighty-five days after sowing. The name refers to the dark maroon soldier's silhouette that marks the eye of each white seed.

'Scarlet Runner Bean'. A pole bean that can climb to 10 feet. 'Scarlet Runner' attracts hummingbirds with its clusters of scarlet blossoms, and bears long pods that may reach a length of 12 inches or more. The pods are tasty when steamed, but the real value in this bean (according to Marty) is its ability to cover up and hide an arbor or trellis within a matter of weeks, thus freeing the gardener from the need to repair or paint for another season.

Steuben Yellow Eye' (aka 'Dot Eye', 'Molasses Bean', 'Yellow Eyed China Bean'). Another old-time bush drying bean, this one also takes eighty-five days from sowing to harvest, and bears white beans dotted with yellow at the eye. This strain germinates well even in cool, damp weather and is notably disease resistant. A traditional favorite for baked beans, soups, and stews.

Cucumbers

Whoever came up with the idea of naming a cucumber the 'Burpless'? Actually, there's also a 'Burpless Muncher' and a 'Burpless No. 26' (which suggests that there were once Burpless numbers 1 through 25, too). It just shows you how one gassy individual can stigmatize a great crop. Cucumbers may be easy to grow, tasty, and prolific: one plant can yield an amazing 30 to 40 pounds of fruits. Yet even so, no one gets passionate about cucumbers (at least, no one admits it, if they do).

But we are straying into risqué territory, and Marty is blushing. So we'll content ourselves with saying that this is a great vegetable, and you really ought to grow it. Cucumbers are especially handy as summer understudies because they are subtropical plants, whose ancestors come from northern India. They relish the kind of hot, humid weather that keeps you hiding in the shade of the porch. Besides, if you use a little imagination you can plant some exotic types that will restore romance to your cucumber patch.

For Marty, however, the main advantage to using cucumbers as summer understudies is that you don't have to start the plants indoors. If you insist on planting cucumbers in the spring and follow the directions on the seed packet, you'll sow the seeds into little peat pots of soil up to a month before you can safely plant them outdoors. Be sure to use peat pots because they will allow you, later on, to transplant the seedlings into the garden without removing the pots—cucumbers have sensitive roots that are easily damaged. That means, of course, a month of catering to the little indoor seedlings. You can eliminate this entirely by planting the seeds right into the warm soil of summer—and that's what Marty does.

Cucumber Basics

· **Build up your soil** by digging in a couple of inches of compost before planting cucumbers. This will help the soil absorb and hold moisture—and cucumbers need that. By bulking up the soil though, and breaking it up, a heavy dose of compost will also speed the rate at which excess moisture drains through and out. Although cucumbers need a moist soil, they do not thrive or bear well on a wet one.

· **Consider growing up.** Cucumbers are sprawling plants, so training them up a trellis (see page 185) saves a lot of space. Remember, according to Marty's first law (or is it his third?), the smaller the space, the less the work.

· **In the North,** plant fast-maturing strains when you are growing cucumbers as understudies. See "Cucumber Favorites" below for specific recommendations.

· **Plant in clusters.** Sow four or five seeds around a circle about 1 foot across, spacing the circles 4 feet apart. This means that by staggering the circles, you can fit three into a standard 4′ × 8′ bed.

· **Cover the clusters** immediately after sowing the seed with a floating row cover (see page 258 for a complete description) or a strip of cheesecloth. Left in place until the plants begin to flower, this will ward off cucumber beetles and the wilt disease that they spread.

· **Thin the clusters** when the seedlings have developed two or three leaves; pull up all but the two healthiest seedlings in each cluster.

· **Mulch** a week or so after thinning.

· **Water regularly.** Cucumbers are 95 percent water, and plants that are thirsty stop growing and produce bitter, deformed fruits.

Soak the soil around the plants a couple of times a week in hot, dry weather.

• **Give the bees a hand** during periods of rainy weather. Most cucumbers bear both female and male flowers, and the females must be pollinated for fruits to form. Bees normally do this job, but may stay in the hive when the weather is wet. That's when you step in: you pluck a male flower (look at the base—the males have no waist), and pull off the petals. Then you stick the exposed sexual parts into a female flower (their bases have waists) and wiggle it around.

• **Pick your cucumbers** before they turn yellow or orange. Even if the vines are sprouting cucumbers faster than you can eat them, keep picking. Leaving the fruits to ripen on the vine will stop the plant from bearing any more.

Cucumber Favorites

'**China Long**' (aka 'China Long Green', 'Chinese Long Jumbo', 'Lungo di Cina'). If size impresses you, you'll be overwhelmed by these cucumbers, which reach a length of up to 36 inches. Slower to mature (sixty-five to seventy-five days from sowing to harvest), this strain is disease resistant and bears over a long season. If you want your cucumbers to be long *and* straight, grow 'China Long' on a trellis so that the fruits can dangle.

'**Lemon**' (aka 'True Lemon', 'White Lemon', 'Lemon Apple', 'Crystal Apple'). A Victorian variety that makes small, round fruits which ripen to a light yellow. Disease and drought resistant, and fast growing—this cucumber matures in sixty days.

'**Mincu**' (aka 'Baby Mincu', 'Mincu Extra Early'). A compact type that may be grown in containers or beds and which bears as soon as forty-eight days after the seed is sown. Plant these closer: set the clusters just 3 feet apart.

'**Vert de Massy Cornichon**'. Marty loves the tiny sour pickles made from these baby cucumbers; Tom thinks they look like something that will turn into a butterfly. This variety reaches harvest in under two months, which makes it a good bet for Northern or high-elevation gardens.

'**White Wonder**'. A quick-bearing sort (thirty-five to sixty days) that remains productive even in very hot weather. The fruits are ivory white and up to 9 inches long.

Luffa

Tom loves okra and Marty thinks it is a particularly insidious plot. This plant, which is often called Chinese okra, is a mutually acceptable compromise. Tom grows it as a vegetable; Marty uses it to scrub his back.

Actually a kind of gourd, luffa (*Luffa acutangula*, to be precise) is a heat-loving annual vine. In the North you should start the seeds indoors, sowing them in pots of moist soil about a month before you transplant them into the garden. That should be done only when the weather has become reliably warm—mid-June is good in New England. If the spring crop isn't quite finished, just pull enough of it to make space for the luffa's planting hole. As the vine recovers from transplanting and starts growing, you can gradually make more room by harvesting the rest of the surrounding cool-weather crop. In the South, you can sow the luffa seeds right into the ground as the spring crops start to fade.

You can train luffas up a trellis or arbor, or just let them sprawl. By mid to late summer, the vines will start bearing their gourds, which really do look like giant okra pods. Picked when 4 to 6 inches long, these gourds have a delicately sweet flavor. Slice off the longitudinal ridges with a potato peeler, and you can slice and simmer the gourds and serve them buttered and dressed with a little lemon juice. Or you can dice them and toss them into a stir-fry.

Marty prefers to leave the gourds on the vines until they dry. Then he picks them and sets them to soak in a bucket of hot water. He changes the water daily until the skin and pulp of the gourds fall away to expose the fibrous luffa "sponges" within. Marty feels that this treatment does little to change the culinary quality of the luffas, but it does make them very invigorating scrubbers. He always wonders, too, as he scrubs, what Tom eats for a second course: the bath mat or, perhaps, the soap?

Luffa Basics

• **Spread two inches of composted manure** over the bed and dig it in before sowing luffa seeds or transplanting luffa seedlings. If the soil is acidic, add a sprinkling of ground limestone.

• **In the North sow seeds indoors,** planting them 1 inch deep in 4-inch peat pots filled with ordinary potting soil. Water well, and place under a light to keep warm until germination. Wait until night temperatures remain at 50°F or above before moving plants out into the garden.

• **In the South sow the seed right into the bed,** clustering three to four seeds together as for cucumbers (see page 201).

• **Fertilize monthly** by scattering a thin layer of composted manure over the ground around the base of each vine.

• **Water twice a week** in dry weather.

Eggplant

We've already discussed eggplants in Chapter 5 (see page 111), so we won't discuss their cultivation in detail again here. Enlisting eggplants as understudies is a bit tricky in cool, Northern areas with short summers. This is not a fast-growing plant and it doesn't thrive in cold or even cool weather, so that a midsummer planting of eggplants in those regions is unlikely to bear fruit before the first fall frost cuts the plants down.

In the South, however, where summers are longer and fall provides some of the best growing weather of the year—warm but not hot, with occasional rains—eggplants are an ideal understudy. Plant them anytime from May through July, and enjoy your eggplant caponata (see page 112 for recipe) for months.

Corn

In the North, summer plantings of corn don't work. Tom has tried, and what you get is stalks but no ears. In the South, though, a July planting of corn, if kept well watered, will produce a good fall harvest.

Marty insists that growing your own sweet corn is a waste of garden space. He set aside a whole 4′ × 8′ bed for this crop one spring, and found out only later that Tom (who had chosen the seed) had ordered a variety called 'Double Standard' (ha, ha). Tom got a great deal of satisfaction from pointing out to all and sundry that Marty was openly cultivating a Double Standard; Marty got tired of this. He was also disappointed by the yield, which totaled enough ears for just a couple of dinners. It was depressing, watching his teenage son wolf down in a few minutes a quarter of his whole corn harvest.

Still, homegrown corn can provide an experience that can be had no other way. Corn was the crop on which this country's agriculture was built, and yet the old-fashioned types are unobtainable today—at least, they are unobtainable as ready-to-eat fresh ears and kernels. All you find at the market or farmstand now are the supersweet types. These have been bred for shelf life. Old-fashioned corns started losing their sweetness as soon as they were picked. For the best flavor, you had to have water boiling on the stove before you went to the field. The new, supersweet corns start out with two to four times more sugar than the older corns, and their sweetness doesn't fade as quickly. The problem is, at least in Tom's opinion, that all that sugar overwhelms their flavor. All you can taste in the supersweet corns is the sweet.

So why don't you try planting some of the great vintage corns of yesteryear? How about 'Country Gentleman', an 1891, white-kerneled sweet corn? Or try a *really* old corn like 'Black Mexican', which Europeans borrowed from the Indians as early as 1493? If Marty would only reconsider, he could have even Martha Stewart angling for a dinner invitation.

Corn Basics

• **For a fall harvest in the South,** plant four months before the average date of the first fall frost.

• **In the North,** plant after the predicted date of the last spring frost, and when the soil has warmed up to about 60°F. Traditional wisdom is that this occurs when the oak leaves are the size of a squirrel's ears. For what that's worth.

• **Plant in a sunny, wind-protected spot.** Corn is tall and so easy to blow over.

• **Enrich the soil** with composted manure—a bucketful per square yard or bed is good.

• **Plant seeds** 1 inch deep in spring, 4 inches deep in summer. Plant three seeds together in each spot, as the germination rate for corn seeds is poor. Space these plantings 15 inches apart.

• **Thin the seedlings** when they reach a height of 6 inches. Leave just one plant per planting spot; remove any extras by snipping them off at ground level.

• **Fertilize** when the corn has reached a height of a foot, and again when the tassels of corn silk appear. Scatter manure over the surface of the ground between the plants, or feed with leftover lawn fertilizer at the rate the label recommends for turf—corn, after all, is a grass. Make sure, however, to use a product that contains no herbicides or pesticides; you don't want to apply "weed 'n' feed" to your vegetable bed.

• **Water regularly.** Corn is a thirsty crop and it needs a deep watering twice a week in hot, dry weather.

• **To tell when the corn is ready** for picking, pull back the shucks along the side of one ear and puncture a couple of kernels with your fingernail. If the juice runs out clear, the corn isn't ready yet. If it runs out milky, it's time to pick.

Corn Favorites

'**Black Mexican**' (aka 'Black Aztec', 'Mexican Sweet', 'Black Sweet', 'Black Iroquois'). Kernels are white when ready for boiling or roasting fresh, blue-black when mature and dried for grinding into meal. A centuries-old variety that tolerates all kinds of weather.

'**Country Gentleman**' (aka 'Shoe Peg'). White kerneled ears, heavy-bearing variety. Introduced in 1891, a favorite for generations.

'**Golden Jubilee**'. A 1950s-vintage, yellow-kerneled variety that grows best in Northern and cool coastal areas. Superb flavor, corn that will convince you that your parents really did know better.

'**Mandan Red Sweet**' (aka 'Red Nuetta Sweet'). Another corn unchanged since Indian days. The long and narrow, red-kerneled cobs are living relics that can take you back centuries. A good choice for Midwestern and Plains states gardeners.

'**Texas Honey June**'. Despite the regional name, this heirloom type grows well in the North as well as the South. White kerneled, 6 inch ears; the extra-tight husks deter hungry insects.

Lettuce

Wait a minute, you say. The collapse of my lettuce is what left a big empty space in my vegetable garden and made it necessary for me to go out looking for understudies. Didn't you guys say that lettuce is a spring crop that can't stand the summer heat? So why are you recommending lettuce now as an understudy?

Well, in the words of Yogi Berra, we didn't say all those things that we said. Yes, lettuce hates summer heat. It's more than just spring crop, though. It grows beautifully in the fall, too, from late-summer planting. That's the time of year when your second string vegetables—like beans—start to look peaked. So consider lettuce as an understudy for your understudies.

For basic information on growing lettuce, we're referring you back to Chapter 4 (see page 81). We just want to add a warning, and one more clever trick.

First the warning: when we say a late-summer planting, we mean *late* summer. Lettuce is sensitive to day length. Actually, what it reacts to is the length of the night, but scientists mixed up the terminology on this years ago and who are we to correct them? The point is, though, that long days (or really, short nights) encourage lettuce plants to bolt, to send up a flower stalk. When they do that, the leaves become bitter and inedible. What this means is that you shouldn't plant your fall crop of lettuce until after Labor Day.

Now, let's move on to the clever trick. There is another problem with late-summer plantings of lettuce, which is that lettuce seeds won't germinate when the soil temperature is above 80°F. The intense sun of summer practically guarantees this temperature throughout most of the United States, even Northern regions, through late summer. However, overcoming this difficulty is easy enough. After planting your lettuce seeds, water the bed well, and then cover it with a sheet of plywood. Then for good measure, wet down the plywood as well. This will keep the soil below cool enough to germinate the lettuce seeds. Keep checking underneath the wood: you have to uncover the lettuce seedlings as soon as they begin to emerge from the soil.

2🕐-MINUTE PROJECT:
Marty's Water Wisdom

Tom, who despises iceberg lettuce, is in the habit of calling it "textured water." As Marty always points out, though, that is an apt description of virtually every vegetable you can grow. Cucumbers, as he noted a few pages back, are more than 95 percent water by weight. Recognition of this fact has had important implications for the 20-minute gardeners. It has robbed Tom of a favorite insult. It has also changed the way Marty waters.

Previously, Marty had treated garden irrigation as the adult equivalent of running through the sprinkler. Whenever he felt hot and dry, he'd put on his Bermudas, wave the hose about, and as he put it, "wet down a whole postal code."

This was fun, but Marty paid a price. The moisture level in his garden beds fluctuated wildly, from soaking wet to near desert, and this had a very direct effect on the produce. The tomatoes, fruits, and cabbage heads would dehydrate during the dry periods, then suddenly swell and split with the arrival of the artificial monsoons. The cucumbers tasted less sweet, the potato tubers stayed small and stingy, and the beans aborted half their flowers—the plants were unwilling to exert themselves in such unpredictable conditions.

Marty could live with this, but he couldn't live with the weeds that his broadcast watering provoked. The basic survival strategy of weeds is one of opportunism: each plant produces seeds by the thousands, or even hundreds of thousands, and spreads them all over the adjacent area, counting on the fact that at least one will find the basics for growth and so the line will continue. The most basic need for weeds is water. They can't grow without it. Keep a weed seed dry, and it may not die—it can lie dormant for decades—but it won't sprout, either. Marty's indiscriminate irrigation was not only supplying water to his vegetable plants, it was also wetting down huge numbers of nearby weed seeds and so it kept him busy hoeing, pulling, and cursing.

After calling friends, hanging out at the local Cooperative Extension office, and thumbing through ancient Chinese agricultural manuals, he came up with three superior watering methods. These ranged from high-tech to no-tech (guess which one Marty prefers?) but they all shared two characteristics. First, they all targeted their water, delivering it directly to the soil around the vegetable plant roots. This meant that the weed seeds remained dormant. The second common characteristic of Marty's new watering systems was that, if used properly, they all resulted in a more or less even level of moisture in the soil: not dry, but not soaking wet. This dramatically improved the quality of the harvest. Marty's first innovation was to invest in a device called a bubbler. This is a round, fist-sized nozzle that screwed on to the end of Marty's hose. By mixing air with the water, this reduced the flow to a gentle flood. Marty was able to moderate the flow even more by tightening the handle of his outdoor faucet so that what emerged from his bubbler was little more than an ooze.

Watering with the bubbler was simple. He'd set the nozzle down in the middle of some area of garden bed and let it slowly flood the surrounding area. Marty would test the depth to which the water had penetrated by pushing a bit of iron rod into the soil. The rod passed easily through the moistened soil but stopped when it reached a drier level. When the rod slipped to a depth of 8 inches, he knew it was time to move the bubbler. In this fashion, he could irrigate both his raised beds with an hour or two of very intermittent attention.

Marty's next purchase was a giant step up the technological ladder. He ordered a drip irrigation kit from a company in California. This arrived as a box full of snap-together plastic tubes and tiny nozzles, and there was an instruction manual, something that Marty will not read. He passed this kit along to Tom, who passed it along to his son, Matthew, and we'll deal with their experience in a minute.

Meanwhile, Marty was deep into the pages of the *Fan Sheng-shih Shu*. This is a 2,100-year-old Chinese agricultural manual, and it described a method for irrigating your garden with unglazed clay pots. Because there were no moving parts, this sounded great to Marty.

Here's how it works: you buy a bunch of 8-inch Italian terra-cotta pots and plug the drainage holes in the bottom with silicone caulking. The Chinese, of course, made their own pitchers, but they were better potters than Marty. Then, after plugging the pot bottoms, you bury them in your garden bed almost up to their lips; you leave just a half inch or so of each pot's top sticking up above the soil surface so that dirt doesn't wash in and fill it.

How you arrange the pots within the bed depends on what you intend to plant there. Where you'll be planting vining crops such as cucumbers or melons, you set the pots 4 feet apart, so that you can plant each cluster of seeds or seedlings right around a pot. In a tomato or eggplant bed, you arrange the pots so that there is a pot beside each seedling that you set out. For crops such as salad greens that you broadcast all over the bed, you set in pots at regular 3-foot intervals throughout.

To irrigate, you simply fill the pots with water and let it

seep out as it will. The sweetest part of this system is that the rate at which the water moves out of the pot and into the soil will be determined by the needs of the plants. On a hot day, when the plant roots are pumping a lot of water out of the soil, water will be drawn more quickly out of the pot. On a cloudy day, the rate of seepage will be less, and on a rainy day, movement out of the pot may stop altogether.

Marty has refined the ancient Chinese method in one respect. He covers each pot with a disposable aluminum pie plate so that it doesn't become a breeding ground for mosquitoes. A couple of rocks in the pie plate keep it from blowing away. A quick check every few days of the water level in the pots tells him if his garden needs watering. Because he puts all the water right into the pots, the weeds get nothing.

2⏰-MINUTE PROJECT:
Tom and Matthew Do the Drip

When Marty offered a brand-new, virtually untouched drip irrigation system to Tom, how could he say no? Tom, after all, is the man who cannot pass up fresh road kill without regret. (*That coon's skin really would make a great hat, and there's a perfectly good drumstick on the unsquashed side of that chicken. . . .*) So Tom accepted Marty's offer with alacrity.

In part he did this because he recognized the snap-together drip system as a distant relative of the Lego, and Tom has a Lego expert on staff. He called in his son, Matthew, as a consultant. Together they read the manual (Matthew does pretty well with technical jargon, for an eight-year-old) and got the thing together and installed. It actually worked. By delivering water drop by drop right to the soil in the vegetable bed, the drip irrigation system practically eliminated weeding. The kit had come with an electronic timer, and by experimenting with this, Tom learned just how long the drip system had to run to moisten his garden soil thoroughly, but not to the point that water pooled on the surface and ran away. In fact, by spreading mulch over the network of drip tubes and emitters, Tom was able to ensure that the garden surface and the above-ground parts of the plants stayed dry even while the watering went on, which seemed to discourage the spread of insects and diseases.

After much experimentation with this kit, and eventually with others, Tom developed a few simple criteria for what makes an effective drip irrigation system. (We've included names and numbers of companies that Tom likes in "Sources for Plants and Seeds" at the end of this book.)

1. Before ordering any drip equipment, call the company and see if they supply technical assistance as well as parts. Most off-the-shelf systems have to be modified somewhat to suit your climate, your soil, and the plants you intend to grow. This needn't be difficult. However, what you'll soon discover is that drip irrigation systems are a bit like computers: theoretically, you can learn how to make them work just by reading the manual. In fact, though, you'll save yourself hours of frustration if you discuss your situation briefly with an expert.

2. Buy only systems with self-cleaning emitters. The emitters are the tiny nozzles that spit water out onto the soil. Any grit or debris that comes down the supply line from the faucet can clog the emitters' tiny apertures. Then what you have is an irrigation system that is no longer irrigating part of your garden. Self-cleaning emitters clear their throats each time you turn them on, blowing out anything that is clogging the apertures. Ordinary emitters must be cleaned manually. This is easy to do, but you may not realize an emitter isn't emitting until a section of your garden has missed a couple of waterings and the plants are withering.

Netafim, an Israeli-designed line of drip irrigation products, offers self-cleaning emitters that are outstandingly reliable, and which are the choice of most professional irrigation experts.

3. Install a filter between the drip irrigation system and your faucet. This will make the self-cleaning emitters' job easier.

4. Install an antisiphon valve between the drip system and the faucet. Otherwise, if for any reason your water pressure should suddenly drop, contaminated water may siphon back from the drip system into your household pipes.

5. Don't rely on an electronic timer to make watering decisions for you. Once you program the timer, it will water at the set interval no matter what the weather is doing. Let the timer supervise the watering, and it will irrigate in the middle of rainstorms. Nor will it recognize the need for an extra watering in the middle of a particularly hot, dry day.

Timers are useful, but you should set them to a manual mode. This means that you tell the timer how long to leave the drip system running, but that you must turn it on each time. The decision to water each time should be based on your daily inspection of the garden. If the soil is getting dry, you decide to irrigate and you set the system to work right away. You don't make the plants wait until the timer is ready.

Chapter 10

The 20-Minute Ultimate

"Imagine," Marty proposed, "that I asked you to design the ultimate edible plant." He leaned back into the shade of a banana tree, and took a pull on his iced tea. "What would it be? And no, it can't be plastic, and yes, it has to be nonalcoholic."

Tom tipped the spout of the watering can into Marty's whitewalled potato planter, and considered. "It would have to be a plant that didn't need watering, that's for sure. Why you won't install a drip irrigation system beats me—this hand watering sure is a pain in the neck. Speaking of which . . ." He reached up to swat the mosquito drilling just above his collar. "It would have to be insectproof, too. At least, if you were going to grow it in this pestilential swamp."

"I think they breed in Martha's lotus pond. But the ultimate plant—it would have to taste good, too, the best, and it would have to be good for you, right?"

"Sure, and it would have to like neglect and abuse if it were going to coexist with *you*."

Marty leaned forward. "I've got it, Tom," he whispered.

"You've got what?"

Marty looked around to make sure that none of the neighbors was watching. Then, getting up, he motioned Tom to follow. Leading him to a sunny spot tucked behind the garage, Marty squatted beside a gnarled little gray-green bush.

"Nice rosemary," Tom remarked.

"What? Well, I didn't know this thing is female, but it figures. Anyway, it's amazing. Just a pinch of its needles and you've got veggie burgers to die for. I don't miss the fats and salt at all."

"It's supposed to stimulate the digestion, too, cure headaches, and strengthen your heart."

"I really think I do feel better. But you know what? The woodchuck doesn't like it. Even the deer leave it alone. No bugs, and it doesn't seem to care whether I water it or not."

"I'll bet you haven't fertilized it."

The familiar look of guilt crept over Marty's face. "I forgot, okay? I'm going to do it. Really. Just as soon as Judy gets more of that stuff that turns the water blue."

"You're better off leaving that plant alone. The flavor is stronger if you don't feed it."

"How do you know that?"

"Because I've grown herbs before, Marty. I hate to admit it, but you are right. It's never occurred to me before, but herbs are the ultimate 20-minute edibles. You're too late to file for a patent, but you have made a discovery. Did you know that rosemary is a traditional flavoring for ale?"

Why are culinary herbs so easy to grow? Essentially, they are weeds. They are the pungent plants that our ancestors found growing wild near the campfires over which they were roasting haunches of cholesterol-rich red meat. The herbs grew in the clearings around the cave mouths and huts because they were tough. Most of the traditional favorites thrive on nutrient-poor, dry, even rocky soils. As Marty had learned, herbs tend to be remarkably drought tolerant, and except in truly arid climates, they get by with little or no watering beyond that provided by natural rainfall.

The herbs were also abundant around the primitive dooryards because of the aromatic oils that give them their fragrances and flavors. In the minute doses we use in cooking, these oils are tasty; actually, most have healthful properties if taken in tiny quantities. However, if we, like insects and grazing animals, ate herbs as a main dish rather than the zest, we would find them to be mildly toxic. The evolutionary function of the flavoring is to ward off diners. In fact, in the days before aerosol cans, many herbs were used as insect repellents.

Marty wants to make it clear that, as far as he is concerned, red meat is as passé as mammoth hunting. He agrees, though, that herbs are more necessary than ever. As a substitute for all those bad things that you would otherwise use to add relish to your food, herbs promote the prolonged life span that modern folk feel is their right. But herbs will not only help you to live longer, they'll let you spend more of your extra time doing what you want.

That's because you don't need many herb plants to transform your diet. You may be too busy to grow enough tomatoes, lettuce, potatoes, and okra to have a significant impact on your diet. The pinchings of a mere half dozen herb plants, though, can radically improve every meal you eat. And if you think you can extract the same benefits from the herbs you buy dried in little cans at the store, well, all we can say is that you haven't tried the real thing.

The 20-Minute Ultimate

Herb Basics

• **A sunny site.** Some herbs will grow in shade or partial shade, but most prefer full sun. If your yard doesn't offer a patch of sunny soil, consider growing your herbs in pots on a sunny deck or terrace, or in a second-story window box that sits above the tree canopy.

• **In the Southwest** and at high altitudes in the Rocky Mountain states, the extra intensity of the sunlight may burn the herbs. Something that will block the afternoon sunlight—the most intense sunlight of the day—such as a tree, fence, or wall to the west of the herb garden, provides useful protection.

• **Loose, well-drained soil.** Some herbs will tolerate a dense, damp soil, but most rot and die if their feet are continually wet. The easiest insurance against this kind of problem is boosting the organic content of the soil. Spread a couple of inches of composted leaves or bark over the soil surface, and a couple of inches of coarse, mason's sand (available at any builder's supply center) and dig these in with a spade or fork.

• **In the South,** high soil temperatures speed the decay of organic matter, making compost a very temporary solution to dense, poorly drained soil. In that region, combine the compost treatment with a heavy dose of coarse sand—the type sold as "sharp" sand at a masonry supply. Layer on the compost, then layer on a couple inches of sand, and dig in both.

• **Don't overfertilize.** Nutrient-rich soils foster lush growth with little flavor. A moderate dose of some slow-release organic fertilizer in early spring should be all the feeding your herbs will need.

• **Buy plants, not seeds.** As a rule, herb seeds are slow to germinate and slow to develop into plants of any size. Even Mr. Do-It-Yourselfer Tom buys his herbs as little potted transplants.

• **Mulch.** A layer of some organic mulch such as shredded bark or leaves will promote herb growth by keeping the soil cooler and slightly moist. As it rots down, such a mulch also provides the kind of slow, sparing feed that herbs prefer. In the Southeast, where summer humidity make herbs prone to disease, mulch also helps by preventing the evaporation of water up and out of the soil; the surface of the mulch stays dry, creating a better environment for the herbs. In North or South, replenish the mulch annually.

• **Water** (as necessary). Okay, so we said that herbs are drought tolerant and survive with little irrigation in all but arid climates. That's true, but there are exceptions. Basil and mint, for example, need weekly irrigation during periods of dry weather.

The point to keep in mind is that plants sweat, just like you do, only plants sweat through their leaves. In general, the herbs with small leaves sweat less and so are more drought tolerant. Fuzzy-leaved or gray-leaved plants are especially drought tolerant. Fuzz shades the leaves, acting as sunblock, while light-gray leaves reflect much of the sun that hits them, rather than absorbing it. Rosemary, thyme, and oregano are all examples of herbs that don't sweat much.

Herbs with more expansive leaves, such as basil and mint, sweat a lot more, and so need more watering. Incidentally, they are also the most shade tolerant. Even the drought-tolerant herbs need some watering during prolonged periods of hot, dry weather. Marty gave his rosemary a couple of drinks when it didn't rain for three weeks last August.

• **Relax.** Don't try to hurry the growth of your herbs or you will end up with large, lush plants with little flavor or fragrance. How much seasoning can you use, anyway?

Herbs in the Humid South

Because so many of the traditional culinary herbs come from the Mediterranean region, these plants tend to have difficulty coping with the combination of heat and humidity found in the South-eastern states. Some flourish. Basil, for example, loved the 105°F temperatures and 100 percent humidity it found in Tom's central-Texas backyard. But the herbs that have adapted to withstand dry conditions, rosemary and lavender, for example, were soon terminated by mildew when not given a bit of special help.

First of all, how can Southerners tell which herbs are going to prove vulnerable? Beware of those with narrow, needlelike leaves, since that (as we mentioned above) is a characteristic they adopted to conserve water. Foliage of that sort is a clue that the herb in question came from a dry climate. Similarly, fuzzy, light-colored leaves are another trouble signal: these are also water-conservation devices that characterize plants from arid climates.

To grow humidity-sensitive perennial herbs, such as rosemary, sage, and thyme, plant them in a raised bed in soil that you have laced heavily with "sharp" sand. By improving soil drainage, these two measures help to reduce the humidity right around the plants. Water with a drip irrigation system or a bubbler. A sprinkler fills the air with water and wets the herbs' foliage, and both of these things promote mildews. Finally, spread a mulch of sand around the plants. This will keep the moisture in the soil from evaporating up into the air during hot weather; at the same time, because the surface of the sand remains dry, it will keep the air around the plant drier and assist in the battle against mildew.

Some of the annual herbs, such as dill and coriander, don't like hot, humid weather, either. In the Southeast, these are best planted in fall for a winter and early-spring harvest.

The Essentials

After a certain amount of polite debate (three days of insults and counterinsults, actually) Tom and Marty settled on the cast of characters they believe should be included in any herb garden. You are welcome to add anything you want to this list, but we believe that unless you are an obsessive chef, or a fan of some special cuisine with exotic ingredients, you'll do fine with no more than the following ten:

1. Basil. This is an annual, which means you must plant it anew every year. There are bunches of different basils, and each has its strength. Given his prejudices, it's not surprising that Tom prefers the Italian basils for culinary use. After extensive testing (he wore out three of his friends' grandmothers), he has come down in favor of the basils from Genoa, such as 'Genovese' or 'Genova Profumatissimo'.

As the inventors of pesto sauce, the *Genovesi* favor an intense, highly perfumed basil. However, the Neapolitan types, such as 'Napoletano', aren't bad either. They have larger leaves with a sweeter flavor, and are wonderful when chopped and sprinkled over fresh tomato slices, or slices of the real buffalo mozzarella.

Marty lusts after novelty. He skips from one basil to another: 'Lemon Basil', 'Cinnamon Basil', 'Licorice Basil', and 'Lime Basil'. He can't wait for the breeders to come out with a 'Lemon-Lime'. For serious cooking, he relies on 'Siam Queen True Thai'.

There are also lots of basils that are primarily ornamental. The stems of 'African Blue' are really a blend of purple and green, but in any event, this basil makes a show in a window box or pot, and is the spice of the flower garden when tucked in among the blossoms. Tom once planted a whole lawn of 'Spicy Globe' basil, a compact, tiny-leaved hybrid, when he lived in central Texas. The result was a tufted, nose-tweaking carpet that became a minor tourist attraction.

20-minute tip: Basil loves hot weather, but requires regular watering during summertime droughts. For the lushest growth of the ornamental types, drench them with a half-strength solution of water-soluble fertilizer every second week. This will spoil the flavor, but that's the price of beauty.

2. Chives. This is a perennial. In general, Marty hates perennials. That's because the plants which come to him under that label almost always behave just like annuals, except that they also make him feel inadequate. He wanders around every spring looking for signs that any of the perennials he planted the previous year have returned, and usually finds very little. What are they, too good to grow in his yard? Who do they think they are, those perennials? But then he finds the chives—green, fresh, and unkillable—and he feels better.

Actually, Marty's chives not only survive from year to year, they flourish. His original clump has multiplied, and now its offspring are multiplying. Each clump gradually expands, so that every few years he has to dig it up with the bread knife (he could use a spade for this if he remembered where he put it). He soaks the roots in a bucket of water and then pulls the big clump apart into several smaller ones. Marty replants a couple of these to maintain the breeding stock, then gives the rest away to apparently grateful underlings at the office.

Tom cannot be content with any pleasure so simple. He has been experimenting with garlic chives. Of Chinese origin, these have, as the name suggests, a stronger, more garlicky flavor. He likes 'Large Broad Leaf', which makes tufts of ribbonlike gray-green leaves, and 'Chinese Leek Flower', whose flower buds have a particularly delicious flavor.

20-minute tip: Chives flourish in sun or shade, and are the easiest of potted plants.

3. **Dill.** This herb actually produces two kinds of flavorings. The feathery leaves can be snipped and chopped to add a light, fresh accent to potato and cucumber salads and fish dishes. Your plants will soon recover from a shearing and if allowed to mature and flower, they will bear seeds that can be used fresh to give a stronger flavor to pickles, or dried and substituted for caraway seeds in cakes and breads.

To harvest seeds, cut the umbrellalike flower heads when the seedpods have begun to appear among the blossoms. Hang these by their stems, upside down, over a clean cloth and collect the seeds as they drop.

20-minute tip: Every time we make a rule, some plant invents an exception. We recommended that you start your herb garden with the plants you find at the nursery, but dill is one of a select group that won't cooperate. Its roots are sensitive, and they don't take well to transplanting. So start your dill by sowing seeds right where you want the plants to grow. Plant the seeds in early spring or early fall, barely covering them with soil. Keep them moist, and they will germinate in ten to twenty days.

Dill is an annual, but it is one that replants itself. If seedpods are left on the plants to scatter their contents, troops of volunteers will spring up the next spring. Depending on your appetite for dill, this can be a blessing or a curse.

'Dukat' is a variety from Finland with an especially sweet, mellow flavor.

4. Garlic. Neither Tom nor Marty can imagine life without garlic. For Marty it is the frontline defense against hypertension, blood clots that might cause strokes, the common cold, cancer, snakebite—all those things that fill his nightmares. For Tom, garlic is the basis of his beloved Italian and Sicilian cuisines, and provides essential protection against cholesterol. At least, so indicate studies published in journals such as *Lancet* and *American Journal of Clinical Nutrition*. As Marty points out, if you eat the way Tom does, you better hope that garlic works.

Of course, you pay a price for garlic's benefits. There is that garlic odor, which in our culture is regarded as a liability. It is persistent and a mere breath mint is no remedy, since the odor-creating compounds are actually absorbed into the bloodstream and exuded through perspiration over a period of days. One S. B. Snell claimed in a letter to *Lancet* that this odor can penetrate even the placental barrier. Snell was not clear as to whether he was narrating from personal experience, but it is difficult to imagine that his letter could come from anything else. At any rate, he wrote of an anonymous obstetrician who claimed that he could detect garlic on the breath of a confirmed garlic eater's newborn. That's okay with us, but apparently it bothered Snell, and it's worth noting that one Spanish king, Alfonso XI of Castile and León, so hated his subjects'

Bruschetta

One way that garlic has made Tom's diet more healthful is by providing a cholesterol-free alternative to his customary break-fast of buttered toast. This alternative toast is called bruschetta. Its inventors, the Italians, eat it at the time of the olive harvest, when the newly pressed oil is freshest and sweetest. Do they eat it for breakfast? Marty says no, claiming that there is a Geneva convention prohibiting morning-time bruschetta consumption by anyone employed outside the home. Luckily, Tom does work at home. Because, if forced to choose between a job and bru-schetta, Tom knows what his decision would be.

To make bruschetta, cut thick slices from a good crusty Italian or French bread. Toast until golden brown on both sides. Peel and cut in half several cloves of garlic, then rub them on both sides of each slice of toast. Meanwhile, warm a cruet of good vir-gin olive oil (first cold pressed) and drizzle this over the anointed toast. Sprinkle with chopped basil if you are feeling extravagant.

garlicky breath that he founded a special order of chivalry whose knights were forbidden to eat the offending bulb.

We aren't going to detail here how to grow garlic, because Marty intends to describe his own unique experiences at chapter's end. However, we do want to strike a blow for diversity. There has been a tendency, especially here in New England, to treat all garlics as part of the same foreign vulgarity. In other words, garlic is gar-lic and need you know more?

Yes, you do. For in fact, there are considerable differences among the 110 types of garlic currently available from North American seed companies. 'Italian Red', for example, has a partic-ularly pungent but especially savory flavor. 'Elephant Garlic' makes huge, baseball-sized bulbs, each of whose cloves may equal in size a whole head of some other strain. The flavor is "mild," according to the catalogs. We call it weak. But if you are just breaking into garlic appreciation, 'Elephant' makes an excellent starter garlic. In contrast, 'German Red Rocambole' is held by many to have the most intense, full-bodied flavor.

One last tip: if you like to festoon your kitchen with braids of garlic, grow a "soft-necked" strain such as 'Gilroy'. Soft-necked garlics don't produce any flower stem during the first year after planting. Harvest comes during the first summer after planting, and at that time, the soft-necks' aboveground growth is still just leaves, which braid easily once they have withered and dried. The "hard-necked" garlics, in contrast, do send up flower stalks during their first spring after planting, and those stiff, brittle stalks do not lend themselves to braid making.

5. Oregano. Marty maintains that the evil people who invented gardening purposely designed it to promote confusion, so that you would have to hire them to do it for you. He may be right. The so-called common oregano (*Origanum vulgare*) would seem to be a likely source of the stuff you find dried and packaged under that name in the supermarket, and called for in recipes. But, no; common oregano has very little flavor and is useless as a culinary herb. If you want oregano flavor, what you have to grow is a different species of plant, *Origanum onites,* the Italian oregano. Unless you want an even stronger oregano flavor, in which case you grow a third species, *Origanum heracleoticum,* Greek oregano. Or Spanish oregano, *Origanum virens.*

This all seems perfectly clear to Tom. Marty, however, insists on tasting the leaves of any oregano plant before he will buy it. This draws stares at the garden center, but it saves him from having to learn all that Latin.

20-minute tip: Where soils tend to be acidic (see page 42), dig a handful of lime into the soil where you plant oregano. It's a perennial, and if it survives from one year to the next, redose every spring, by sprinkling lime around the plant.

6. Parsley. Parsley leaves are an aid to digestion, according to Marty's research, which would make this herb worth growing, even if it weren't so useful. It's pretty in the garden, a rich green, and if left in place over winter so that it blooms (parsley takes its time with this, and doesn't finish the business until its second year), the flowers attract predatory insects who prey on the herbivorous insects that prey on your plants. In addition, parsley is a traditional garnish. A sprig of it laid out beside a chop really does seem to sharpen the appetite.

Does it taste good? Marty says yes, Tom says not really. Marty likes the fresh, "healthful" flavor of parsley. Tom says anything would enhance the flavor of Marty's tofus and health foods, even clippings from the lawn. To be fair, though, every chef we have ever consulted voted with Marty. They also agree, however, that a cook's arsenal should include two kinds of parsley: a visually plainer but more flavorful, flat-leaved sort such as 'Single-Leaf Italian' for seasoning, and a prettier, curly-leaved variety such as 'Forest Green' for decorating the plate.

20-minute tip: To help parsley plants through a Northern winter, so that they will survive to bloom the following summer, bury them with shredded leaves in fall. A blanket of straw works, too, but it will look messy unless you remove it the following spring. The brown-leaf confetti you can just pull aside as your plants are beginning to emerge from dormancy. Leave the leaves, is Tom's motto, to compost in place.

7. Rosemary. We've already touched on the virtues of rosemary. But did Marty mention that rosemary is, aside from chives, his only reliable perennial? This, Marty says, proves that Tom is wrong. He *is* capable of sustaining a long-term relationship.

Of course, it is Marty's wife, Judy, who is the caregiver in this case. She keeps the rosemary bush planted in a large clay pot. It spends the colder months in an unheated but frost-free sun porch. Every year in mid spring, Judy slips the plant out of its pot and with a pair of nail scissors, she prunes back the roots. Then she eases the plant back into its pot. A month or so later, after the danger of frost is past, she takes the plant outside and buries it to the top of its pot in a sunny patch of soil, so that the rosemary can enjoy the outdoor sunlight and air, and so that the soil around the roots stays cool and moist. When frost threatens in the fall, she pops the pot out of the ground and brings the rosemary back indoors.

If Marty and Judy lived south of the Mason-Dixon line, or better yet in the Southwest, they could grow their rosemary outdoors year-round. Particularly in the Southwest, rosemary is a gardening mainstay, and many distinctive varieties have been developed. There's a creeping rosemary, 'Prostratus', that looks fine spilling over a rock; 'Tuscan Blue', which bears tiny but clear blue flowers; and 'Majorca Pink', which has light-pink flowers. The bottom line, though, is that any rosemary looks good and tastes great.

20-minute tip: If rosemary doesn't quite make it through your winters outdoors, try the varieties 'Salem' or 'Arp'. Though not exactly hardy, they will stand more frost than other rosemaries.

8. **Tarragon.** This is an herb to handle with respect. The strong-flavored, bitter leaves add character to salads, omelettes, and fish dishes when just a few are applied. Mix in more than that, however, and all you'll taste is tarragon.

Actually, the most convenient way of seasoning with tarragon is to add the herb as a flavoring in olive oil or vinegar. To do this, first get a light, mild-flavored olive oil or a good-quality cider or wine vinegar (not balsamic). The vinegars are easy to flavor: you simply slip sprigs of tarragon into the bottle and leave them to steep for a couple of weeks.

Flavoring the oil takes a little more technique. Bruise a little bouquet of tarragon sprigs and put it in a glass jar. Fill the container with oil and cover it with a paper towel held in place with a rubber band. Set the jar on a sunny windowsill to warm and, once a day, stir its contents with a wooden spoon. After two weeks, strain out the herbs and store the oil in a corked or stoppered bottle.

20-minute tip: There are actually two kinds of tarragon: French tarragon (Artemisia dracunculus var. sativa*) and winter tarragon (*Tagetes lucida*), which is actually a kind of marigold (see why gardeners make Marty cranky?).*

French tarragon has the better flavor, but it's particular. Where summers are warm, it goes dormant ("aestivation" is what Tom calls this, to distinguish it from that wintertime sleep, hibernation). That means your French tarragons won't be producing new leaves then, and won't react well to pinching and shearing. In addition, though French tarragon is supposed to be perennial, it isn't in really cold climates or really warm ones.

All in all, you may throw up your hands and opt for the winter tarragon, which despite its name stands summer heat much better, and which is an annual. That means any outdoor planting is going to die every fall, so you don't have to worry about how it likes your winter. To take you through the cold months (life without tarragon?) you can grow it in a pot on a sunny windowsill.

9. Sage. Designer sages—"salvias," as the initiates call them—have flooded the more fashionable gardens in recent years. What good are these plants? Sure, they're nice to look at. But can you stuff a chicken with them? Go ahead and try. We'll stick to the good old garden-variety sage (though Tom takes comfort in calling it *Salvia officinalis*).

Marty favors this plant because the old-timers (a group which he is rapidly joining) believed that it could heal both an upset stomach and memory loss. It's also quite attractive. Garden sage makes a shrub up to 2 feet tall and 3 feet across, with pebbled green leaves and violet-blue flowers that appear in mid to late spring. Marty maintains that *this* would be the fashionable sage, if only its name were more difficult to pronounce.

Besides serving as an essential ingredient of poultry stuffings, sage has a clean bite to it that goes well with pork or veal, and it makes an outstanding flavoring for vinegars. Marty brews it up as a tea he claims relieves his abundant tension.

There are lots of "improved" varieties of garden sage—strains with purplish or golden-streaked leaves, dwarf strains, white and red-flowered types. None taste as good or perform as reliably as the good old garden variety, however.

20-minute tip: Sage is a hardy perennial that may persist in your garden (though not in Marty's) for many years. To keep a plant compact and covered with tasty young leaves, cut the stems back annually in early spring.

10. Thyme. How tough is this plant? Listen: it flourishes as a weed on the cold, stony hillsides of western Massachusetts, where Tom's wife, Suzanne, grew up. It grows where even grass won't thrive.

Take a tip from Nature, then, when you plant thyme. Tuck the plant into a crack at the edge of a stone patio or path or, better yet, plant it among the boulders in that hideous rock garden that your home's previous owner created along the slope running down to the driveway. Of course, if you want to *spoil* your thyme, you can turn it loose to creep around any sunny, well-drained parts of your herb garden.

There are lots of different varieties and species of thyme, but what you want is the common thyme: *Thymus vulgaris*. It's common because it flourishes without any help from you, which of course is what any sensible person (like Marty) wants. Actually, this is a good tip in general when shopping for herbs: given a choice, take those that are labeled as *communis* or *vulgaris*. In the garden, as in most other arenas, vulgar wins out.

Lamb and beef stews are traditional uses for thyme. Tom has found it goes particularly well with rabbit, a meat that is available very reasonably wherever there are gardens.*

20-minute tip: This is another herb that prefers a lime soil.

---

* One time when Tom was manning the plant information desk at a flower show, a lady asked him what he used for rabbits in his garden. "Onions, potatoes, a cup of red wine, and a few sprigs of thyme" was Tom's immediate response. "One treatment provides permanent relief."

Those are the ten essentials. Inevitably, Tom cannot be satisfied with just the necessary, and he insists on adding coriander and fennel. Both are relatives of dill and are grown the same way. Coriander, which Tom calls cilantro (and some other people call Chinese parsley), is a two-fer. The leaves are an essential ingredient of any self-respecting salsa (Suzanne chops them into salads), while the seeds are a basic spice for Indian cuisine.

Marty wonders why Tom wastes his time on these unnecessary refinements. He, however, would not be without a pot of peppermint. He wouldn't let this loose in his garden, however, because its roots spread so aggressively through sunny or shady areas that he would soon be the proprietor of a 20-minute julep farm. If confined in a pot, though, the mint poses no threat, and a sprig of its leaves is a necessary part of Marty's iced teas. The mint also proves essential when he or Judy is in the mood to make tabouli.

Marty also would not be without a plant of catnip. This is his gift to his "American shorthair," Max. Max finds this plant . . . stimulating. Marty has grown up a good deal since the year he spent in San Francisco (remember the Summer of Love?) and he is a firm believer in responsible behavior, for humans. But vicarious pleasures are harmless, and watching Max wallow around the catnip patch fills him with sweet nostalgia.

2⊕-MINUTE PROJECT:
Herb-Ball Remedy

A couple of years ago, Tom's wife, Suzanne, took her sabbatical at the Massachusetts Institute of Technology, and suddenly Tom found himself with the pied-à-terre in Cambridge that aspiring writers dream about. He spent his days sipping cappuccinos in Harvard Square, when he wasn't musing by the banks of the Charles River. At night he ate. Sometimes he went to the ethnic restaurants run by the hustling immigrants who, it turns out, own most of Cambridge. Or he cooked, making meals from the intriguing ingredients he found at the immigrants' groceries. The only problem was, Tom had a native-born American landlady.

She didn't seem to care what anybody ate as long as it was neat. Neatness she regarded as a virtue second only to equity. Plants, even herbs, were intrusions on her paved-over, stainless habitat. Any time Tom placed a pot of some great new acquisition into the little yard around the house, it suffered a fatal accident. The flat of tomato seedlings, for example, that Tom grew from seed and set out for a few hours to harden off—well, his landlady accidentally dropped a door on *them*. This behavior frustrated Tom because it meant he could not grow the herbs he needed to complement the intriguing exotic ingredients he was getting at the food co-ops. Until he invented the herb ball.

This he did one morning as he was sitting and sulking in his bright, sunny kitchen. He was sitting there because he feared that if he lounged on the porch, his landlady would tidy him away. Then he considered: the sanctuary that was safe for him was safe for plants, too. Of course, there wasn't any plantable soil in his kitchen, but that was easily fixed. Though he had better be careful, he reflected, or Suzanne might join the landlady's camp. So, Tom decided that what he needed was a compact, self-contained and, yes, *neat* herb garden.

What Tom created had all these virtues and one more: it was National Basketball Association regulation sized. Tom knew this because he made the garden by molding chicken wire around his son's basketball. He trimmed off the overlapping edges of the wire with shears. Once the shaping was completed, he slipped the ball out and twisted the wire ends together to seal the sphere, leaving a hand-sized opening. Then, working through the hole, he lined the wire sphere with "sheet moss." Sold at most craft stores and garden centers, sheet moss is a sort of ragged green carpeting made from dried sphagnum moss that flower arrangers use for something or other.

After lining the wire sphere, Tom filled it with some off-the-shelf potting soil. Actually, to reduce the weight of the herb ball, he used a "soil-less" potting mix in which sphagnum peat had been substituted for soil. Peat, even when wet, is considerably lighter than real soil. Once the herb ball was filled with soil, right up to the top, Tom sealed the hand hole, again by twisting wire ends at the edge around the network of the rest of the ball.

He planted his herb garden next. With a sharpened pencil, he poked five holes in through the wire and moss skin at even intervals around the sphere. By wiggling his finger in through these holes, he was able to excavate small cavities in the potting mix inside. Into these cavities he slipped the roots of five herb seedlings that he had bought: a chive, an oregano, a parsley, a thyme, and a creeping rosemary. To fit the root masses of the plants in through the holes in the wire mesh, Tom had to trim them, and he did this with a sharp knife.

Finally, Tom tied a trio of sturdy strings to the herb ball, and then hung it up by the sunny window over his kitchen sink. There he was able to water it with the diverter, and any drips fell harmlessly into the sink (this he explained to a very dubious landlady). Once a day he spun the ball halfway around so that all the herbs got full exposure to the sun. Because there are no plant nutrients in peat, Tom had to fertilize these herbs. He did this by soaking the ball with a half-strength solution of houseplant fertilizer every second week.

This indoor herb garden proved a great success. Because herbs are so drought tolerant, they actually seemed to like the arid atmosphere of the centrally heated apartment. Perhaps it reminded them of the Mediterranean hillsides from which they hail. In any event, the pinches they provided revitalized Tom's cooking, and this seasoning process never failed to impress dinner guests, though being Bostonian they were too polite to say so.

When the sabbatical came to an end, the herb ball moved back to Connecticut, where it spent the summer hanging from the arbor outside the kitchen door. Though its contribution wasn't essential there (at home, Tom can be as un-neat as he likes), still, it made for a good story. It is, as Tom is fond of pointing out, a real horticultural slam dunk, an herb garden that is even proof against flying doors.

2🕐-MINUTE PROJECT:
The Garlic of Benign Neglect

As far as Marty can tell, his family did not originate in Transylvania. They were Brooklynites as far back as anyone remembers (which is the winter of 1952). The only bloodsuckers Marty worried about while he was growing up were loan sharks, and Westport, his current home, is too well bred to allow those. So his decision to ring his garden with garlic had nothing to do with superstition.

Marty planted garlic because 1) he had time and because 2) garlic takes care of itself.

Marty had the time to plant garlic because its planting season doesn't coincide with much of anything besides tulips and daffodils. In the chillier parts of the North and in most of the South, garlic is planted in mid to late fall; only in climates with both mild winters and summers is it planted in spring (early spring). Marty happened to have some cloves to plant, because Tom had ordered a couple of heads of both 'New York White' and 'German Extra-Hardy'. Can you guess which type Marty chose to plant?

He broke up the heads of 'New York White' into individual cloves. On October 27th, he planted these all around the outside of his garden beds, setting the cloves out 4 inches apart and poking each 1 or 2 inches deep. Thereafter he did nothing. Tom, meanwhile, divided and planted his heads of 'German Extra-Hardy' in the same fashion. He watered his new planting assiduously, irrigating about twice a week until the ground froze. He also mulched his planting under a couple of inches of straw to keep the soil temperature evenly cold—alternate freezing and thawing can heave the buried cloves up out of the ground.

Come spring, the garlics' long, straight leaves pushed up out of the ground. Marty's 'New York' garlics, which were a soft-neck type, produced a luxuriant growth of leaves; Tom's 'German' garlics, a hard-neck type, sprouted leaves and then tall flower stems that topped themselves with pretty blue-purple, sunburst-shaped flowers. Tom removed most of the mulch with which he had covered his garlic, leaving just enough of a blanket to keep down the weeds. Marty continued to do nothing.

By late July, the bottom leaves of the garlic plants had yellowed. This is the signal that harvest time has arrived. Tom took his garden fork and loosened the soil around the garlic plants; then he carefully lifted the plants out whole. Marty grabbed handfuls of garlic leaves and yanked. Marty filled a basket with his fat, white heads; Tom's garlic heads were fine, but markedly smaller than Marty's.

This confirmed two points. First, that Tom should have pinched off the flower stalks on his hard-neck garlics as soon as they appeared, so that the plants would have devoted all their strength to fattening the bulbs, rather than to seed making. The second point that this confirmed is that there is no justice in this world. After gardening with Marty for several years, though, Tom already knew that.

Chapter 11

Our Own Private Enemies List

Weeds and wildlife: both have their points. Deer and rabbits and woodchucks and thistles can all be quite attractive. In their place. But that place should not include your vegetable garden. It's hard to appreciate the majesty of that eight-point buck, for example, if he happens to be devouring your lettuce. Likewise, those little blue thistle flowers are a lot less appealing if you know their purpose is to sow gazillions of thistle seeds all over your beds and keep you on your hands and knees most of the following summer.

So we are going to tell you how to banish these annoyances. Or at least, you will so confuse them that frustration will be the main thing they take away from a visit to your garden. What's more, we are going to tell you how to do this without chemical sprays. If you have read the ingredients on food packaging lately, you'll know that you are getting plenty of chemicals in your diet anyway. Tom and Marty don't believe in adding to the list on a do-it-yourself basis.

Weeds

Let's begin the enemies list with weeds, as they are the easiest garden pests to exclude. Exclusion is easy, that is, if you understand how weeds operate.

Over the years, Dr. Asher (pH) has examined the weeds in his yard at some length and up close, and he has arrived at a diagnosis. He has found weeds to be classic passive-aggressive types: their whole lifestyle is calculated upon getting you to do their work for them. Refuse to cooperate, and the weeds fade away. How simple. Except that like all passive-aggressives, weeds have a genius for enlisting you as their helper.

For instance, what is your first impulse when you see a dense thicket of pigweed springing up in your garden bed? If you are Marty, of course, your first impulse is to assume that the pigweeds are potatoes—that's what you planted in that spot—and you undertake a dutiful program of fertilization and watering. The pigweeds respond by flourishing and spreading through the rest of the garden.

Chances are, though, that *you* know enough to recognize a pigweed as a weed, even if you do not know what type it is. So you pull the invaders and then, for good measure, you spade up the soil to expose any roots. That's good, right?

Wrong! What you are doing is exactly what the weeds, all the weeds and not just the pigweeds, want you to do. They have laced that bed with tens of thousands of dormant seeds. On average, cultivated land contains about 10 million weed seeds per acre in the top 6 inches of soil. In some areas, the total is more like 100 million seeds per acre. In fact, it's safe to say that the only thing that makes gardening possible at all is that most of these seeds do not germinate.

They don't germinate because most weed seeds need exposure to light before they can germinate, and the majority of those in your yard have been covered up by topsoil and the natural debris that accumulates on top of it. But when you spade up an area of soil, you stir it up, and you expose the weed seeds in it to the light. Even if the seed ends up back underground, just having been exposed for a fraction of a second is enough to start it growing. In short, spading up your garden is about the best thing you can do for your weeds. That's one reason why traditional gardening, with its emphasis on digging and cultivating, is so much work.

What's the answer, then? Stop digging altogether? Actually, that's not such a bad idea, according to Lee Reich, a horticultural consultant and writer based in New Paltz, New York. Lee really knows his stuff. He has a Ph.D. in horticulture (really) and a master's degree in soil science. His book about pruning* is the best guide to that subject, just as Lee's vegetable garden is the lushest we have seen. It's also virtually weed free, and he hasn't dug the soil, he says, in fifteen years.

His success, according to Lee, is a result of getting off to a good start. He creates new beds by mowing closely the area he wants to plant, and then covering it with newspaper in a layer four sheets thick. Overlap the edges of the newspapers so that you make a continuous blanket and then cover that with 3 to 4 inches of compost. He plants right into the compost.

The cover of paper and compost smothers any weeds that are actively growing, and by burying the weed seeds, it ensures that they don't sprout. Worms do the work of cultivating the soil in the beds. Lee helps out these creatures by making the beds narrow enough that he can reach into their centers without stepping into them. Never, ever step onto your beds, he stresses (remember when we told you that?). Top them up with a couple more inches of com-

* Lee Reich, *The Pruning Book,* The Taunton Press, 1997.

Compost Cuisine

When it comes to composting, Marty has two rules. *Rule No. 1:* No meat or dairy goes into the heap. To add these things means your compost will not be kosher, and besides, it will turn your compost heap into a magnet for stray dogs, possums, rats, vultures, etc. *Rule No. 2:* Compost happens. Turning old leaves and vegetable scraps into compost is Nature's business, and Marty doesn't interfere. He just keeps adding more stuff to the top of the heap, and when he needs some finished compost, he takes a shovel and digs it out from the bottom.

Tom, predictably, has lots more rules about composting. He wants to produce high-grade compost, the weed-free kind that Lee Reich spreads on his vegetable beds. To do this, Tom has to help Nature along.

To begin with he uses a recipe. For each basketful of green and juicy stuff such as grass clippings, fresh manure, or vegetable peelings that he adds to his heap, he adds two basketfuls of some brown and dry stuff such as old leaves or hay (he shreds these first by running them over with a power mower). He stacks these materials in piles three feet wide and three feet tall, and then he waters the piles until they are evenly moist.

Within a couple of days, the piles start to heat up. In fact, they reach a temperature of 150°F. in their centers, and Tom once baked a chicken by burying it in the heap overnight (he dined alone). The heat is a sign that the bacteria and fungi are really busy, digesting all the materials in the heap and turning them into compost.

After a week or two, the heaps cool, and Tom turns them. He uses a fork to remix all the materials, and then rebuilds them into 3' × 3' piles. This causes the heaps to heat up again. After turning the heaps twice, Tom lets them rest for a couple of months and then the compost is ready to use. What's more, it's free of weed seeds, because the heat has cooked all of them.

post once a year (Lee does this in fall) and you'll bury any weed seeds that happen to have blown in.

In fact, if you keep adding compost, you shouldn't have any serious problems with weeds. Lee says that he spends about five minutes a week on weeding. He kind of enjoys it. He says his garden-making technique turned his daughter off to gardening, though. She wanted to *do* things, and after the planting there wasn't much of anything to do until harvesttime. She decided that gardening is boring.

One caution Lee adds is that for his method to work, you have to have really good compost. It must come from a heap in which the ingredients were properly blended and which was turned periodically so that the materials heated up as they decayed. That cooks any weed seeds, Lee explains. If you just dump debris to rot in a back corner of your yard (as Marty does), the result will be a compost full of weed seeds. It will benefit the garden in many other ways: such sloppy compost will improve the structure of the soil, nourish the plants, even help discourage soilborne diseases and pests. But it isn't suitable for mulch in a no-dig garden.

If you don't want to manage your compost heap scientifically (that seems suspiciously like work to Marty), then Lee suggests that for topping up the vegetable beds you buy commercially made compost, the kind of compost you'll find in bags at the garden center. That, of course, is the kind that Marty used to create the soil in his off-the-shelf beds. This gave his garden the advantage of starting out weed free.

We know of one other way to start a garden weed free. Actually this method also starts the garden free of soilborne insect pests and diseases, too. This involves some digging, but the hard work is done by the sun. That's why it's called "solarizing."

This technique involves planning ahead, which is another thing that Marty refuses to do when he's not at the office. You want me to keep an agenda, he insists, then you pay me by the hour. Tom, though, would rather plan ahead than pull weeds.

When he wants to start a new garden bed, or even clean up an old one that has become a haven for weeds and pests, Tom waits until the hottest part of the summer. Then he tills up the area, or spades it up by hand. His purpose in doing this is partly to mix in compost or sphagnum peat, fertilizer, etc. However, he is also anxious to expose as many of the weed seeds to sunlight as he can, and so start them growing. That's why, right after raking the bed smooth, he waters it thoroughly.

After turning and irrigating the soil, Tom covers the bed with a sheet of clear plastic 1 to 4 mils thick. He fastens this down by burying its edges in a shallow trench that runs all around the bed's perimeter. This plastic film traps solar energy and causes the soil within the bed to heat up to as much as 120°F. Left in place for 4 to 6 weeks, the plastic kills not only weed seeds but also the plant diseases and parasites that tend to become entrenched in vegetable gardens.

This is why solarizing your beds is a good idea for an older garden as well as a new one. Particularly in the South, where nematodes are common in the soil, a garden that has been productive may slip into an inexplicable decline. You treat the plants the same way as you always did, but they just don't seem to thrive. Try solarizing the beds, and see if that helps.

Keeping the Door Closed

Once you have exterminated or suppressed the weeds already in your garden, the next step is to keep them from creeping back. Weeds are opportunists, and they will seize on any opening you leave. Soil that is not occupied by something else is an invitation to weeds. So your best strategy is to keep your garden small and keep it filled up.

All through this book, we have advocated planting your vegetables closer together than other gardening gurus recommend. In part, that's because closer planting produces more harvest per square foot, as long as you take good care of your soil. Tom and Marty also prefer close planting, though, because it leaves less room for weeds. A conventional vegetable garden, which is planted in widely spaced rows, invites weeds. Planting in blocks as Tom and Marty do, so that the vegetables spread in continuous sheets, makes the beds weed-unfriendly.

In Chapter 9, Marty recommended targeting your watering (see page 210). By delivering irrigation right to the vegetable plants, and not spilling any over the surrounding soil, you deny weeds a vital resource. They can't live without water any more than you can. So targeting your watering reduces your weeding problems.

You can enhance the effect of targeted watering by covering your beds with a few inches of mulch. The mulch helps your vegetables by keeping the soil below moist, cool, and loose. The top of the mulch, in contrast, stays hot and dry, so if weed seeds drift or fall onto this, they stay dormant.

Pests

Holes begin appearing in the leaves of your plants, and this time, you are reasonably certain it isn't the little sharpshooter next door, practicing with his BB gun. Thoroughly distraught, or maybe just enraged, you turn to a gardening book. And what do you get? Well, if you haven't been smart enough to turn to us, what you get is a short course in insect identification. After spending a week or two learning how to play horticultural Sherlock Holmes—"I can tell by the mark of the incisors, Watson, that it is the lesser flea beetle who is attacking your cabbages"—you probably find that the problem is probably moot. The cabbages are gone.

But maybe there is a gnawed stump or two still remaining. At this point, your conventional garden guide declares war. Before you know it, you are suited up in rubber, spraying death over the landscape. Or, if it is an organic gardening guide, it has you crouched over some blender, pureeing bugs to create a homemade repellent. Either way, it doesn't sound like much fun.

Are we recommending surrender? Certainly not! At least, Tom isn't recommending surrender. Marty seems to find a strange comfort in defeat. By confirming his vision of this as a basically hostile universe, one created to crush innocent Ashers, defeat reassures him. He is happiest while wringing his hands.

In contrast with Marty, Tom hates to lose to insects, rabbits, birds, or woodchucks. Unfortunately, he has found that once the battle is joined, the wildlife commonly prove far more persistent and wily than he. That's why he declines to become involved.

Tom has a rule: he doesn't fight pests, he excludes them. How does he do this? Two ways. First, he uses a variety of physical barriers to keep pests out of the vegetable garden. Then, too, he plants the garden in such a way that if the pests do gain entry, they cannot easily find the flora they like. It's important to keep in mind that while pests may be persistent and good at what they do, they aren't rational thinkers. You can outsmart them.

Critters

The pests with the biggest and most indiscriminate appetites are the four-legged ones. This makes them the most dangerous. A woodchuck or rabbit or, worse yet, deer can swallow weeks' worth of work in a matter of hours.

They are also creatures of habit. Once a critter gets used to dining on your fruits and vegetables, it will be very difficult to make it stop. Deer are particularly troublesome in this respect. As a rule, they follow a regular route, traveling along a circular path that, with stops for eating and resting, takes a couple of days to complete. Once your garden becomes one of their regular stops, it will be very difficult to keep them from returning. So with deer, and to a lesser extent with all mammalian pests, the key to successful exclusion is to keep them from ever entering. This means that, ideally, you should erect a barrier before you plant your first garden bed. What type of barrier you install depends on where you live, the type of pests you anticipate, and your tolerance for ugliness.

Tolerance for ugliness? Yes, that's important because the most effective fences tend to be obvious. This makes barrier design a balancing act. You may achieve complete critter exclusion by turning your yard into something that looks like a gulag, but is it worth it?

Suburban Guilt

It's odd, but Marty never seems to feel guilty about pulling weeds. Nor does he worry about terminating a few bugs. But he drives Tom crazy with his agonizing over the larger pests. Fundamentally, he believes that four-legged pests, anything mammalian and non-human, have more right to his garden than he does. Let a wood-chuck into Marty's garden and he (Marty) will complain. He won't do anything that might inconvenience the woodchuck, though.

The problem is that Marty is paralyzed by guilt. As he has told Tom, he feels like an intruder in his own yard. He cannot look at any kind of critter without thinking that he, Marty, has stolen that creature's habitat. Apparently, it is Marty's belief that Westport looked like a set from *Bambi* before he and his fellow commuters arrived on the first evening express. They destroyed this idyll when they built their houses, so now the deer and rabbits et al are homeless. Surely, even Tom believes that we must take care of the homeless.

Tom does. But he has also pursued his research into wildlife management a bit farther than Disney movies. He has actually spoken to a few wildlife management experts. What he learned from them has given him a very different view of the situation.

First of all, there were no deer a generation ago in most areas now occupied by suburbs. The farmers and ranchers extermi-nated them decades previously. New Jersey, for example, which now boasts a deer herd of 175,000, was home to an estimated two hundred individuals at the turn of the century. So it wasn't the suburbanites who displaced the deer.

Au contraire—suburbs, it turns out, are a deer habitat more hospitable than anything Nature provides. Deer don't like deep forest; they find their food and the kind of cover they like at the edges of such growth, in clearings, meadows, or in the drier, open uplands that emerge amid swamps and marshes. The Native Americans used to burn large tracts of forest to create similar habitat and attract deer to their area. Suburbanites, by creating a lushly planted, heavily irrigated patchwork of open space, shrubbery, and woods, have improved on this. They have created the ideal deer nursery.

Recent studies have revealed that young does in woodland habitats routinely give birth to one fawn at a time, many of which are stillborn, though when they are fully mature, the does may sometimes bear twins. But in many suburban areas, does are producing their first live birth at one year of age and thereafter often bear triplets on an annual basis. Ecologists attribute the change in fertility to improved nutrition. The average adult deer eats about seven pounds of greenery a day, and has a far easier time finding this in your backyard than in the forest. The effect of this more abundant diet is that local deer populations sometimes double in a single year.

Deer, incidentally, aren't the only garden pests to have profited by suburbanization. Raccoons and squirrels have found the suburbs to be much more comfortable than the wild wood. Opossums, which used to be a Southern species, have moved North to fill the suburbs, too. Rabbits have benefitted by the extermination of predators such as foxes and wolves, and in many areas their population has exploded.

As best we can estimate, there were probably some 53 million deer living on this continent when the first European settlers arrived; 40 million of these were of the Eastern species, the whitetail deer. Today, state wildlife departments estimate the total deer population at 30 to 35 million, with 25 to 30 million of these being whitetail deer. That's a decline in numbers of 25 to 37.5 percent in the Eastern United States, and considerably more in the Western states. But given that ranching, farming, and urban development have excluded deer from vast tracts, it's safe to say that populations in many suburban areas are higher than ever before.

That may be cold comfort to you, if deer have just destroyed your garden. However, it should release you from any feelings of guilt. You still may not want to try Tom's recipes. (Bambi en brochette, anyone?) But you can take measures to exclude the deer (and the raccoons, squirrels, and opossums) from your garden without feeling like a monster. The deer will do just fine without your help.

Where you live is important because it will determine which pests are likely to become a problem. Tom, for example, lives close to the center of a small city, so the only critter he has to worry about is raccoons. Marty lives in an older suburb, so while he sees few deer, he does have to cope with rabbits and woodchucks. Western friends tell us that gophers are the most destructive pests in their area. Where you live will also help determine what sort of barrier you employ.

Types of Barriers

• **Electric fences.** These are among the most effective barriers and the least obtrusive. They are also among the easiest barriers to erect, because electric wires don't have to be particularly strong or

The Natural Calendar for Exclusion

Barring pests before they get in the habit of dining *chez vous* makes an obvious kind of sense. In addition, though, you want to make sure that barriers are in place before the critters feel their most intense hunger pangs. When they are hungry is when they are most likely to come marauding into your backyard.

Fortunately, the timing for this is predictable. Mammals are most hungry in early spring. That's when the woodchucks and rabbits emerge from a winter's sleep, not having eaten for months. The deer, though they don't go dormant in winter, typically find that a hungry season. They retreat from their usual ranges to more protected ones, often "yarding up" in some spot where the snow doesn't drift and accumulate. Come spring, they are often on the point of starvation. That makes them particularly aggressive garden pests.

The message in all of this is to get your barriers in place before the last thaw. Don't do the usual thing and wait until you find the starving hordes actually in your garden. By then, they'll have you down in their dining guide.

securely supported; the animals won't lean on them and push against them as they do with an unelectrified fence. For this reason you don't need securely planted wooden posts to string an electric fence; light fiberglass stakes that you simply push into the ground will usually do the job.

The number of wires you must include in an electric fence depends on what you are trying to exclude, and on the climate. A single strand of wire stretched 30 inches above the ground is enough to repel deer in most circumstances, as long as your climate is reasonably moist. If there is moisture in the soil, it will work as the "ground," and the deer will get a shock if it touches one live wire. In areas with arid climates, however, there may not be enough moisture in the soil for a single-wire fence to work. There, you must stretch a second, unelectrified wire parallel to the hot one, so that the deer will touch both at once to complete the circuit.

You'll also need two wires to repel rabbits and woodchucks. You need one wire running 4 inches above the ground to keep these critters from sneaking under the fence, and a second wire 8 inches high to keep them from stepping over it.

Consult the local electric-fencing supplier to find out what arrangement works best in your area. However you design your fence, though, be sure not to forget the peanut butter. This is as irresistibly attractive to critters as it is to the average kid, and smearing it over the wire (before you electrify it) encourages invaders to make intimate contact. That will impress invaders with the fact that your garden tastes bad.

One disadvantage of an electric fence is that it requires continual maintenance. You have to keep the vegetation below the wires cut down, for if a stem or branch contacts a hot wire, the result is likely to be a short circuit and a temporary end of the fence's electrification. Another problem is that in areas of deer overpopulation, a single-strand fence may not do the job. In such locations, you may have to stretch three or four wires or even five wires, one over the other at intervals of a foot. To do this, you'll need to set wooden fence posts, and that makes the fence expensive to install.

The real problem with electric fences, though, is one of perception. Any time Tom mentions them, a look of horror and disdain comes over Marty's face. This makes Tom feel like one of the gun-toting, degenerate prison guards in *Cool Hand Luke*. Which is not fair, as the shock a fence carries is designed to sting and not to injure, and Tom could argue that the farmer's barbed wire is really far more brutal. That explanation hasn't changed Marty's mind, though, and it probably won't change the minds of your neighbors. As a result, electric fences are only suited, really, to gardens on large properties or in rural areas where neighbors don't live cheek by jowl.

• **Deer netting.** Conventional, nonelectrified wire fencing can be quite effective at stopping deer, too, but the fences have to be quite tall—8 feet is the standard height for upright, woven-wire fencing. This is ruinously expensive to maintain and extremely unaesthetic.

Fortunately, a less expensive and less visually obtrusive fencing material has come on to the market in the last few years. This is the sturdy, black plastic netting that is made specifically for deer exclusion. Because of its dark color, this material blends in with a leafy background, and can be almost invisible from a distance of a dozen yards. Because it is so flexible, this netting is also easy to install. You can, of course, staple it to fence posts set up around the vegetable garden, but often it is quicker and simpler to tie the netting to trees along the perimeter of your yard.

• **Fishing line.** You can make an impromptu but effective fence by tying ordinary, heavy-duty monofilament line to trees or stakes. Stretch a cordon of line a foot above the ground, another a foot higher, etc., continuing until you reach a height of eight feet. Mark the fence by tying lengths of yellow ribbon to the lines at four-foot intervals.

Why does a fishing-line fence work? Wildlife experts speculate that deer, whose eyesight is poor, fear becoming entangled in something they cannot see. Which is why Marty won't employ this defense; he refuses to put on reading glasses every time he goes out into the garden.

• **Noisemakers.** We have also heard good reports about strings of clanging pie pans or bunches of tin cans suspended around the garden on sturdy twine. If you connect these junkyard wind chimes one to another with horizontal lines, then you create a sort of obnoxious burglar alarm. Those who rely on this device swear it works; we only hope that it annoys deer more than it annoys you.

• **Fences for diggers.** Deer are certainly the most destructive mammalian pests; their huge stomachs and indiscriminate appetites (if they are hungry enough, deer will eat almost anything green) have led to the nickname "Agent Orange on the Hoof." And though it takes smaller mouthfuls, a persistent rabbit, woodchuck, or gopher can, over time, achieve almost as much damage.

Because these creatures rely more on digging than on leaping, the type of barrier you must use to exclude them is fundamentally different. You don't need the sturdy fences that are necessary for use against deer. A light (and inexpensive) woven-wire fencing commonly sold as "chicken wire" works well at barring these smaller animals. You have to run it down into the ground, though, as well as up into the air.

You'll find the chicken wire at most hardware stores. What you want is a roll of the 4-foot-tall kind. To install this, first drive 5-foot-tall stakes at 5-foot-intervals all around the outside of the vegetable garden. Then, just outside the line of stakes dig a 6-inch-deep, 6-inch-wide trench just outside the line of stakes.

Next, lay out a strip of chicken wire as long as the whole perimeter of the garden and fold up the bottom 6 inches so that it sticks out at a right angle like a foot or shelf. When you've finished your folding, take the wire and set it into the trench so that the foot rests on the trench's bottom and reaches outward—the rest of the wire, the upright sheet that will be the fence, should be on the inside of the trench, next to the stakes. Wrapping the chicken wire around the corners of the garden will involve cutting slits through the fence's foot so that these can spread at the angles.

With a heavy-duty staple gun, fasten the upright part of the chicken wire to the stakes, but leave the top foot of wire loose. Then refill the trench with soil and tamp this down firmly.

You now have a fence which is virtually impregnable to the smaller quadrupeds. The aboveground part stands 3 feet tall, which is higher than the most active rabbit can jump. A particularly active young woodchuck may try climbing the fence, but when he or she reaches the unsecured top foot of the wire, this will flip down and outward, dumping the woodchuck back onto the ground. Both rabbits and woodchucks may try to burrow under the fence, but they will begin their tunneling right at the fence's foot and so will run up against the buried, outward-reaching wire foot.

The only creature who may dig under such a fence is a gopher. Common in many parts of the West, these creatures tunnel deep, 6 to 18 inches down, and so are likely to pass under your fence's foundation. Where gophers are troublesome, we advise lining the entire bottom of your garden with chicken wire. Lay down strips of chicken wire under raised beds as you build them, and under the paths, too.

The Threat from Above

Marty always thought birds were sweet, but that's because his only interactions had been around the bird feeder. As soon as he became a vegetable gardener, he discovered that Alfred Hitchcock had it right. You thought that the bird sitting up in a tree, singing, was just trying to pick up a female bird, or maybe expressing pleasure at the beautiful weather. What they are actually doing, though, is watching. They watch all the time, and as soon as anything edible appears in the garden—a block of tender, young corn seedlings, a ripening tomato, or a bunch of grapes—the birds swoop in to snack.

The "Natural Gardeners," a sect that claims Nature will create and maintain the perfect garden if you, the homeowner, stay out of the way,* claim that birds earn their keep by eating insects and slugs, etc. Birds do eat these pests, but only out of self-interest. They don't want the slugs to eat a berry or seedling that by rights belongs to a bird. Our response is, fine. Let the birds eat pests. But make sure the birds are really hungry so that they eat all the pests. Keep the birds hungry by making sure that they don't eat any of your harvest as well.

Getting the best of the birds requires a different strategy than the one you use with other sorts of critters. Obviously, conventional fencing won't exclude birds. In fact, because they can attack barriers from so many different angles, you really can't exclude them from the garden, unless you cage the whole thing in chicken wire. We have seen that done, and it's *really* ugly. It's also terrifically expensive to erect a structure of this sort. Besides, who can have fun gardening in a prison?

Anyway, it isn't necessary to keep birds out of the garden all the time. They won't bother your unripe berries; they won't attack the corn after the seedlings turn into stalks, at least, not until the ears

---

* Because he loves the idea of something for nothing, Tom was initially quite smitten with the idea of natural gardening. Why not let Nature do all the work? Unfortunately, what he has found through his own experiments, and through visits to the homesteads of noted natural gardeners, is that Nature has its own ideas about what makes the perfect landscape, and they aren't based on your comfort or convenience. After all, poison ivy, briars, ragweed, and rattlesnakes should all have their place in a truly natural landscape. On the other hand, a place for the kids to play or a spot for you to sit out and eat supper really isn't natural. Nor is a vegetable garden, for that matter.

What it comes down to is the fact that a human house and the accompanying accessories like driveways, paths, and hammocks are all artificial and so intrinsically unnatural. Tom has seen a few truly beautiful natural gardens, but most were the result of cheating: the gardener had made a lot of decisions about what plants would be included and where they would be put, and who would be declared a weed and so hounded out. In short, these natural gardeners had chosen to garden and spent as much time at it as anyone else.

We admire wildflowers and are passionate advocates of native plants. We belong to the Nature Conservancy, and have experimented with woodland plantings, even patches of reconstructed prairie. But we don't fool ourselves that just by ceasing to involve ourselves with the yard, we can return it to a garden of Eden.

ripen. Birds won't damage the tomatoes while they are small and green and hard. If the birds want to hang around eating slugs and bugs in the meantime, why not let them?

Because bird attacks are intermittent, what you need are defenses that are easy to erect and take down. You want something you can drop into place when the birds become a problem, and then remove again when that particular crop is harvested. The light plastic mesh sold as "bird netting" fits this bill perfectly—if you modify it just slightly.

This netting was created for protecting fruit crops and it is designed to be wrapped around fruit trees and berry bushes, and then tied in place so that the birds don't find their way in under the edges. You do want to tie the netting securely, too, because if birds do find their way in, they have difficulty finding their way out. That's because the netting is so light as to be practically invisible. A trapped bird soon dies, and to find a casualty of that sort takes the pleasure out of gardening.

Unfortunately, putting the netting in place is a lot of work, if you use it as intended. We don't. Instead, we rely on the birds' characteristic paranoia. Birds are light and delicate creatures and they are keenly aware of their own vulnerability. Anything that could be interpreted as a potential trap, they regard with extreme suspicion. They won't even approach the "trap" until they have watched it for a period of days or even weeks.

This is why we don't install bird netting until a crop is just at the point of ripening, or just after we sow seeds. We want the netting to be unfamiliar and unnerving. Then, to make sure that the birds see it, we tie tinsel along the netting's edges.

Once the netting has been adorned in this fashion, we can achieve complete bird exclusion by just draping it loosely over whatever we want to protect—ripening grapes, emerging seedlings, berries, whatever. The birds sit in nearby branches whispering about that flickering silver stuff, and the netting that the gardener thought they couldn't see. By the time they screw up their nerve to actually approach the trap, the fruit is picked, the seedlings grown, and the tomatoes safely in a salad. Then we can remove the netting to let the birds back to their bug hunting.

Insect Pests

Speaking of bugs, what does a 20-minute gardener do about them? Not much in the flower garden. As Tom and Marty pointed out in their previous encounter, *The 20-Minute Gardener,* insect pests are typically a minor problem there. However, the situation is very different in the vegetable garden. Flowers are a minor but acceptable food source; fruits and vegetables, though, which have been bred for their nutritional value, are real prizes. Hungry insects are sure to home in on an unprotected food crop. Fortunately, this particular group of predators is easy to outsmart. A few basic measures should be enough to confuse them so that they don't do any serious damage.

• **Interplant.** In *The 20-Minute Gardener* we recommended a "cottage garden" as a naturally insect-resistant kind of planting, and *The 20-Minute Vegetable Gardener* is recommending that you create something similar in your vegetable garden.

So what is a cottage garden? It's the type of garden that Marty tends toward naturally. It's spontaneous and unplanned, and cheerfully disorganized. There is no definable plan to a cottage garden, except that plants are set where the conditions of sunlight and terrain will suit them. Typically, they are set out in ones and twos, and the different types of flowers are all intermingled.

Cottage gardens are very fashionable these days. Their informal tousled appearance has an Old World charm, and they help gardeners like Marty throw off the tyranny of pompous experts like Tom. From a practical perspective, however, the greatest virtue of a cottage garden is that it presents insects with a smaller target. That's why we are recommending that you follow this style in your vegetable garden, too.

Most insects are fairly specific in what they eat. A given species of grazing insect tends to rely on a particular family of plants for its food. Cabbage looper caterpillars, for example, home in on members of the cabbage family, such as cabbages, broccoli, and brussels sprouts. Afterward, they may move on to other greens, but it is the cabbages that usually bring them to the garden. Colorado potato beetles restrict their dining to potatoes and their relatives, tomatoes, eggplants, and peppers.

Plant a lot of the preferred plants together in an extended mass, and you create a big target that draws the corresponding pests from far and wide. So keep each block of plants small, and intermingle them whenever possible. Mix up different kinds of plants, keep the clumps of any given plant small, and you create a much less distinct target. Roaming insects may never spot the attractive plants in your garden and even if they do, chances are they may find only some of the potatoes or broccoli, and that the other clumps of these plants you have tucked away elsewhere will escape the pests' notice.

In the German communities of rural Texas, Tom has seen authentic cottage gardens whose elderly owners took intermingling of the plants to the extreme. They mixed their strawberries and lettuces right in with the flowers. This made a walk around their gardens a continual series of surprises for human visitors, and for insects, too.

• **Rotate your crops.** This phrase has a pleasantly bucolic sound to it, and it makes you an instant expert. Explain to your neighbor that you intend to rotate your crops this year, and you are sure to impress him. *You* will be impressed when you find out how much trouble this simple act will save you.

Tom sneered at Marty when he asked if rotating your crops is anything like rotating your tires. In fact, though, the concept is similar. In its most basic form, crop rotation means that you never plant the same plant, or its close relatives, in the same spot two years running. In other words, if you set your tomatoes in the front bed one year, you don't plant them there the next one. Nor do you put potatoes, eggplants, or peppers (all tomato relatives) in that front bed, either. You don't have to move each crop very far—you just don't put it in the exact same spot.

The reason you don't keep planting the same things in the same spot year after year is that monotony is too congenial to insects and diseases. Never vary your garden plan, and each kind of pest will eventually find the type of vegetable or fruit that it likes, and then it will settle in so that you will have pest problems forever. Even in fall, when you clear the frost-killed debris from the beds, the pests won't leave. They'll just lay eggs in the soil or burrow down deep to wait for spring, when they know that the predictable clod who plants this space is going to bring them their favorite food.

Move each kind of plant to a different spot each spring, however, and you frustrate those overwintering pests. They emerge in spring looking for food, and their food is gone. The disease organisms starve and the insects wander off and most get lost or eaten by birds (remember them?) or by predatory insects.

Tom always rotates his plantings. At least, he has done this ever since he lost all his Chinese cabbages to the blight one year—the third year running that he had planted them in the same bed. Marty, incidentally, was kind enough not to laugh.

Actually, to get the most benefit out of crop rotation, you should allow an interval of at least two years or, better yet, three, before you replant a particular crop back into the spot you grew it in this year. The reason for this is that some disease pathogens can survive in a dormant state for more than a single year, and you want to make sure that your cabbage blight or whatever is all dead before you return cabbages to that spot.

An added benefit of crop rotation is that it helps to prevent soil exhaustion. Different types of plants tend to draw different mixes of minerals and nutrients from the soil. If you plant the same thing in the same spot for several years running, that crop may suck its particular favorites out of the soil entirely. Switch the plantings around, and the effect is that the withdrawals are more balanced. That means you can recharge the soil with any average fertilizer such as composted manure or even just compost.

Remember: KISS (Keep It Simple, Stupid) is the 20-minute gardener's motto.

This is not the motto of traditional gardening gurus, and they like to prescribe elaborate schemes about which crop should follow which. Their theory is that the particular withdrawals that one type of plant makes from the soil leaves that spot ready for some other type of plant. Carrots, for example, should always be followed by beans or peas. These horticultural minuets confuse even Tom. He, like Marty, contents himself with random transfers, and that works just fine for him (and Marty).

• **Floating row covers.** These are strips of gauzy plastic fabric that allow light, air, and water to penetrate down to your plants, but which exclude insects. They are called "row covers" because the material typically comes in rolls three or four feet wide, which are wide enough to cover a row of most vegetables. Such rolls are not wide enough to cover a 4-foot-wide raised bed, but if you ask the manager at the garden center, he or she can get wider strips of this material for you.

Some gardeners routinely enclose trouble-prone crops in a protective cocoon of row-cover material. If beetles always attack the young beans, then the gardeners cover the beans right after sowing with a row cover. The most useful aspect of this material is that it is so light that seedlings lift it easily as they emerge from the soil, and the plants continue to push it upward as they grow. Usually, you must remove the row covers when your plants begin to flower, because if you exclude the insects then, the blossoms don't get pollinated and you get no fruit. Marty, incidentally, used this fact as the basis of a thoroughly incomprehensible lecture that he delivered to his teenage son.

To install a row cover, you loosely drape the strip of material over the newly seeded area or the newly transplanted seedlings. Leave plenty of slack so that the plants under the cover will have room to expand. Be sure to bury the edges of the row cover. Otherwise, pests may find their way in, and birds and the insects who prey on them won't, in which case the pests will graze undisturbed.

Marty, whose style of gardening is purely reactive, doesn't use row covers to ward off insects. To foresee a possible insect infestation while he is just planting seeds would require an impossible leap of the imagination. He has, however, used row covers in his ongoing campaign against squirrels. Draped over tomato vines when the fruits are ripening, the row covers hide the fruit from view and so help to fool the bushy-tailed rodents. Of course, the vista of white veils does give the garden the appearance of a convent, a sight that Marty finds unnerving.

· **The sprays.** No, we aren't going back on our commitment to avoid chemicals. But there are times when despite all your cunning arrangements, a plague of insects does discover some fruit or vegetable crop. For those occasions we reserve a couple of homemade, nonchemical sprays.

The first of these is a solution of dishwashing soap and water. We use Ivory Liquid for this, and we mix it at a rate of 2 teaspoons per gallon of water. This is lethal to a variety of plant-eating insects, including white flies, aphids, and mites. Spray the soapy water onto the plants until it covers and runs off the leaves, and repeat this treatment again two to three days later. For stubborn infestations, you may have to repeat the sprays over a period of two weeks. Do not apply this soap spray during periods of extreme heat, during the middle of the day when the sun is most intense, or when your plants are stressed from drought. If applied then, the soap spray may "burn" the leaves.

If this soap-and-water spray doesn't work, then we move on to our second formula, the vegetable-oil-and-water one. One application of this kills all sorts of plant eaters, including mealybugs and many types of caterpillars.

To make this spray, pour four-fifths cup of cooking oil (Tom uses corn oil; Marty insists on olive oil, first virgin cold press) into a gallon of water, and add a teaspoon of liquid soap to let the other two ingredients mix. Shake to mix and spray onto the plants, if the temperature outside isn't over 85°F. If the temperature is higher, this spray, too, may injure your plants.

20-minute tip: Spray in early morning. The air is usually calm then, which means that your spray won't be blown away before it can hit the plants. Early-morning temperatures are cooler, which reduces the risk of injury to the plants. In addition, insects that fly by day aren't active yet. This means you will kill more of the insects that are afflicting your plants, and won't injure honeybees, because they haven't yet left their hives.

• **Attracting the predators.** It's always best to get someone else to do your dirty work. This is especially true of insect control. Fortunately, there are mobs of insects who support themselves and their families by preying on the insects who prey on your plants. Boosting the numbers of these insect hit men (*And hit women, Tom, don't forget the women*—M.A.) is the most effective and easiest way to protect your vegetables and fruits from insect damage.

Avoiding the use of chemical insecticides is the best way to encourage the predatory insects. When you poison the insects on which they feed, you pass the toxins up the food chain to the predators and kill them, too—that's basic ecology.

There are also a few simple things you can do to make your garden more predator friendly. Fill a shallow bowl to the lip with pebbles, top it up with water, and set it out in the garden to give the flying predators a drinking place. Plant pollen- and nectar-rich flowers among your fruits and vegetables, too; many predators eat other insects when they are in their immature stages, but feed on pollen and nectar as adults. Catnip, dill, and yarrow are especially effective as food sources. Finally, cover paths with an organic mulch such as wood chips or shredded bark. They can then serve as hiding places for the predators when you are tearing up their usual hunting grounds to replant or cultivate.

Blights, Smuts, Rots, Rusts, Etc.

Your potato plants are flourishing, and you are already debating with yourself: mashed or baked, or maybe scalloped? Then, one morning, gray spots are covering the leaves like a case of albino acne. Next thing you know, the leaves are browning and whole plants are collapsing.

What happened? A disease: the "late blight" has found your potato patch. Isn't there anything you can do? Yes. If you had read another kind of gardening book and trained yourself to recognize the first symptom, the leaf acne, you could have started spraying fungicides over the potatoes on a weekly basis until you harvested the chemical impregnated crop.

Do you want to do this? Hopefully, no. You certainly don't want to eat those toxic tubers, and the sprays would probably drift onto other, nearby fruits and vegetables. Besides, those chemicals are likely to persist in the soil and add to the toxic soup already polluting your environment.

So what do Tom and Marty do when a plant starts to wither mysteriously?

First of all, we don't worry too much, because this is not a common occurrence in our gardens. We start with disease-free seeds and plants and we rotate our plantings. We take care to keep the soil healthy, too, by giving it regular doses of compost.

Next, we assume that the problem is probably not a disease, because it is far more likely that it is a result of some cultural problem. We feed any failing plant with a drench of some balanced water-soluble fertilizer, the type that turns the water blue or green, the kind you use for your houseplants. If we want to take stronger measures, we drench the plant with seaweed extract mixed with water.

And if those things have no effect, we pull the plant up and dispose of it with the trash. That way, it can't infect its neighbors.

One more thing that Tom does is to read the labels and catalog descriptions before he buys any plants or seeds. Given a choice, he always buys the variety that is described as "disease resistant."

Marty won't read labels and he makes his catalog choices based on which names he finds most appealing. He says that he does this because he likes to be surprised. Certainly, it is a shock when the plant he had purchased as an eggplant starts bearing hot peppers. Once, by some miracle, the carrot seeds he had planted were transformed into radishes. This sort of experience is what gives his gardening a sense of childlike wonder. Marty has adventures in his garden that Tom cannot even imagine. He also has more diseases, though.

Loosen Up

Ultimately, the most effective technique for coping with plant pests and diseases is to learn not to take their damage too seriously. Fence the garden if you must to exclude the critters. Do what you can to confuse the bugs. Then recognize that if you lose half your lettuces, you won't starve. Concentrate on enjoying the half you do harvest.

If a particular crop turns out to be unusually trouble-prone, year after year, forget it. Plant something else. Or plant the pest- and disease-attractive plant in a container of some sort and set it off by itself somewhere, apart from the rest of the fruits and vegetables. If, for example, your tomatoes always develop the wilt by mid-summer, try growing them in tubs. Set these in a sunny corner of the driveway and fill them with soil brought in from off-site. If the slugs always get your strawberries, grow them in hanging baskets suspended from an end of the porch roof. If the woodchuck always finds a way to get into your lettuce, grow it in a window box, where he'll need a ladder to reach it.

Tom has one other solution for pest control. Borrow an old copy of *The Joy of Cooking* from your local library. It has recipes in it for everything from venison to raccoon. It is Tom's belief that these creatures have a sort of right to your vegetables—they are higher up on the food chain than summer squash and tomatoes. But gardeners are higher yet, and they have a right to harvest those further down the chain. This is why Marty brings his own lunch when he visits Tom.

2🕐-MINUTE PROJECT:
Designer Pumpkins

Earlier in this book (on page 92, to be nitpickingly exact) we alluded to Marty's discovery that less is less. Now we are going to examine Tom's discovery of the corollary. More is definitely more.

We are talking pumpkins, the easiest, most rewarding vegetable we know. Tom had been aware, vaguely, that these were a vegetable crop but he had never grown them. Then he saw them under cultivation in the Bronx, and he knew he was falling behind the curve.

Where Tom saw the pumpkins was at Wave Hill, a former estate on the Hudson River's shore in the Fieldstone area of the Bronx. Wave Hill had been a summer residence for folks like Teddy Roosevelt, Mark Twain, and Arturo Toscanini (an odd assemblage if you think about it; can you imagine Mark Twain showing T.R. around?).

But in 1960, Wave Hill was donated to the City of New York, and under the impassioned guidance of horticulturist Marco Polo Stufano, it has evolved into the finest public garden in the United States. If you don't believe us, just visit.

Anyway, a year or two ago, when Tom visited Wave Hill,

he took his usual course through the wild garden and the various flower borders, the summer garden of annuals, and then came upon a sunny hillside that Marco had buried under a rampant, huge-leaved vine. Upon closer inspection, Tom found nestled into the bed of leaves some huge fruits. These were what botanists (for inscrutable reasons of their own) insist on calling "berries," though to Tom they looked remarkably like pumpkins. They looked like pumpkins, except that they were a pale, smooth bluish-white in color.

This was slick. But there was a sense of humor to this planting, too; a fun-house sensation about the display. The size of the fruits and the leaves was so much bigger than that of the average ground cover that the view made Tom feel like a dwarf by comparison.

When Tom tracked down Marco, he learned that these were 'Lumina' pumpkins. He had to have them. Besides, he admired the nerve of anyone who could plant pumpkins amid all those hyper-sophisticated phloxes, delphiniums, and other aristocratic flowers.

Needless to say, Tom's first stop when he got home was his waist-high heap of seed catalogs. In digging through these, he found that he had been missing a lot. There were early American pumpkins, such as 'Connecticut Field', which the New England Indians had been growing before 1700. There was 'Hopi Pumpkin', a green-skinned kind from Arizona. 'Lady Godiva' was grown for its naked, hull-less seeds, which can be eaten roasted or raw, and 'Little Gem', an African pumpkin, can make apple-sized fruits that can be baked whole. 'Small Sugar' is the classic pie pumpkin, though 'Sugar Baby' is the traditional Midwestern favorite, and 'Flat White' from South Africa is supposed to be sweetest. 'Acoma' is a blue-skinned pumpkin that has been growing in the Southwestern pueblos for the past thousand years. Tom ended up ordering seeds of 'Rouge Vif d'Etampes', a French-heirloom type. He liked to imagine those Frenchmen passing down pumpkins from father to son, and finally to him.

The only requirements for pumpkin growing are a rich soil, which Tom had, and a sunny spot, which Tom did not. So he decided to give his pumpkins to his mother-in-law, Gige. She lives out in the country and has lots of room.

Because his mother-in-law lives in a chilly area of New England, and pumpkins require from two to three months of frost-free weather to produce a harvest, Tom knew he had to give this planting a head start. He sowed his pumpkin seeds into 3-inch peat pots filled with seed-starting mix (two seeds for each pot) in early May. The seeds germinated within a matter of days, and grew like Jack's beanstalk. The seedlings were already outgrowing the pots three weeks later when Tom took them with him on his Memorial Day pilgrimage to Gige's house. He had a rendezvous with a hamburger scheduled, but first he took time out to plant the patient Gige's pumpkin patch.

Digging up a patch of her backyard and enriching the soil with a bucket of compost per square yard, Tom scooped out planting pits: shallow, saucer-shaped depressions at 6-foot intervals. Because his mother-in-law had expressed reservations about living on a pumpkin farm, Tom had room for only two of these excavations. Into the bottom of each he dug in a handful of 5-10-5 fertilizer, and then into the center, the lowest points of the pit, he planted a peat pot of pumpkin seedlings. He watered them, covered the surrounding soil with a mulch of shredded leaves, and then went back to the family picnic.

Subsequent care was mostly provided by Nature. Whenever Tom visited his mother-in-law, he watered the pumpkins. Twice in the course of the summer he weeded. For the most part, though, the huge-leaved pumpkins took care of weeds themselves. The vining stems climbed over them, and the foliage spread a dense canopy of shade that smothered all but the most persistent weeds.

On October 12th, when Tom's in-laws had all assembled to help him press cider from the neighbor's apples, the younger members of the party harvested the pumpkins. The total pick was just four fruits, but since the largest of these weighed 18 pounds (measured on the bathroom scale), the harvest was still considerable. Just in time for Halloween, this was definitely the gardening experience of the year for the younger set. Though Tom's pumpkins didn't look like jack-o'-lantern material. Shiny, almost blood red, they were flattened, drum-shaped. So what if these French berries wouldn't impress the trick-or-treaters? Tom thought. He had no intention of leaving them out on a doorstep.

Instead, he lined them up on the kitchen counter and then, one at a time, he cooked them. First he split them latitudinally with a knife. Then he scooped out the guts and dumped these into a sieve to separate out the seeds. Finally, he placed the pumpkin halves cut-side down on foil on a cookie sheet and baked them in a 350°F oven for one hour.

This left the flesh tender and moist. And delicious, too. Botanically speaking (something Marty won't have in his house), pumpkins are indistinguishable from winter squash. This baked meat of 'Rouge Vif d'Etampes' tasted like squash, all right, but a sweeter and richer squash than that to which Tom was accustomed.

The pumpkin meat was quite good as a side dish at dinner, and was superb in pies (Tom gave Gige some of these, too). Its apotheosis, though, came in the pumpkin soup that Suzanne made.

Suzanne's Pumpkin Soup

4 tablespoons butter
2 onions, chopped
2 to 3 garlic cloves,
    minced
1 teaspoon cumin
1 cardamom clove seed,
    crushed
½ teaspoon cinnamon
1 teaspoon celery seeds
5 to 6 cups pumpkin
    puree

6 cups soup stock (bouillon,
    chicken or vegetable)
1 to 2 tablespoons fresh
    ground pepper
1 teaspoon salt
1 cup diced pumpkin
½ cup thinly sliced celery
    stalk
1 cup tart apples, diced
½ cup sherry
1 cup heavy cream

Melt butter in large saucepan. Sauté onions and garlic until soft. Add cumin, cardamom, cinnamon, and celery seeds. Cook another 1 to 2 minutes.

Add pumpkin puree, soup stock, pepper, and salt. Bring to a boil and then let simmer until soft (10 to 15 minutes).

Make sure soup is smooth—it may be necessary to either beat with rotary beater or run through a blender.

Return soup to pot and add diced pumpkin and celery. Cook until almost soft (this will depend upon the size of your cubes). When they are almost soft, add apples and cook until they, too, are almost soft.

Just before serving, heat soup, stir in sherry, then cream.

May be cooled and placed in the refrigerator until ready to use.

Options: Just before serving, core apples and add thin slices to top of soup, or whip some cream and add it to the top of soup.

Tom's insatiable curiosity (the elephant child had nothing on him) later drove him to experiment with the pumpkins he found for sale at local farmer's markets. The jack-o'-lantern type he found at the garden center yielded a bland and stringy meat, not in the same league with his heirloom French berries. Later, Tom learned that this had almost certainly been a 'Connecticut Field Pumpkin', and that aside from seasonal decorations this is used principally as the feed for cattle and pigs.

The 'Sugar Baby' pumpkin he found at a farmer's market, supposedly prime material for pies, was also disappointing, with a dry and rather tasteless flesh. The 'Lumina' pumpkin he begged off the folks at Wave Hill, though—that was quite good. The flesh was pale, greenish yellow rather than the standard orange, and moist, with a sweet, subtle flavor. It was too delicate for pie making, perhaps, but a good alternative for serving baked and topped with a pat of butter. The 'Lumina' seeds were winners, too: large and plump, and excellent when baked until crunchy.

Tom's harvest would have been larger had he given his pumpkins better care. The plants would have appreciated more conscientious watering during dry spells. He should have pinched off the tips of the vines after the first little green fruits appeared—that would have encouraged the plant to make more pumpkins and fewer leaves. Still, Tom suspects that the increase in yield would not have matched the increased effort. Besides, there is something so pure about a vegetable that you plant and then forget until you eat it. It's the ultimate 20-minute crop.

More, most definitely, is more.

2🕐-MINUTE PROJECT:
The Backyard Brewmaster

The ultimate skill of the 20-minute gardener (we've been saving the best for last) is learning how to leverage your harvests. Leveraging is something invented by the financial industry and it means that you use a little bit of your assets to persuade someone else to give you the use of a whole lot of theirs. That may sound opportunistic and unfair, but the sharpies down on Wall Street claim that it is not. According to them, you the leverager are investing more than money. You are supplying the precious imagination and vision. What we know is that, in the garden, if you leverage right, everybody makes out.

It's like beer. If that seems like a non sequitur to you, that's because you are not yet wise in the ways of 20-minute gardening. We have already alluded to the role that beer has always played in Tom's vegetable gardening (see Chapter 2, page 12). But since Marty revolutionized the craft, beer has become even more important. It's become more important because it has also become much better.

This is the consequence of a revelation that struck while Tom was browsing through an English gardening book. This quaint and stodgy text proposed for the reader's consideration *Humulus lupulus* 'Aurea'—the golden hop. Tom didn't care for the photograph of this plant's lurid yellow foliage, but the name was suggestive. Hops, he knew, are the herbs that give beer its pleasantly bitter flavor. Tom's brother Nick makes beer, and he had told Tom about how he steeps dried hop flowers in his brews before he adds the yeast.

Of course, no one uses the golden hop for beer making. Unless you are aesthetically impaired, that vine is wholly useless. But Tom reasoned that where you could grow useless hops, you might well be able to grow useful ones. In fact, a little research proved that this hunch was correct. Hops—brew-quality hops—will grow in every state of the Union except Alaska, and they thrive in every sort of habitat from desert to elevations of 7,000 feet up in the mountains. What's more, hops are ridiculously easy to grow.

You order "rhizomes," which look like roots but are actually underground stems, from a mail-order supplier (see Appendix), who offer all sorts of different varieties: German hops for making German-type beers, English hops for making an authentic English bitter, Bohemian pilsner hops, American hops for stocking your own microbrewery, etc. Unless you are truly hung up on authenticity, however, what you will go for is a disease-resistant, hardy hop such as 'Nugget' or 'Cascade'. Make sure, too, that you order only female roots, since it is unfertilized female flowers that you want for your harvest.

The roots will be shipped to you while still dormant in early spring. If you can't plant them right away, seal them into a plastic bag with a couple of handfuls of moistened (not wet) peat moss, and store them in the refrigerator. Meanwhile, find a sunny spot next to a fence or shed, and dig a hole about a foot deep and two feet across. Mix a handful of 5-10-5 fertilizer and a bucketful of compost with the soil you take out of the hole; if you live in an area of acid soil (see page 40), add a handful of ground limestone, too, since hops prefer a neutral to alkaline pH (see page 42 for an explanation). If the soil seems sticky and dense, mix in a half bucket of coarse sand, too.

Replace the soil in the hole, and just before you finish this task, plant the rhizome, setting it horizontally about 1 inch below the soil surface. Water well, and then wait. Shoots may be slow to emerge in the first weeks after planting, though once established, hops are usually up and going by the time the daffodils are blooming. Keep the soil moist by watering it at least once a week during dry weather, but take care not to drown the hops.

Make sure to provide something for the hops to climb, too, because soon the new shoots may be growing by as much as a foot a day, and by midsummer they can reach to a height of 35 feet. Hop farmers train their hops up strings suspended from tall poles, but it's easier to let your hops wind their way up through a fence. Tom has trained his hops up through a panel of wooden latticework that he attached to the west wall of his garage. He set 2-inch blocks of wood between the latticework and the garage, so that the hop vines can wind all the way around this homemade trellis, and so that air can circulate between the wall and hops. Otherwise, the wooden clapboards might rot and the vine might fall prey to mildew.

Hops are cold hardy to −35°F, and once they have settled in, they are genuinely perennial, so you shouldn't have to plant more than once. Care is simple: feed the vine by sprinkling ordinary vegetable-garden fertilizer around its base in early spring (feed at the rate recommended on the fertilizer bag). Water the vine whenever a week passes during the growing season without significant rainfall, and when you do water, thoroughly moisten the soil to a depth of a foot.

Tom's vine bloomed during its second summer in his garden, and by late August he had snipped a lunch bag full of aromatic, papery flowers. He dried these indoors by spreading them out on sheets of newspaper in an airy spot away from direct sunlight. Meanwhile he called his brother, offering to share the harvest. Nick accepted the challenge, and played alchemist. Within weeks, he had transmuted Tom's dried blossoms into a rich, smoky brew that he generously shared with his brother.

Then came an unanticipated bit of luck. Tom had long admired the beer-making skills of his neighbor, Dr. Marc Eisner. The world lost a great brewmaster when Marc became a professor of political science. But the world's loss is his friends' gain, for Marc makes more beer, on an amateur basis, than he himself can drink, and he, too, shares generously. Tom had already tried Marc's "Toad Spit Stout." It left him speechless (Tom has since learned moderation).

When Tom offered to share his harvest with Marc, he asked instead for the address of the hop nursery. Soon Marc had hops climbing the side of *his* house, and with their yield he crafted a varied stream of new brews: Tom feels like a Germanic Johnny Appleseed.

For those who have talents in the field of brewing, we've included below a simple recipe for Nick's creation. But if you don't feel up to making your own, do not despair. With the current craze for home brewing, you can surely find someone local who will transform your harvest for you. Ask around at the nearest brew supply store. You'll find that most home brewers are intrigued by the idea of incorporating a truly local flavor into their beers, ales, and stouts. You'll also find that they are generous people.

Nick's Philadelphia Stout
(makes 6 gallons)

EQUIPMENT NEEDED:
Cheesecloth
4-gallon stainless steel kettle
Plastic brew bucket with
  airlock installed in top
INGREDIENTS:
1 pound crystal malt
⅓ pound roasted barley
Spoonful of espresso coffee
  grounds

2 cans John Bull Dark Malt
  Extract
Boiling hops: 1½ ounce
  cluster hop pellets, Alpha
  7.0
Finishing hops: handful of
  Tom's homegrown
Yeast: 1 packet of WYEAST
  Ale, Irish 1084
¾ cup corn sugar

Heat 2 gallons of water to 160°F.

Turn off heat. Put crystal malt, roasted barley, and espresso grounds into leg cut from old panty hose, knot closed, and steep in hot water for 20 minutes. Remove, and add both cans of malt extract and the boiling hops. Return to heat and boil for 50 minutes. Add finishing hops, and boil an additional 10 minutes. Remove mixture from heat and strain through cheesecloth. Pour into sterile plastic brew bucket, and let cool to 65°, then add yeast. Cover, and let sit for a week to ten days, until the bubbles emerging through the airlock in the brew-bucket lid slow to a rate of one bubble every five minutes. Add ¾ cup of corn sugar to liquid in brew bucket, pour into sterile bottles, and cap. Store bottles upright in cool, dark basement for 3 to 4 weeks, for the stout to clear and mature.

Epilogue

It was late June again, and summer was settling in like a fat bottom on a comfortable chair. Tom had planned a morning of fishing. At the last minute, though, he was overwhelmed with a wave of benevolence. It must have been the weather. Putting rod and reel back in the closet, he instead picked a bagful of delicate red and green lettuce leaves to give to Marty.

All through the drive to Westport, Tom imagined how pleased poor Marty would be to get the fresh greens. Why, Tom bet that Marty hadn't even ordered his seeds yet. Poor guy—if it weren't for Tom's charity and the odd can of peas, Marty would have died of scurvy by now. The warm, smug feeling that enveloped Tom was the perfect complement to the blue-skied perfection of the day.

When he arrived, however, he found Marty's yard in an uproar. There were sport utility vehicles parked all over the lawn; it looked like a reunion for Operation Desert Storm. Tom fought his way through the milling herd of taut-skinned men and women to the spot where Marty presided over a stand roughly fashioned from a cardboard refrigerator carton. Before Tom could utter a word, Marty had snatched the bag from his hands to peer inside.

"No arugula! I need arugula, and you bring me lettuce. Do you know what lettuce is going for a pound? I practically have to give it away. Anyway, what my customers want is arugula!"

Tom staggered, shouldered aside by a woman in Lycra who began grabbing French horticultural beans from a basket at Marty's side.

"Marty, I'm shocked. I didn't know—"

"Yeah, well, it's the height of the season. Next week, half these people will be on their way to the Hamptons. Thank goodness for that, because I've got to get this place cleaned up before the photographer from *Forbes* gets here. We're doing a feature on market trends in upscale vegetables."

Marty slapped Tom's hand as he reached to squeeze a tomato (how had Marty ripened those so early in the season?). Then Marty gasped and pointed. A stretched Humvee bristling with antennas had just turned into the drive.

"Oh, my God, it's Martha! Listen, Tom, I've got to go. But I'll call you, okay? Maybe next week. . . . We'll do a few sprouts. *Ciao.*"

Tom watched Marty's back disappear into the crowd. Then, with a thoughtful look, he began pocketing the tomatoes.

Sources for Plants and Seeds

Nurseries and seed companies are continually changing their stock, and gardeners have little choice but to adapt. The most useful resources for those in search of a particular fruit or vegetable are two guides published by The Seed Savers Exchange: *Fruit, Berry and Nut Inventory* (an itemized list of cultivars with commercial sources for each) and *Garden Seed Inventory* (an equivalent guide to vegetable seed sources). These are updated regularly, and may be purchased from:

Seed Saver Publications
3076 North Winn Road
Decorah, IA 52101

Listed below are current sources for all the vegetables and fruits recommended in this book. For convenience sake, our guide begins with a list of sources, each of which is numbered. The vegetables and fruits follow, in alphabetical order. The sources for each of these plants is indicated by the numbers following that entry; these numbers correspond to those of the nursery or seed catalogs that sell those items.

1. A Bamboo Shoot Nursery
   P.O. Box 121
   12001 Eel River Road
   Potter Valley, CA 95469
   707-743-1710
   free catalog

2. Bear Creek Nursery
   P.O. Box 411H
   Northport, WA 99157
   free catalog

3. Burgess Seed and Plant Co.
   905 Four Seasons Road
   Bloomington, IL 61701
   free catalog

4. Burpee Gardens
   W. Atlee Burpee & Co.
   Warminster, PA 18974
   800-888-1447
   free catalog

5. Carroll Gardens, Inc.
   444 East Main Street
   P.O. Box 310
   Westminster, MD 21158
   410-848-5422
   catalog $3.00

6. Fedco Trees
   P.O. Box 520
   Waterville, ME 04903
   catalog $2.00

7. Filaree Farm
   182 Conconully Highway
   Okanogan, WA 98840
   509-422-6940
   catalog, $2.00, offers 100-
   plus types of garlic

8. Foundation Plant Materials
   Service
   University of California
   Davis, CA 95616
   916-752-3590
   free price list

9. Freshops
   36180 Kings Valley Highway
   Philomath, OR 97370
   541-929-2702
   free catalog

10. Gleckler's Seedmen
    Metamora, OH 43540
    free catalog

11. Goodwin Creek Gardens
    P.O. Box 83
    Williams, OR 97544
    541-846-7357
    free catalog

12. Greenleaf Farm & Nursery
    Route 3, Box 398
    Wendell, NC 27591
    free catalog

13. Johnny's Selected Seeds
    310 Foss Hill Road
    Albion, ME 04910
    207-437-9294
    free catalog

14. Miller Nursery
    5060 West Lake Road
    Canandaigua, NY 14424
    716-396-2647
    free catalog

15. Native Seeds/SEARCH
    2509 North Campbell Av-
    enue, No. 325
    Tucson, AZ 85719
    520-327-9123
    seed list $1.00

16. Nichols Garden Nursery
    1190 North Pacific High-
    way
    Albany, OR 97321
    503-928-9280
    free catalog

17. Pacific Tree Farms
    4301 Lynwood Drive
    Chula Vista, CA 91910
    760-422-2400
    catalog $2.00

18. Peaceful Valley Farm
      Supply
    P.O. Box 2209
    Grass Valley, CA 95945
    916-272-4769
    free catalog

19. Pinetree Garden Seeds
    Box 300
    New Gloucester, ME
      04260
    207-926-3400
    free catalog

20. R. H. Shumway's
    P.O. Box 1
    Graniteville, SC 29829
    803-663-9771
    free catalog

21. Redwood City Seed Co.
    P.O. Box 361
    Redwood City, CA 94064
    415-325-7333
    catalog $1.00

22. Richters Herbs
    357 Highway 47
    Goodwood, Ontario LOC
      1AO
    Canada
    905-640-6677
    free catalog

23. Ronniger's Seed & Potato
      Co.
    P.O. Box 307
    Ellensburg, WA 98926
    catalog $1.00

24. Seeds Blum
    Idaho City Stage
    Boise, ID 83706
    catalog $3.00

25. Seeds of Change
    621 Old Santa Fe Trail,
      No. 10
    Santa Fe, NM 87501
    505-438-7052
    free catalog

26. Shepherd's Garden Seeds
    30 Irene Street
    Torrington, CT 06790
    860-482-3638
    free catalog

27. Sonoma Antique Apple
      Nursery
    4395 Westside Road
    Healdsburg, CA 95448
    707-433-6420
    catalog $1.00

28. Sonoma Grapevines, Inc.
    1919 Dennis Lane
    Santa Rosa, CA 95403
    707-542-5510
    free catalog

29. Southern Exposure Seed
    Exchange
    P.O. Box 170
    Earlysville, VA 22936
    804-973-4703
    catalog $2.00

30. Southern Seeds
    P.O. Box 803
    Tampa, FL 33548
    catalog $2.00

31. Sunrise Enterprises
    P.O. Box 1960
    Chesterfield, VA 23832
    804-796-5796
    catalog $2.00

32. The Cook's Garden
    P.O. Box 535
    Londonderry, VT 05148
    800-457-9703
    free catalog

33. Thompson & Morgan
    P.O. Box 1308
    Jackson, NJ 08527
    800-274-7333
    free catalog

34. Tomato Growers Supply
    Company
    P.O. Box 2237
    Fort Myers, FL 33902
    888-478-7333
    free catalog

35. Vermont Bean Seed Com-
    pany
    Garden Lane
    Fair Haven, VT 05743
    803-663-0217
    free catalog

36. White Flower Farm
    P.O. Box 50
    Litchfield, CT 06759
    800-503-9624
    free catalog

37. Worcester County Horti-
    cultural Society
    Tower Hill Botanic Garden
    P.O. Box 598
    Boylston, MA 01505
    508-869-6111
    free list

Cucumber 'Armenian Cucumber': 26
    'China Long': 24
    'Lemon': 13, 26, 32
    'Vert de Massy Cornichon': 19
    'White Wonder': 20
Curly Cress: 26, 32
Garlic 'Elephant Garlic': 33
    'Italian Red': 7, 18
    'German Extra-Hardy': 13
    'New York White': 13
Gourd, 'Bottle Gourd' and 'Cucuzzi': 19
Grape 'Carlos': 3, 12
    'Edelweiss': 6
    'Foch': 14
    'French Columbard': 8, 28
    'Noble': 3
    'Petite Sirah': 8, 28
    'Seyval Blanc': 14

Herbs
Basil 'African Blue': 22
    'Cinnamon': 22
    'Genova Profumatissimo': 26
    'Genovese': 13
    'Lemon': 32
    'Licorice': 32
    'Lime': 13
    'Napoletano': 26
    'Siam Queen True Thai': 26
    'Spicy Globe': 22
Catnip: 19
Dill 'Dukat': 32
Coriander/Cilantro: 13
Fennel: 13
Garlic Chives (all types cited): 31

Oregano, Greek: 13
Oregano, Italian: 22
Oregano, Spanish: 11
Parsley 'Forest Green': 13
Parsley 'Single-Leaf Italian': 26
Rosemary (all types cited): 11
Sage: 13
Tarragon, French: 13
Thyme: 13
Hops: 9
Horseradish: 4, 13
Jerusalem Artichokes: 13
Kale 'Vates': 19
Luffa: 31
Lettuce (all types cited): 32
Mâche—*see* Corn Salad
Malabar Spinach: 31
Mizuna: 26, 30, 32
Mustard Greens 'Green in Snow': 31
Pea 'Sugar Snap': 13
Peanut 'Spanish Type': 20
Pepper (all types cited): 34
Potato, Irish: 23
Potato, Sweet (all types cited): 4, 23
Pumpkin, 'Connecticut Field': 13
    'Hopi': 15
    'Lady Godiva': 10
    'Little Gem': 10
    'Rouge Vif d'Etampes': 32
    'Sugar Baby': 29
    'Small Sugar': 13, 19, 32
Radish, Asian 'China Rose': 19, 31
    'Shogoin': 16
Radish, Spring 'D'Avignon': 13
    'Easter Egg': 13, 26, 32
    'Shunkyo': 13

Rhubarb 'Canada Red': 2
    'Crimson Red': 18
Sprouts: seeds and supplies available from Johnny's Selected Seeds, 13
Strawberry, Alpine, 'Alexandria': 13, 33
    'Charles V': 36
    'Pineapple Crush': 5
    'Ruegen': 4, 16
Swiss Chard 'Rhubarb'/'Ruby Red': 13, 20

Tomato (all types cited): 34 except:
    'Chiapas Wild Tomato' and 'Punta Banda Tomato' which may be purchased (as seed) from Native Seeds/SEARCH, 15
Turnip 'Purple Top White Globe': 13
    'Shogoin': 20
Zucchini (all types cited): 26

Nurseries That Specialize in Heirloom Vegetables and Fruits

Abundant Life Seed Foundation
    P.O. Box 772
    930 Lawrence Street
    Port Townsend, WA 98368
    360-385-5660
    catalog $2.00
    nonprofit educational foundation specializing in heirloom and Native American vegetables

Heirloom Seeds
    P.O. Box 245
    West Elizabeth, PA 15088
    412-384-0852
    catalog $1.00
    family-owned business specializing in heirloom vegetables

High Altitude Gardens
    P.O. Box 1048
    4150 B Black Oak Drive
    Hailey, ID 83333
    208-788-4363
    free catalog
    many heirloom vegetables adapted to the climate of the mountain West

Native Seeds/SEARCH
    2509 N. Campbell Ave., No. 325
    Tucson, AZ 85719
    520-327-9123
    seed list $1.00
    foundation that specializes in collecting, preserving, and redistributing seeds of traditional vegetables of the Southwest

Sand Hill Preservation Center
   1878 230 Street
   Calamus, IA 52729
   319-244-2299
   free catalog
      heirloom vegetable seeds,
      specializes in tomatoes—
      174 kinds

Seeds Blum
   Idaho City Stage
   Boise, ID 83706
   catalog $3.00
   outstanding collection of
      heirloom vegetable seeds

Seeds of Change
   621 Old Santa Fe Trail,
      No. 10
   Santa Fe, NM 87501
   505-438-7052
   free catalog
   organically grown heir-
      loom and Native Ameri-
      can vegetables

Sonoma Antique Apple Nursery
   4395 Westside Road
   Healdsburg, CA 95448
   707-433-6420
   catalog $1.00
   superb collection of old-
      fashioned apple trees,
      available as plants or as
      scionwood for the do-it-
      yourself grafter

Sources for Garden Supplies

Deer repellents, fencing,
electrical fencing supplies:
   Deer Busters
   9735-A Bethel Road
   Frederick, MD 21702
   800-248-3337
   free catalog

Drip irrigation kits and equip-
ment:
   Gardener's Supply Com-
      pany
   128 Intervale Road
   Burlington, VT 05401
   800-234-6630
   free catalog

Dripworks
380 Maple Street
Willits, CA 95490
800-522-3747
free catalog

pH testing supplies:
Pinetree Garden Seeds
Box 300
New Gloucester, ME
   04260
207-926-3400
free catalog

Row covers:
Gardens Alive!
5100 Schenley Place
Lawrenceburg, IN 47025
812-537-8650
free catalog

Seed starting supplies:
The Cook's Garden
P.O. Box 535
Londonderry, VT 05148
800-457-9703
free catalog

Vegetable seedlings by mail order:
Santa Barbara Heirloom
    Nursery, Inc.
P.O. Box 4235
Santa Barbara, CA 93140
805-968-5444
catalog $2.00
an extensive collection of
    unusual varieties,
    shipped ready to plant

ABOUT THE AUTHORS

TOM CHRISTOPHER is a professional horticulturist. His first book, *In Search of Lost Roses,* won the 1990 Quill and Trowel Award of Excellence of the Garden Writers Association of America. He has written for publications such as *The New York Times* and *Martha Stewart Living,* given programs at botanic gardens, arboreta, and museums all over the United States, and has been featured on National Public Radio. He lives in Middletown, Connecticut.

MARTY ASHER is editor in chief of Vintage Books. He is the author of a novel, *Shelter* (Arbor House), and *57 Reasons Not to Have a Nuclear War* (Warner Books). His humor pieces have appeared on *The New York Times* op-ed page and in *Newsday.* He lives in Westport, Connecticut.

ABOUT THE TYPE

This book was set in Sabon, a typeface designed by the well-known German typographer Jan Tschichold (1902–74). Sabon's design is based on the original letterforms of Claude Garamond and was created specifically to be used for three sources: foundry type for hand composition, Linotype, and Monotype. Tschichold named his typeface for the famous Frankfurt typefounder Jacques Sabon, who died in 1580.